Medical Work in America

Medical Work in America

Essays on Health Care

ELIOT FREIDSON

Yale University Press

NEW HAVEN AND LONDON

The empirical research reported in chapters 4, 7, 8, 9, and 10 was supported in part by U.S. Public Health Service grants RG-7882, GM-07882, CH-00025, CH-00414, and HS-00104.

Designed by Barbara Werden
and set in Linotron Sabon type by The Composing Room of Michigan.
Printed in the United States of America by Vail-Ballou Press, Binghamton, New York.

Library of Congress Cataloging-in-Publication Data
Freidson, Eliot, 1923–
    Medical work in America: essays on health care / Eliot Freidson.
        p.   cm.
    Bibliography: p.
    Includes index.
    ISBN 0-300-04157-8 (alk. paper). — ISBN 0-300-04158-6 (pbk. : alk. paper)
    1. Medicine — Philosophy.   2. Medicine — United States.
3. Physician and patient.   I. Title.
R690.F735   1989
610.69'6'0973 — dc19   89-5448
                            CIP

The paper in this book meets the guidelines for permanence and durability of the Committee on Production Guidelines for Book Longevity of the Council on Library Resources.

10 9 8 7 6 5 4 3 2 1

For Sammy

CONTENTS

IV. HEALTH CARE IN THE FUTURE

Now and in the future, what happens to practicing physicians and their work affects all who need health care. This is not to say that only doctors provide care or that only they are important. But in the division of labor in health care, medicine has the central place, and even if other professions should take over some of its present tasks, medicine will remain central. For this reason, while its concern is with health care in general, this book focuses on the medical profession and the medical practitioner in particular. Its essays address the social characteristics of medical work in America, how today's economic and administrative pressures are changing that work, and what choices both the public and the medical profession now face. They analyze physicians' relations with patients, with their colleagues, with the institutions in which they work, and with those who pay for their patients' care, all of which shape the content and the quality of health care.

One policy issue that has guided my thinking in these essays is the quality of the health care that is and will be provided to the public. I fear that many present-day policies designed to reduce costs and assure a minimal technical standard of care will lead to a system that reduces patients and their ills to standardized bureaucratic categories and discourages practitioners from dealing with them as individuals with unique problems and needs. Health service in a decent society should serve the idiosyncratic needs of individuals and seek the realization of individual potential.

To deal with patients as people rather than objects, those who serve them must be allowed to exercise considerable discretion. Mechanical and narrow standards for evaluating and controlling medical performance, administered at a distance and dominated by financial considerations, undermine and discourage the capacity and incentive of physicians to provide individualized care. Public policy must find ways to organize health care that avoid its industrialization.

Underlying the policy issue of the human quality of care is a theoretical point. Direct interaction between people constitutes the reality of human life. Important changes in people's behavior are far more likely to stem from changes in their interaction with others than from changes in administrative rules intended to govern their activities. Thus, if we wish to create circumstances in which physicians can employ the discretionary judgment necessary for dealing with patients as individuals while at the same time maintaining the accountability and discipline that public policy rightly demands, we must change the way medical practice is organized and the way colleagues interact at work.

The essays in this book are arranged to develop these themes. Those in the first section deal with the most enduring and ubiquitous element of health care: the doctor–patient relationship. My introductory essay attempts to make explicit the issues of both theory and policy that are embedded in that relationship. This is followed by papers analyzing how the human experience of obtaining health care is structured by a variety of social factors, such as the culture, status, role, and education of patients and physicians, the position of each in community and professional networks, and the way new contractual relationships are changing the way they interact.

The papers in the next section analyze the social organization of medical practice. The introductory paper addresses the central problem of controlling medical performance in the public interest. After reviewing recent innovations in the organization and financing of practice, it discusses how the social organization of practice can influence the nature of health care. This is followed by a paper that presents a logical typology by which variation in the organization of practice can be analyzed. A series of papers then reports the findings of my early studies of an organized form of practice that would now be called Health Maintenance Organization (HMO) and is much favored by recent public policy. One reports a study of how the relations among physicians in such a practice limited the possibility for the exercise of control over each other's performance, while another reports the kind of control the physicians did in fact exercise and suggests why it took that form. Other papers describe the markedly different ways in which group practices were organized at the time and how physicians reacted to participating in those practices.

The third section turns to the broad cultural, political, social, and economic forces in America that are now changing the conditions of medical practice. The first paper sketches the characteristics of the major institutions and organized interests that create and sustain the framework within which medical work goes on. Those following it are concerned with appraising the present status of the medical profession. They attempt to make sense of rapidly changing circumstances whose lasting consequences are not yet clear, first by examining the application of theories of "proletarianization" and "deprofessionalization" to what is happening to practitioners today, and then by suggesting my own more modest but, I believe, more useful theory.

The final section includes a paper that describes and analyzes the theoretical models that are implicit in various policy positions and the major organized interests involved in health care. It predicts the likelihood of a recurrent cycle of partial and ultimately unsatisfactory change in the health care system during the remainder of this century. Such a cycle creates the danger of drifting into a thoroughly undesirable system, one that industrializes both doctor and patient. In conclusion, therefore, I present a paper suggesting that our goal should be health care that serves all in need, but in ways that preserve and enhance individual potential. I discuss both the principles that should guide policy and some of the concrete means by which they might be realized. While my suggestions are reformist rather than revolutionary, they are unlikely to be welcomed by most vested interests. In the case of medicine, however, I firmly believe that the importance of what it can lose is far outweighed by what it can gain—the preservation of its privilege to exercise considerable discretion in its work and to control itself. That privilege is now at risk. Without it, the challenge, pleasure, and pride in work that has been lost by most other occupations will be lost by medicine as well. Should this occur, we will all be the poorer.

Finally, I want to thank Helen Giambruni for her meticulous and demanding editorial work on several drafts of all the new essays in this book, Buford Rhea and John H. Mann for their earlier collaborative efforts, Dorothy Nelkin for her critical reading of one chapter, and Patricia Hartman for putting it all together.

PART ONE

Doctor-Patient Relations

Growing Constraints on Doctor-Patient Relations

The doctor-patient relationship is the primary foundation of all modern health care. It is where we start and ultimately where we finish. From its beginnings to the present day, health care has involved interaction between two kinds of people—one who seeks help and a consultant who is believed capable of helping. In other times and places consultants were not medical doctors and were not equipped with the knowledge, skill, and technology of today's physicians. Nonetheless, they were set apart by being believed to possess an inherited or learned capacity to help that was not available to ordinary people. Given that relationship of client to specialist, interaction between the two parties has always been more structured than is the case for the informal self-diagnosis and consultation with friends and family that often precede it. Indeed, one can think of it in purely formal terms, as a relationship that can be defined by the social characteristics of its members.

As I note in chapter 2, this relationship is intrinsically problematic. While it may appear that both participants desire the same outcome and so should be cooperating in order to attain it, the characteristics and perspectives of each can differ so markedly that each can have a different conception of the problem for which help is being sought, of the possible and acceptable solutions to the problem, and of the authority each is willing to grant the other. It is thus no accident that both lay people and consultants have joked and complained about each other. Lay people have complained of consultants' arrogance or inability to cure; consultants have complained of patients' lack of respect,

3

ignorant preference for inappropriate methods of treatment, and failure to follow the recommended treatment.

While the general parameters of the doctor-patient relationship have been constant throughout history, important elements vary in time and place. Furthermore, the social and economic structure within which the relationship takes place also varies. Here I wish to discuss those variables and their implication for the nature of the doctor-patient relationship in the United States today. Essentially, I will suggest that changes in the characteristics of patients, in conjunction with changes in the social and economic context of health care, are introducing circumstances that will make it more and more difficult for present-day physicians to deal with their patients in ways that are mutually satisfying. While part of that problem will be solved by both becoming accustomed to the new contractual terms of their relationship and new modes of organizing practice, enough of a problem will remain to warrant more attention to the role of the patient in medical decision making than has lately been the case.

TRENDS IN RESEARCH

During the golden age of medicine (and medical sociology)—the period between the end of World War II and the introduction of Medicare and Medicaid—sociologists paid a great deal of attention to the doctor-patient relationship. They were concerned that many patients were not receiving adequate care. Some people were not seeking health care when it was actually needed. Others endangered their health by failing to comply with medical recommendations. Sociologists and anthropologists studied particular ethnic and underprivileged populations thought to be prone to underutilization or noncompliance. They sought data on familiarity with and understanding of medical conceptions of illness, on lay conceptions of health and illness (including which symptoms were considered trivial and which serious), on the diagnostic and curative techniques appropriate to particular ailments, and on other issues germane to understanding how and why the target populations use medical care. They also sought data on attitudes toward physicians and health care institutions—whether physicians were respected and trusted, for example.

Most of those studies took place in the community and relied on survey and interviewing techniques to determine the opinions and attitudes of patient populations. Due to the difficulty of penetrating the privacy of the consulting room, only a few examined doctor-patient interaction directly. Those that did justified themselves in large part by purporting to learn why patients did or did not obey the physician's instructions. In those studies the focus was on how the physician explained the diagnosis and the treatment plan, what patients were able to understand, how sensitive the doctor was to occasions when the patient did not understand, and the like. There was virtually no attention paid to the role of the economic and contractual terms of the relationship.

A steady shift in the emphasis of research began in the 1960s. Where earlier studies concerned themselves with showing the way differences in status, knowledge, and culture influenced what went on between doctor and patient, those of the 1960s began to document the way doctors and health care institutions withheld information and forced on patients their own arbitrarily chosen modes of treatment. The issue was no longer why patients did not comply but rather how patients were not adequately informed and how decisions were imposed on them by medical personnel. That research showed, furthermore, that particular kinds of patients—for example, members of scorned ethnic groups, the poor, and women—were treated prejudicially. Consonant with the political and cultural climate of the time, the emphasis was on arbitrary and ostensibly unjust and discriminatory domination of patients by physicians rather than on sources of variation in the interaction between physician and patient.

Perhaps the most influential commentary on physician domination stemmed from special groups within the women's movement. They sought to gain some control over their ordinary gynecological and obstetrical care, arguing that those specialties were practiced in such a way as to sustain a patriarchal status of doctors over women and to impose on female patients male prejudices about women and the female body in the guise of objective medical science. As in the women's movement itself, the issues investigated sprang from the interests and preferences of educated middle-class women of child-bearing age as well as from the ambitious leaders of female-dominated occupations like midwifery and nursing, who sought higher status and greater freedom to practice autonomously.

Members of the women's movement have continued to publish prolifically, the historians among them showing how male domination of obstetric and gynecological concepts and practices emerged during the nineteenth century. Nonetheless, in recent years a new emphasis has engaged health care research. From the end of World War II until the late 1960s the concern was with the *under*utilization of health facilities by particular populations. But as the cost of health care mounted astronomically and showed no signs of slowing, the concern came to be with *over*utilization. The content of the interaction between patient and doctor became less important than its cost.

Beginning early in the 1970s but intensifying in the 1980s, priority was given to reducing cost. Both legislation and private insurer policies designed to control costs advanced a conception of the medical encounter that was almost wholly economistic in character. That is, on the surface, policy recommendations were predicated on the assumption that the behavior of both doctor and patient is influenced primarily by economic considerations. The preconceptions each has of the other, their different conceptions of the presenting problems, the structuring of their interaction, and the substance of their interaction in the consulting room were ignored as factors shaping decisions. The outcome alone, in the form of a claim for reimbursement, was taken to be the only necessary datum, to be explained by assuming rational calculation of economic self-interest on the part of doctor and patient. Other influences on decisions were either ignored or treated as random variables, selected and directed by economic considerations.

This approach is no doubt useful on a gross aggregate level, but it does not have the conceptual or empirical resources to deal with the variety of factors concealed in that aggregate. Many factors, even the inclination to rationally calculate economic self-interest, are variables rather than constants, so that if they change so will the aggregate results. Indeed, not even those policies designed to control cost are based on economistic assumptions, for if it were truly believed that economic self-interest was the sole basis for medical decision making—untempered by social, ethical, and medical considerations—then the incentives and constraints of policy would have to be much different than they have been. Policy actually (and rightly) assumes that doctors' decisions are mostly honest and concerned, and that economic self-interest may tilt decisions one way or another, but largely within the limits posed by professionalism. Nonetheless, even though those extra-economic considerations are assumed, they are not systematically taken into account in the formulation of policy and have not been receiving much attention in today's research.

Reliance on the assumptions of the economic model of human behavior also leads to neglecting the possibility of finding more desirable solutions to the problem of cost than the manipulation of economic incentives. Studies do show that changes in reimbursement policies are associated with changes in the treatment employed by physicians, a linkage which supports the assumptions of the economic model. But such findings are statistical, which means that some doctors—even a large proportion of them—do *not* behave the way the model assumes. Since it is desirable that doctors be concerned more with serving the good of others than with material self-interest, surely those whose decisions are not immediately responsive to economic incentives challenge the model, and surely they should be studied as a potential source of instruction on the influence of other factors in medical decision making.

Virtually exclusive preoccupation with the gross issue of controlling cost will not continue indefinitely: when the focus shifts more toward concern with improving the health of all the people, with preventing where possible and otherwise treating effectively particular health problems, and with improving the social and psychological process of consultation and treatment, then the variables influencing interaction will become critical elements for investigation and analysis. Some of those variables are changing now, and they will have important effects on the utilization of health services, on the behavior of both physician and patient in the course of such utilization, and on the kinds of decisions that doctors ultimately make in their practice.

CHANGES IN THE BALANCE OF THE RELATIONSHIP

The events of the past twenty years in the United States have transformed the traditional doctor-patient relationship in ways that have not yet become entirely clear. Chapter 2, "Dilemmas in the Doctor-Patient Relationship," addresses some timeless factors of that relationship— the differential social status of doctor and patient, the conventional roles of each that weight the balance of their interaction, and the cultural understandings, specialized knowledge, and experience with health, illness, and treatment that each brings to the interaction. Chapter 3, "Client Control and Medical Practice," attempts to conceptualize how those factors are organized in both lay and professional communities.

The elements I address in those chapters are always to be found in the doctor-patient relationship, but their content and structure varies, and variation leaves its mark on the interaction that takes place. However, some vary less than others. A relatively constant source of asymmetry in their interaction is the gap in technical knowledge, experience, and skill between client and consultant. In the vast majority of encounters it is the consultant who is superior to the client in knowledge, skill, and experience and who therefore exercises the greater influence. If this were not the case, why would a client seek help? But this difference is neither absolute nor always of the same magnitude. In the case of those with chronic illnesses, for example, many have the time, opportunity, and motivation to learn a great deal about diagnosis, treatment, and "management" of their particular complaint, and they become very active in their relations with doctors. Prospective patients vary in the depth and extent of their knowledge about health and illness, the physician-as-patient being the ideal example of how sophisticated a patient may be.

Certainly we can assume that the better educated the consumers of health services, the more capable they are of playing an active role in the relationship with those they consult. And during this century, but particularly since World War II, the proportion of the population of the United States with postsecondary education has increased markedly. This means that doctors today have to contend with more patients who can question their recommendations intelligently and who may try to adopt an active role in choosing their diagnosis and treatment. This does not mean that the intrinsic asymmetry in technical knowledge has vanished. It has been and will be reduced in the encounters of the educated middle class, but it will come nowhere near to being eliminated as a significant element in the relationship.

The same may be said for another source of asymmetry in the relationship—namely, the role each plays in it. As has been observed by many writers from those of the Hippocratic corpus down to the present day, patients are often gravely concerned about their health, perhaps in pain, and not entirely in normal command of their faculties. This handicaps their capacity to use what knowledge they have in the course of their interaction with the doctor who, in contrast, is not suffering but is engaged in a routine occupational role. Such a role difference provides the physician with additional weight in the balance of the relationship.

However, that difference is not great in routine circumstances involving minor and familiar complaints, and it need not exist at all in such circumstances as prenatal and preventive care, when the patient is not ill, let alone incapacitated. Contemporary efforts to normalize or "demedicalize" particular conditions, problems, or disabilities (or to instill a sort of aggressive pride or self-assertion among those who have them) will certainly narrow the range of circumstances in which an asymmetrical relationship may exist between doctor and patient, but they cannot eliminate all such circumstances or prevent new ones from being created by "medicalization."

These sources of asymmetry intrinsic to the relationship interact with others that are more variable. The physician's social rather than functional status in the relationship varies with the patient's, being quite different when the patient is lower class or female than when the patient is powerful or even simply middle class and male. Recent changes in the United States have altered the status balance between doctor and patient. Some women, for example, particularly educated middle-class women, have revolted against their traditional status and resisted what have been called patriarchal elements of domination in their relationships with male health personnel. And apart from changes in the willingness of women to accept their traditionally subordinate role as patients in the doctor-patient relationship, women themselves are becoming physicians in ever-greater numbers. It will be interesting to see how that contradiction between gender status and functional status will influence the doctor-patient relationship of both men and women.

Finally, I might note that the considerable growth in the educated middle class has created a large number of relatively well-informed patients who also consider themselves to be the doctor's equal in status. From them doctors cannot expect the outward passivity and deference that mark lower-status patients. Rather, those patients are likely to expect the doctor to give them more information and to allow them more choice than was previously the norm.

Taken together, these shifts in both objective status and status consciousness have contributed significantly to the changes that have been going on in the interaction between doctor and patient. They play an important part in influencing initial utilization, diagnosis, therapeutic choices, and in general the temporal and substantive demands made of the physician by the patient. And their role has been intensified by changes that have been taking place in the social and economic milieu in which everyday care is provided.

THE CHANGING QUALITY OF DEMAND FOR
HEALTH CARE

Until World War I it was possible to make sense of most of what went on in the provision of health services by analyzing the interpersonal variables I have been discussing. In earlier times people consulted individual physicians in private consulting rooms or in their own homes. There was little specialization and physicians were heavily dependent on their patients' good will and testimonials. Physicians' practices were embedded in what chapter 3 calls lay referral systems. As hospital treatment became more common, the difference between care by a variety of health personnel in hospital and care by solitary physicians in their offices in the community became marked. So did the difference between hospital-dependent and community practice, particularly in light of the massive growth of elaborate technologies and the continued proliferation of medical and paramedical specialties. A system of specialized practice grew up in which many physicians became more dependent on colleagues than on their patients for referral. This system was built around the hospital.

In the hospital, patients are likely to be considerably more helpless and passive by virtue of the difficulty that brought them there and of having to deal with a large number of staff responsible not to them but to the hospital and the doctor who ordered their services. The present trend toward treating more complaints on an ambulatory basis will intensify the distinction between the two modes of care. Patients remaining in the hospital will be those absolutely dependent on its staff and technology and thus will be in a considerably less powerful position to influence what happens to them than those being treated on an ambulatory basis.

In ambulatory care it is still possible to see the treatment situation as one in which two individuals interact with each other. Before the rise of health insurance patients were nominally free to choose any available physician so long as they were able to pay the established fee. Private health insurance plans and then Medicare and Medicaid seemed at first to eliminate most economic constraints over choice without otherwise changing the relationship between doctor and patient. The utilization of health services increased, as did the income of physicians and the overall cost of health care to public and private insurers.

However, the availability of health insurance is not the only

factor that has encouraged people to seek health care. Equally important are the public perception of health care as something of great value
and the way many more complaints today are "medicalized" so as to
require medical treatment (and have the cost reimbursed by insurance
funds). There are many factors that make health care such an attractive
commodity to Americans. There is first the weakness of both political
and medical efforts to gain support for preventive policies, that is,
attempts to remove the causes of illness and disability from the environment, the workplace, the home, and the marketplace. Instead the emphasis falls on curative and repair techniques. As I shall note in chapter
II, that emphasis is created by the intellectual interests of physicians
themselves, the economic interest of pharmaceutical and other health-
related manufacturers, and public concern with particular illnesses or
disabilities.

Furthermore, the mass media subject the American public to a
barrage of information about new methods of diagnosis and treatment, new hope, new cures. They do so aggressively, in a manner
designed to attract and hold the attention of readers and viewers. Indeed, they are driven to do so by their need for sufficient circulation to
attract the advertisers who supply them with their profits. The media,
I believe, are as responsible as the availability of health insurance for
the massive and expanding American demand for health care.
Equipped by the media, the educated middle class can specify and
articulate its interest in new diagnostic alternatives and more advanced procedures; the less well educated may express only a sus-
picious concern that what has been offered them does not exhaust all
miraculous possibilities. In both cases, patients are often led to expect
more than they can actually receive from their physicians.

To this pervasive and aggressive publicizing and merchandising of health care and related products must be added an entirely different element that stimulates patients to be aggressive and calculating in
their relationship to physicians. I refer to social and economic pressure
that virtually forces patients to try to become the rationally calculating
consumer dear to the hearts of economists. At present the pressure
seems to be exerted primarily by large firms that are trying to lower the
cost of the health benefits they provide their employees. In some cases
they present them with a choice between a prepaid service contract or
"discount" plan (which limits their choice of physicians but provides
comprehensive benefits for a single sum) and a fee-for-service plan that

is more limited in its coverage and that requires consumers to pay whatever difference may exist between the fee their physician charges and the fixed sum for which they will be reimbursed. The conscious exercise of choice requires consumers to pay close attention to the detailed terms of each plan, something that is especially important to those who choose a contract that offers ostensibly comprehensive health services with no significant out-of-pocket cost. It is in the context of just such a plan that chapter 4 discusses the new "demanding" patient.

The significance of a prepaid service contract lies in the fact that it joins doctor and patient together over a period of time in such a way that negotiation, if not actually conflict, cannot be avoided. In the traditional, uninsured fee-for-service encounter, the relationship between doctor and patient is reestablished from one visit to another; the unhappy patient need not return after an unsatisfactory consultation. Doctors in turn can encourage patients to go elsewhere, and they are free to manipulate both fee and availability as barriers to undesirable patients. There is no contract entailing an obligation to provide a defined range of services over a given period of time at a given price. Under those conditions, many potential sources of tension are simply avoided. However, with a prepaid service contract such as that provided today by health maintenance organizations (HMOs), doctor and patient are bound to each other and have no choice but to arrive at some accommodation. The demands on both, but more particularly on doctors, represent a new and unsettling element in the relationship.

Furthermore, both prepaid service contract plans and those involving "preferred providers," who have agreed to accept discounted fees in return for the patronage of the patients who are covered, add another weight to the balance of the doctor-patient relationship. Insofar as they involve a defined group of physicians who depend on each other's cooperation for their practice, their commitments to each other may reduce their immediate responsiveness to individual patients. And they may be more responsive to the third party that creates the contract, does the accounting, and pays the bills than they are to the patient. However, this is a complex matter that cannot be addressed intelligently by employing crude dichotomies: in some ways patients are empowered by having a third party to act as their agent and court of appeal; in others they are weakened by loss of their capacity to exercise direct, personal, and immediate choice. But without doubt these developments have the potential of affecting utilization, the substance of treatment, and patient compliance.

HEALTH CARE AND THE NEW MIDDLE CLASS

These new elements in the doctor-patient relationship are not likely to influence the responses of all patients to the same degree. Those of lower status than the doctor, who lack the resources of a higher education, who are not exposed to a broad range of media information, and who are not forced to make calculated choices are not likely to become troublesome for the doctor. On the other hand, those who consider themselves to be of equal or higher social status than the doctor, who consider themselves to be well informed about the latest diagnoses, prognoses, and treatments for what ails them, and who are experienced in reading the language of contracts and dealing with bureaucratic procedures have the potential to become serious problems of management.

Without the constraints of a service contract, much potential conflict is drained off by mutual self-selection and fee barriers. But given the continuing effort by insurers to stop or at least slow increases in the cost of care by reducing the proportion of the physician's fee for which they will provide reimbursement, I suspect that fewer and fewer people will feel able to afford fee-for-service plans and an increasing number will turn to prepaid service contract plans instead. It will not be the truly affluent, for their health insurance plans are very generous and they can afford increases in out-of-pocket costs. It will be the blue- and white-collar sectors and those often called the new middle class—the growing proportion of the labor force that fills professional, technical, and middle-management positions in our institutions.

It is precisely the new middle class that is in a position to introduce new difficulties into the doctor-patient relationship. If present trends in the polarization of the distribution of income in the United States continue, more and more of the new middle class will find themselves no longer among the affluent. While they are likely to remain better off than the working class, the savings anticipated from prepaid service contract plans will become more and more attractive. But when dissatisfied with their care—and their better education and higher status predispose them to dissatisfaction—they will not be able to afford to go outside the prepaid service plan and pay out of pocket for the care they want for particular complaints. They will have to try to get it from those with whom they have a contract. Constrained by their economic status, relying on the letter of the terms of their contract, sustained by their own social status and sophistication, many of them are likely to pose serious challenges to the authority of physicians and their capacity to control the amount and kind of care they given.

Notwithstanding the rhetoric of those who speak of physician domination of the doctor-patient relationship, the patient is not without influence. And contractual schemes provide patients with new resources with which to struggle for what, right or wrong, they believe they need. In order for the doctor to persuade the patient otherwise, however, requires time for discussion and negotiation. But since the major methods of controlling cost today lie in denying "unnecessary" services and reducing the amount of time for each consultation, neither participating physicians nor their practice organizations have much leeway. They must refuse services that they or third-party payers believe are unnecessary, but they may not have the time to persuade patients that their refusal is reasonable and appropriate even though the services are, when necessary, covered by the contract. It is not yet clear how much of a problem this new factor will be in coloring the doctor-patient relationship of the future.

Dilemmas in the Doctor-Patient Relationship

Almost 2500 years ago, the Hippocratic corpus presented doctors' complaints about the nonprofessional criteria that people use to select their physicians (Jones, 1943: II, 67, 281, 311), criticism of patients for insisting on "out of the way and doubtful remedies" (Jones, 1943: I, 317) or on overconventional remedies like "barley water, wine and hydromel" (Jones, 1943: II, 67) and for disobeying the doctor's orders (Jones, 1943: II, 201, 297). The physicians who have left us historical documents largely treat the patient as an obstacle, a problem of "management." From their point of view the patient is very troublesome, full of anxiety, doubt, and fear, insisting upon using his own scanty knowledge to evaluate the practitioner.

The patients who have left us documents often treat the physician as a potential danger to which one must respond cautiously and whom one must always be ready to evade. Patients have circulated stories about the occasions on which they successfully cured themselves or continued to live for a long time in defiance of medical prognoses. This sort of literature may be represented by the Roman "epigram about a doctor Marcus who touched a statue of Zeus, and although Zeus was made of stone he nevertheless died" (Pondoev, 1959: 87), and by Benvenuto Cellini's mild little story:

An earlier version of this chapter appeared in *Patients' Views of Medical Practice: A Study of Subscribers to a Prepaid Medical Plan in the Bronx,* © Russell Sage Foundation, 1961. Used with permission of the Russell Sage Foundation.

I put myself once more under doctor's orders, and attended to their directions, but grew always worse. When fever fell upon me, I resolved on having recourse again to the wood: but the doctors forbade it, saying that if I took it with the fever on me, I should not have a week to live. However, I made my mind up to disobey their orders, observed the same diet as I had formerly adopted, and after drinking the decoction four days, was wholly rid of fever. . . . After fifty days my health was re-established. (Cellini, n.d.: 128)

The struggle between physician and patient has continued into modern times. The cases recorded in Paul's volume (Paul & Miller, 1955), in the work of Saunders, (1954) Clark, (1959) Koos (1954), and in my own study (Freidson, 1961) have indicated that on important occasions patients do not necessarily do what they are told by physicians. They persist in diagnosing and dosing themselves and in assigning heavy weight to lay advice and their own personal dispositions. It is difficult to get them to cooperate wholly with health programs that professionals believe are for their own good (e.g., Cobb et al., 1957).

That the problem continues today is somewhat paradoxical, for it seems unquestionable that the medical practitioner has reached an all-time peak of prestige and authority in the eyes of the public. The physician of today is an essentially new kind of professional whose scientific body of knowledge and occupational freedom are quite recent acquisitions. His knowledge is far more precise and effective than it has ever been, since for the first time in history it could be said that from "'about the year 1910 or 1912 . . . [in the United States] a random patient with a random disease consulting a doctor chosen at random stood better than a 50-50 chance of benefitting from the encounter'" (Gregg, 1956: 13). The physician has obtained unrivaled power to control his own practice and the affairs that impinge upon it, and the patient now has severely limited access to drugs for self-treatment and to nonmedical practitioners for alternative treatment. But the ancient problem continues.

THE CLASH OF PERSPECTIVES

It is my thesis that the separate worlds of experience and reference of the layman and the professional worker are always in potential conflict with each other (cf. Becker, 1953; Merton, 1957). This seems to be inherent in the very situation of professional practice. The practitioner, looking from his professional vantage point, preserves his detachment by seeing the patient as a case to which he applies the general rules and categories learned during his protracted professional training. The client, being personally involved in what happens, feels obliged to try to judge and control what is happening to him. Since he does not have the same perspective as the practitioner, he must judge what is being done to him from other than a professional point of view. While both professional worker and client are theoretically in accord with the end of their relationship—solving the client's problems—the means by which this solution is to be accomplished and the definitions of the problem itself are sources of potential difference.

The very nature of professional practice seems to stimulate the patient on occasion to be especially wary and questioning. Professional knowledge is never complete, and so diagnosis, made with the greatest of care and the best of contemporary skill, may turn out to be inappropriate for any particular case. These mistakes may occur in two basic ways (cf. Hughes, 1958: 88–101).

First of all, it is obvious that in every age, including our own, there are likely to be worthless diagnostic categories and associated treatments—sometimes merely harmless without contributing anything to cure, sometimes downright dangerous. As Shryock put it for an earlier time, "No one will ever know just what impact heroic practice [heavy bleeding and dosing with calomel] had on American vital statistics: therapy was never listed among the causes of death" (Shryock, 1960: 111). In addition, in every age, including our own, there are likely to be diseases unrecognized by contemporary diagnostic categories—as typhoid and typhus were not distinguished before 1820, as gonorrhea and syphilis were once confused, and as mental diseases are no doubt being confused today. Thus, the best, most well-intentioned contemporary knowledge may on occasion be misdirected or false and some of the patient's complaints wrongly ignored.

Second, however, is a considerably more complex source of error that flows not from knowledge so much as from the enterprise of applying knowledge to everyday life. Insofar as knowledge consists in general and objective diagnostic categories by which the physician sorts the concrete signs and complaints confronting him, it follows that work assumes a routine character. This is the routine of classifying the flow of reality into a limited number of categories so that the individual items of that flow become reduced to mere instances of a class, each individual instance being considered the same as every other in its class.

The routine of practice not only makes varied elements of experience equivalent—it also makes them *ordinary*. This seems to be the case particularly in general medical practice. In general medical practice, while the range of complaints may indeed be unusually wide, the number of complaints falling within a rather narrow range seems to be overwhelming. In our day, for example, complaints that are categorized as upper respiratory infections are exceedingly common. Like malaria in the nineteenth century, they are so common that they are considered ordinary. And insofar as they are considered ordinary it is not legitimate for the patient to make a great fuss about the suffering they involve. His subjectively real pain is given little attention or sympathy because it is too ordinary to worry about. His likely response to this may be gauged by reading Dr. Raffel's account of the reception of his complaint of acute sinusitis (Pinner & Miller, 1952: 236–41).

What also happens is that more of reality than proves to be appropriate tends to be subsumed under the ordinary and commonly used categories. This agains seems to be in the very nature of professional practice—if *most* patients have upper respiratory infections when they complain of sneezing, sounds in the head, a running nose, and fatigue, then it is probable that it is an upper respiratory infection that is involved when *one* particular person makes the complaint. It may indeed be an allergy or even approaching deafness (Pinner & Miller, 1952: 62–72), but it is not probable—that is to say, it has not commonly been the case in the past. The physician cannot do otherwise than make such assumptions, but by the statistical nature of the case he cannot do otherwise than to be sometimes wrong.

THE PATIENT'S PROBLEM

These problems of diagnosis are not only problems for the doctor but also problems for the patient. All the patient knows is what he feels and what he has heard. He feels terrible, his doctor tells him that there's nothing to worry about, and a friend tells him about someone who felt the same way and dropped dead as he was leaving the consulting room with a clean bill of health. The problem for the patient is determining when the doctor is mistaken. When are subjective sensations so reliable that one should insist on special attention, and when can one reasonably allow them to be waved away as tangential, ordinary, and unimportant? The answer to this question is never definite for any individual case and indeed cannot be resolved decisively except by subsequent events. All of us know of events that have contradicted the judgment of the physician[1] and of course many others that have contradicted the patient.

The situation of consultation thus proves to involve ambiguities that provide grounds for doubt by the patient. Furthermore, those ambiguities are objective. Most reasonable people will agree that the doctor is sometimes wrong, whether by virtue of overlooking the signs that convert an ordinary-appearing case into a special case or by virtue of the deficiencies of the knowledge of his time. He is less often wrong now than he was a hundred years ago, but frequency is not really the problem for the individual. Even if failure occurs once in ten thousand cases, the question for the patient is whether or not it is he who is to be that one case, a question that no one can answer in advance. If the evidence of his senses and the evidence of his knowledge and that of his intimate consultants are contradicted by the physician, the patient may feel it prudent to seek another physician or simply to evade the prescriptions he has already obtained.

THE ROLE OF CONFIDENCE

If it is true that the very practice of medicine, through the process of diagnosis, is permeated with objective uncertainty of which the patient

1. In discussing one of the mammoth but well-intentioned and probably competent "professional" mistakes of the past, St. Theresa calls the practitioner's routine and easygoing attitude a temptation by the devil of the client: "[A spiritual director must not be] of the kind that teaches us to be like toads, content if our souls show themselves just capable of catching small lizards. . . . I believe the devil is very successful in preventing those who practice prayer from advancing further by giving them false notions of humility. He persuades us that it is pride that gives us such great aims, and that makes us wish to imitate the saints and desire martyrdom" (Cohen, 1957:89).

Most of the sensible priests who devoted themselves to soothing underemployed women who fear for their souls have been lost to history. St. Theresa, however, has left them a monument in her ungrateful remarks about one of their harried colleagues, for they all ran the same risk of assuming that they were confronted by a hysterical lady rather than by a future saint. She, like the cancerophobic patient who actually turned out to have a sensational tumor, is the symbolic case that stiffens the backbones of those who wish to imitate the saints in spite of being told they are quite holy or healthy enough.

may become aware, it is at least as important to understand why patients do cooperate with doctors as to understand why they do not. One reason seems to be the ignorance of the patient—he may not be aware of or be sensitive to the contingencies of practice. Another reason seems to be the kind of situation with which the patient is confronted— whether it is a crisis situation that motivates him to be sensitive to uncertainties or a routine situation that blunts his sensitivity and attention. There is still another possible reason, however, which, if true, is more strategic than the patient's ignorance or the variable context of consultation. I refer to the special status of the professional in society that (unlike the businessman with his motto, caveat emptor) supposedly entitles him to a priori trust and confidence (Gross, 1958: 78).

The usual conception of confidence seems to be shallow and parochial. It is indeed true that under ordinary circumstances one goes to a doctor assuming that the doctor knows his business and that his judgment may be trusted, but it is no less true of the ordinary use of other services. It is a mistake to assume that the title "profession" confers a kind of expert authority on the practitioner that is greatly different from the authority of any fairly esoteric craftsman. Simmel pointed out some time ago that "our modern life is based to a much larger extent than is usually realized upon the faith in the honesty of the other. . . . We base our gravest decisions on a complex system of conceptions, most of which presuppose the confidence that we will not be betrayed" (Wolff, 1950: 313). Under normal circumstances we have confidence in a mechanic's ability to grease our car properly just as we have confidence in a physician's ability to prescribe the right drug for us and a pharmacist's ability to fill the prescription accurately. In the same fashion we have confidence in a variety of other service workers— appliance repairmen, bank clerks, carpenters, fitting-room tailors, and so on. Faith in the honest application of specialized ability by a consultant seems to be connected not only with the use of those who are called professionals but also with the use of any kind of consultant whose work is fairly esoteric. Such confidence must exist if life is to function smoothly, routinely.

However, there seems to be a generic distinction in the way the definition of the situation of consultation varies. On the one hand, there is an unthinking and fundamentally superficial sort of confidence that is automatically attached to any routine consultation. It is manifested in uncritical cooperation with the consultant. This sort of confidence sustains the doctor-patient relationship in about the same way it sustains any consultant-client relationship. It appears to waver when the client's expectations are not fulfilled by the consultant and when the problem of consultation comes to be seen as critical (that is, nonroutine) to the patient. Questions arise when the consultant does not act as he is expected to, when the diagnosis seems implausible, when the prescription seems intolerable and unnecessary, and when "cure" is slow or imperceptible. They become pressing when the problem of consultation assumes what seem to be serious proportions. Under such circumstances what is needed to sustain the relationship is at least a different quantity if not a different quality of confidence.

It may be that it is this latter sort of confidence that is in the minds of those who make a special connection between professions and client confidence. Certainly it is true that three of the old, established professions deal with some of the most anxiety-laden topics of existence—the body, the soul, and human relations and property. Plumbing, internal combustion engines, and clothing are not likely to occasion as much anxiety. In this sense doctors, clergymen, and lawyers are more likely to require for their practice a special kind of confidence than are plumbers, mechanics, and fitting-room tailors. But, we may observe, it is precisely this special sort of confidence that is problematic for professions in general and medicine in particular; it is precisely this sort of confidence that does *not* flow automatically from professional status. Routine confidence is automatic but grants no special advantage to the professions. Confidence in crises, however, is demanded but not necessarily obtained by consultants with professional standing.

THE ROLE OF CULTURE

One of the things that breaks routine and thereby suspends routine confidence is an occasion in which the patient's expectations are not met. Instead of prescribing what seems to the patient to be a good sensible remedy like barley water, wine and hydromel, or penicillin, the physician suggests that the patient go on a dietary regimen or simply take aspirin. Obviously, we have in essence a clash of culture or education. The patient's culture leads him to expect what the doctor's culture does not suggest.

Cultural differences between patient and doctor have received a great deal of attention. The tenor of contemporary writings suggests that much patient-doctor conflict can be eliminated by reducing the differences between the two.

Some—particularly those writing about fairly exotic patients who cannot be expected to become "educated" quickly (Mead, 1955)—suggest that the physician should be able to get patients in to see him and to reduce conflict during consultation by adjusting himself to the patient's expectations. If, for example, his prospective patients interpret the professional attitude of detachment and impersonality to be hostile, the doctor should be prepared to behave in a less "professional" and more sociable way (Clark, 1959: 215). On the whole, the recent movement to bring social science into American medical schools seems to share this perspective: by teaching the prospective physician more about "the patient as a person," it is presumed that when he starts to practice he will be better equipped to understand, tolerate, and adjust himself to those expectations of the patient that contradict his own.

But how far can be we expect the physician to adjust himself to the patient's lay (and sometimes bizarre) expectations without ceasing to practice modern medicine? There is of course a great practical difference between automatic and rigid compliance to a set of scholastic propositions and a more flexible kind of behavior, and certainly professionals would agree that the latter is likely to produce the better practitioner. But flexibility must remain within limits or it becomes irresponsible. The physician can listen closely to the patient and adjust to him only so far. If his adjustment is too great, the physician must deny the heritage of special knowledge that marks him off as a professional—in effect, he ceases to be a professional. Thus, we may say that some conflict in the physician-patient relationship may indeed be forestalled by educating physicians to be somewhat more understanding and flexible with patients, but that there is a line beyond which the physician cannot go and remain a physician. Some patients' expectations cannot be met.

It might be suggested that at the point where the physician must stop adjusting, the patient must begin. After the physician has accommodated himself to the patient as far as he can, the patient should make all further accommodation if conflict is to be forestalled without destroying medical authority. With the proper health education it is believed that the patient will understand and believe sufficiently in modern medicine to be able to approach his illness from the same perspective as the physician. Thus, *patients* are to be changed so as to conform to the expectations of the doctor.[2]

The relation of health education to the reduction of conflict is, however, by no means clear. As one way of assessing it we might contrast the consequences of two extremes. First, we may ask, what sort of conflict exists when the patient has no health education at all—that is to say, no culturally determined expectations of the doctor. Situations like this are often found in veterinary and pediatric medicine—at least when the parent or owner of the patient does not take a surrogate sick role. Patients in both cases lack any health education. As such, they lack any of the knowledge that would lead them, when ill, to seek a physician. Unassisted, they are likely either to seek a familiar sympathetic person or, like the lion in the fable, lie helpless somewhere waiting for the chance and professionally unqualified kindness of an Androcles. If they should happen to strike upon a treatment situation, they prove incapable of indicating by any but the crudest and largely involuntary means—like a swollen paw and roars of distress—what is wrong with them. Nor can they themselves be counted upon to follow or even to submit to the treatment prescribed; indeed, it often happens that they must be physically restrained to be treated.

It is patent that there are shortcomings in working with patients with no health education at all, but are there any virtues? One is that while the patient may be incapable of illuminating his complaint due to his lack of education, he is also incapable of obscuring it by irrelevancies and misinformation or compounding it by imaginative anticipation. Another is that he has no expectations about treatment, so that once the consultant establishes control there is no contradiction of his authority. Another is that simply by reason of the fact that the patient cannot cooperate it is permissible to use physical restraint, a very convenient device for practice that cannot be used on people who theoretically can but will not cooperate. And finally, apocryphal but worth citing nonetheless, the ignorant client, once won over, may, like Androcles' lion, show undying gratitude and devotion to his healer. If this is true, it is no mean virtue.

2. Talcott Parsons (1951) in fact seems to define the role of the patient by reference to the expectations of the physician, for what he describes is not at all typical of what empirical studies show to be the expectations of patients and their lay consultants.

However, the virtues of the completely ignorant patient may seem small in the face of the shortcomings. After all, patients who are educated in health affairs will have the knowledge to allow them to recognize symptoms so as to come in to see the doctor in time, to give a useful history, and to cooperate intelligently with treatment. Surely people with the most health education will be more cooperative and will not struggle with the doctor.

It does not seem to be so simple. The physician is the one with the greatest possible health education, but there are good grounds for believing that he is not a very cooperative patient at all. The physician is reputed to be given to a great deal of self-diagnosis and treatment. This follows in part from his advanced health education, which makes him feel competent to diagnose himself "scientifically," and in part, like his susceptibility to drug addiction, from his privileged access to the medication that his self-diagnosis calls for. And when, after the long delay caused by self-diagnosis and treatment, the physician does seek the aid of another, he is reputed to be an argumentative and uncooperative patient incapable of repressing his own opinions in favor of those of his consultant.[3] This too seems to follow from his very health education, for it gives him a "scientific" position in which to stand and counter that of his consultant, and it gives him a clear insight into the uncertainties of practice such that he may feel strongly justified in holding to his own opinion.

This view of physicians as patients is supported only by the plausibility of what is essentially gossip. It is made substantially more credible, however, when we look at the behavior of well-educated middle-class patients. Fairly well versed in modern medicine, they can on occasion cooperate beautifully with the physician, but on occasion they are also quite active in evaluating the physician on the basis of their own knowledge and shopping around for diagnoses or prescriptions consonant with their knowledge. They are more confident and cooperative on a routine basis, perhaps, but they are also more confident of their own ability to judge the physician and dispose themselves accordingly.

3. The bad reputation of the doctor as patient is not limited to the United States. From the Soviet Union, Pondoev (1959: 104–05) observes, "If we ask any doctor he will agree with any other that the most difficult patient is a sick doctor. No other patient interferes so much with the doctor in his work as does the ailing doctor. . . . Nothing is more difficult than to convince the sick doctor that he is mistaken in his own diagnosis."

Whether health education resolves or encourages conflict in the doctor-patient relationship, then, seems to depend upon the situation. Where the well-educated, acculturated patient's expectations are being met (and they are more likely to be met by a physician than are those of worse-educated patients), his cooperation can be full and intelligent by virtue of the correspondence between his conceptions and those of the doctor. But by the nature of the case, so much of diagnosis and particularly treatment being a matter of opinion even within the profession itself, the patient's expectations will on occasion be violated: here his education is more likely to encourage conflict than to resolve it, for it allows the conflict to be justified by the same authoritative norms as those of the physician himself. A worse-educated patient may be far more manageable.

THE ROLE OF LATENT STATUS

Thus far, the only clear way by which professional authority seems able to sustain itself consistently appears to lie in an at least partial compromise of the *content* of the authority—by taking patients' expectations into account and adjusting practice to them. At the point of adjustment to the patient beyond which professional authority must be sacrificed, however, an additional nonmedical element may work to control the patient without compromise. In political affairs we would call it power; in professional affairs we lack an adequate term but might call it ability to intimidate.[4] This mode of resolving conflict flows not from the expert status of the physician but from the relation of his status in the community to that of his patient.

In the consulting room the physician may be said to have the manifest status of expert consultant and the latent status (cf. Gouldner, 1957) of his prestige in the lay community. His latent status has no necessary relationship to his technical qualification to be an expert but obviously impinges upon his relation to his patients. Indeed, latent

---

4. I find myself severely handicapped by this terminological problem. The physician has no administrative authority or power such as is attached to an office in an organization. The "authority" of his expert status is, as we have seen, problematic. But if he is, say, upper middle class, and his patient lower class, he has leverage over his patient that does not rest on authority or expertness as such and that exists in spite of the fact that the patient is paying him for his service. To my knowledge there is no analytically appropriate term for this type of influence.

status seems crucial for sustaining the force of manifest or professional status, for while many occupations possess expert knowledge, few have been able to control the terms of their work. The established professions, however, have obtained both the political power requisite for controlling the sociolegal framework of practice and the social prestige for controlling the client in consultation. Both the power of the profession and the prestige of the practitioner are quite separate from the "authority" inherent in technical expertness. They seem to be critical conditions for reducing doctor-patient conflict *without* compromising expert knowledge. However, even when professional power and technical expertness are high, the relative prestige of the practitioner varies. It is not a constant. It has varied through history; within any particular society it varies from one practitioner to another; within any particular practice it can vary from one patient to another. What are the consequences of variation in relative latent status for the doctor-patient relationship?

When the physician has had a lower standing than his patient, "more on a footing with the servants" (Eliot, n.d.: 91), he is likely to have to be either complaisant or nimble or both to preserve the relationship. This necessity is clearest in instances in which social standing is accompanied by absolute power and in which the severest result could ensue from failure. For example: "Astragasilde, Queen of France, on her death bed had begged her husband, Gontrano, to throw her doctor out the window immediately after her death, which was done with the greatest punctuality. . . . In the fifteenth century, John XXII burned an unsuccessful physician at Florence and, on this Pope's death, his friends flayed the surgeon who had failed to keep him alive" (Riesman, 1935: 365). Under such circumstances the difficulties of practice according to strictly professional standards must be very great indeed—beyond fear of severe punishment for failure, considerable frustration could be caused by the way a patient of relatively high standing could effectively refuse to cooperate, as the difficulties of Dr. Henry Atkins, physician to Charles, duke of Albany, indicated (Keevil, 1954).

Even today it seems plausible to think that physicians of eminent and powerful men have a trying practice and that their behavior in the presence of superordinate patients will differ considerably from their behavior in the presence of "charity" patients in a hospital outpatient clinic (cf. Turner, 1959: 211). Indeed, Hollingshead and Redlich observed that upper-class patients and their families make more demands of psychiatrists than other patients. . . . These patients and their families usually view the physician as middle class. In such relationships the psychiatrist is not in a position to exert social power; he is lucky if he is able to rely on professional techniques successfully. All too often he has to carry out complicated maneuvers vis-à-vis a critical, demanding, sometimes informed, and sometimes very uninformed "VIP." Some VIP's push the physician into the role of lackey or comforter, and some psychiatrists fall into such a role. (Hollingshead & Redlich, 1958: 353)

Obviously, where the relative latent status of the physician is below that of the patient, he is not in a very good position to obtain cooperation. Overt or covert conflict seems likely to ensue.

On the other side we have a situation in which the physician has considerably higher standing than his patient. The most extreme example illustrating this is found in the case of James IV, king of Scotland, who practiced on his subjects. Here, while the physician's behavior might be qualified by his sense of paternalistic or professional responsibility, we should expect that his standing is sufficiently intimidating to the patient that, while the patient is in his hands, he will be in a position to impose the full weight of his professional knowledge. However, in response to his lack of control over his own fate, the patient seems to be inclined to adopt the defense of evasiveness. He may avoid coming in to see the physician in the first place—King James, as a matter of fact, paid his patients a fee to get them into his consulting room—or he may play dumb, listen politely while in the consulting room, and, once outside, ignore the physician's advice. Evasive techniques seem to be very common in instances where the physician is in a position to intimidate his patients. As Simmons has observed: "The deference doctors receive as upper-status persons can easily be mistaken for voluntary respect and confidence. This error could prevent perception of substantial resentments and resistances of patients" (Simmons, 1958: 22).

I have argued that objective differences in perspective between physician and patient and uncertainties inherent in the routine application of knowledge to human affairs make for incipient conflict between patient and physician. Conflict occurs especially when the patient, on the basis of his own lay perspective, tries in some way to control what the physi-

28   DOCTOR–PATIENT RELATIONS

cian does to him. It is more likely to occur when the patient defines his illness as potentially critical than when he sees it as minor and ordinary. There seem to be three ways by which conflict may be fore-stalled, but each is problematic. The doctor may accommodate to the demands of the patient, but if he should do so extensively he ceases to be the doctor. The patient may be educated in health affairs so as to be more in agreement with the doctor, but education also equips him to be more self-confident and self-assertive in evaluating the doctor's work and seeking to control it. Finally, the physician may attain such relatively high social standing as to gain an extraprofessional source of leverage for controlling the patient, but the patient tends to answer by only superficial cooperation and covert evasiveness.

In the light of these dilemmas it might be asked how it is that medical practice can even persist, let alone grow as much as it has over the past fifty years. Pain and desire for its relief are the basic motives of the patient, and they are not diminished by any of the elements of contradiction in the doctor-patient relationship. The prospective patient will not stop seeking help, but the way these dilemmas are managed will figure in what he seeks help for, when he seeks help, the way in which he seeks help, whom he seeks help from, and how he will behave in consultation. How some of the dilemmas are managed, of course, also involves the physician—his willingness and ability to accommodate to the patient, and the presence of situations in which he must accommodate if he is to keep his practice. They are reflected in the way he tries to deal with the patient. Thus, the doctor-patient relationship is not a constant, as Parsons (1951) seems to imply, but obviously a variable. As I have tried to show elsewhere (see chap. 3), systematic differences in the doctor-patient relationship such as Szasz and Hollander (1956) discuss may be seen to flow from historical and situational variability in the strength and content of struggling lay and professional systems.

REFERENCES

Becker, H. S.
1953   Some contingencies of the professional dance musician's career. *Human Organization* 12:22–26.
Cellini, B.
N.d.   *The autobiography of Benvenuto Cellini.* Trans. John A. Symonds. New York: Modern Library.

Clark, M.
  1959.   *Health in the Mexican-American community.* Berkeley: University of California Press.
Cobb, S., S. King, and E. Chen.
  1957.   Differences between respondents and nonrespondents in a morbidity survey involving clinical examination. *Journal of Chronic Diseases* 6:95–108.
Cohen, J. M., trans.
  1957.   *The life of Saint Theresa.* Harmondsworth: Penguin Books.
Eliot, G.
  N.d.   *Middlemarch: A study of provincial life.* New York: A.L. Burt.
Freidson, E.
  1961.   *Patients' views of medical practice.* New York: Russell Sage Foundation.
Gouldner, A. W.
  1957.   Cosmopolitans and locals: Toward an analysis of latent social roles–I. *Administrative Science Quarterly* 2:281–86.
Gregg, A.
  1956.   *Challenges to contemporary medicine.* New York: Columbia University Press.
Gross, E.
  1958.   *Work and society.* New York: Thomas Y. Crowell.
Hollingshead, A. B., and F. C. Redlich.
  1958.   *Social class and mental illness.* New York: John Wiley & Sons.
Hughes, E. C.
  1958.   *Men and their work.* New York: Free Press.
Jones, W. H. S., trans.
  1943.   *Hippocrates.* London: William Heinemann.
Keevil, J. J.
  1954.   The illness of Charles, duke of Albany (Charles I), from 1600 to 1612: An historical case of rickets. *Journal of the History of Medicine and Allied Sciences* 9:410–14.
Koos, E. L.
  1954.   *The health of regionville.* New York: Columbia University Press.
Mead, M., ed.
  1955.   *Cultural patterns and technical change.* New York: International Documents Service (UNESCO), Columbia University Press.
Merton, R. K.
  1957.   The role-set: Problems in sociological theory. *British Journal of Sociology* 8:106–20.
Parsons, T.
  1951.   *The social system.* Glencoe, Ill.: Free Press.
Paul, B. D., and W. B. Miller, eds.
  1955.   *Health, culture and community.* New York: Russell Sage Foundation.
Pinner, M., and B. F. Miller, eds.
  1952.   *When doctors are patients.* New York: W.W. Norton.

Pondoev, G. S.
    1959.   *Notes of a Soviet doctor*. New York: Consultants Bureau.
Riesman, D.
    1935.   *The story of medicine in the Middle Ages*. New York: Paul B. Hoeber.
Saunders, L. W.
    1954.   *Cultural differences and medical care*. New York: Russell Sage Foundation.
Shryock, R. H.
    1960.   *Medicine and society in America*. New York: New York University Press.
Simmons, O. G.
    1958.   Social status and public health. Social Science Research Council Pamphlets, no. 13. New York: Social Science Research Council.
Szasz, T. S., and M. H. Hollander.
    1956.   A contribution to the philosophy of medicine. *A.M.A. Archives of Internal Medicine* 97:585–92.
Turner, E. S.
    1959.   *Call the doctor*. New York: St. Martin's Press.
Wolff, K. H., ed. and trans.
    1950.   *The sociology of Georg Simmel*. Glencoe, Ill.: Free Press.

THREE

Client Control and
Medical Practice

That the medical practitioner is typically a colleague in a structure of institutions and organizations, the patient being an essentially minor contingency, is the picture presented in the general discussions of Carr-Saunders and Wilson (1933), Parsons (1949), Merton (1957), and Goode (1957), as well as in studies of medical practice by Hall (1946, 1948, 1949), Solomon (1952), Hyde (1954), Peterson (1956), and Menzel, Katz, and Coleman (1955–56, 1957, 1959). The nature of medical practice is seen as determined largely by the practitioner's relation to his colleagues and their institutions and by the profession's relation to the state.

But practice cannot exist without clients, and clients often have ideas about what they want that differ markedly from those supposedly held by the professionals they consult. As anthropologists have so copiously illustrated (Paul, 1955; Foster, 1958), the client's choice is guided by norms that differ from culture to culture and even within a single complex culture (Koos, 1954; Simmons, 1958). And, after the client has exercised his choice to see a practitioner, normative or cultural differences between patient and physician qualify the relationship considerably (Saunders, 1954). These characteristics, in the client, obviously are a systematic source of pressure on the practitioner. To understand medical practice, therefore, one must learn the circum-

© 1960 by the University of Chicago Press. Reprinted from *American Journal of Sociology* 65 (January 1960) by permission.

stances in which the pressure is initiated and sustained, and this requires regarding the client and the practitioner in a single analytical system in which one explores the sources of strength of each.

To bring the two together, analysis must proceed on a model of society that is more common to anthropological than to sociological studies. Practice seems usefully analyzed not only as a set of practitioners interacting with each other[1] but as a concrete local situation in which two systems touch to form a larger whole in which there are characteristic norms, positions, and movements. To isolate the whole, the model is not that of a society within which there are practitioners and clients (Goode, 1957) or of a consultation room in which there are a practitioner and a client (Parsons, 1954) but of a system in which representatives of the medical profession practice in consultation rooms located in local communities of prospective clients. In recognizing practitioners as members of a profession, reference may be made to their organization and culture. In recognizing clients as members of a specific local community, reference may be made to their own organization and culture. In joining the two within a community, instances studied by anthropologists in which professional practitioners find it difficult to get clients can find as much of a place in the analysis as instances in which professional practice is so thoroughly accepted by clients as to be almost (but never quite) routine.

It is the purpose of this paper to use such a model to organize analysis of aspects of client experience that may significantly affect medical practice and to outline a descriptive typology of such practice, the analysis being put in a sufficiently general fashion to allow application to other types of professional practice.

Characteristically, the professional practitioner claims that his skills are so esoteric that the client is in no position to evaluate them. From this stems his privilege to be somewhat removed from the marketplace and to accept the evaluation of his colleagues rather than of his clients (Hughes, 1958). And this claim is one mark of his separation as a member of a professional "community."[2]

1. Hall's (1946) stress on the "inner fraternity" implies this even though he has some important things to say about clients. He is primarily concerned with how a physician obtains a clientele already organized into practices.

2. Goode uses the term *community* in the sense of shared interests and identity. Thus, all American physicians belong to the medical community, just as all American Catholics belong to the Catholic community. I use the term to mean locality.

But, while his own "community" may be without physical locus, he must practice in a spatially located community among more or less organized potential clients. Thus, while he is a member of a professional "community," accepting its norms and formally dependent on its institutions, the practitioner is always a kind of stranger in the community of his practice, for his reference group is his colleagues, not his clients.

However, while the physician may share special knowledge, identity, and loyalty with his colleagues rather than with laymen, he is dependent upon laymen for his livelihood. Where he does not have the power to force them to use his services, he depends upon the free choice of prospective patients.[3] But, since these prospective clients are in no position to evaluate his services as would his colleagues, and insofar as they do exercise choice, it follows that they must evaluate him by nonprofessional criteria and that they will interact with him on the basis of nonprofessional norms. Hence practice generically consists in interaction between two different, sometimes conflicting, sets of norms.

Consequently, we have two systems, the professional and the lay. In any concrete situation the two touch: the local physician may be seen as the "hinge" between a local lay system and an "outside" professional system. Structurally, the practitioner's support theoretically lies outside the community in which he practices, in the hands of his colleagues, while his prospective clientele are organized by the community itself. Culturally, the professional's referent is by definition "the great tradition" of his supralocal profession, while his prospective clientele's referent is the "little tradition" of the local community or neighborhood.[4] The lay tradition of the local community may, in one place or another, absorb varying amounts of the professional tradition, but by the nature of the case, as Saunders and Hewes have so persuasively argued (1953), lay medical culture seems unlikely ever to become identical with professional medical culture.

How are the physician and his prospective clientele brought

3. It is not predicated here that clients choose particular practitioners—that is, that practice is characteristically solo, fee-for-service in nature. Choice of physician is made to some degree by clients in the United States but hardly in other countries. (Cf. Ben-David, 1958, for Israel.) The choice the client must make everywhere is not which doctor to see but whether to see one at all.

4. The terms and image are those of Robert Redfield (1955, 1956). In industrial society the "little tradition" seems less stable than in peasant society and more dependent upon the "great tradition" for its content.

together? How is consultation initiated and sustained? Obviously, the prospective client must perceive some need for help and believe that it is a physician who can help him. And, if solo practice is the rule, he must determine who is a "good" practitioner. These perceptions seem to emerge from a process of interpersonal influence similar to that studied in other areas of life, a process organized by the culture and structure of the community or neighborhood through which "outside" knowledge and evaluation is strained.

In one locality, conceiving the need for "outside" help for a physical disorder seems to be initiated by purely personal, tentative self-diagnoses that stress the temporary character of the symptoms and to end by the prescribing of delay to see what happens.[5] If the symptoms persist, simple home remedies such as rest, aspirin, antacids, laxatives, and change of diet will be tried. AT the point of trying some remedy, however, the potential patient attracts the attention of his household, if he has not asked for attention already. Diagnosis is then shared, and new remedies or a visit to a physician may be suggested. If a practitioner is not seen but the symptoms continue (and in most cases the symptoms do *not* continue), the diagnostic resources of friends, neighbors, relatives, and fellow workers may be explored. This is rarely very deliberate; it takes place in daily intercourse, initiated first by inquiries about health and only afterward about the weather.

This casual exploration of diagnoses, when it is drawn out and not stopped early by the cessation of symptoms or by resort to a physician, typically takes the form of referrals through a hierarchy of authority. Discussion of symptoms and their remedies is referral as much as prescription—referral to some other layman who himself had and cured the same symptoms, to someone who was once a nurse and therefore knows about such things, to a druggist who once fixed someone up with a wonderful brown tonic, and, of course, to a marvelous doctor who treated the very same thing successfully.

5. The following sketch stems from intensive interviews with seventy-one patients of a metropolitan medical group in which they were asked to give detailed chronological accounts of the way in which they were led to seek medical care. It is not intended to describe the average experience but is a synthetic construct designed to portray the full length to which the process may go before professional practice is reached. The data suggest that the longer the process that intervenes between first perception of difficulty and contact with a practitioner, the greater the likelihood that the symptoms are ambiguous and not unbearable: a broken leg has different consequences than does a cold of excessive duration.

Indeed, the whole process of seeking help involves a network of potential consultants, from the intimate and informal confines of the nuclear family through successively more select, distant, and authoritative laymen, until the "professional" is reached. This network of consultants, which is part of the structure of the local lay community and which imposes form on the seeking of help, might be called the "lay referral structure." Taken together with the cultural understandings involved in the process, we may speak of it as the "lay referral system."

There are as many lay referral systems as there are communities, but it is possible to classify all systems by two critical variables—the degree of congruence between the culture of the clientele and that of the profession and the relative number of lay consultants who are interposed between the first perception of symptoms and the decision to see a professional. Considerations of culture have relevance to the diagnoses and prescriptions that are meaningful to the client and to the kinds of consultants considered authoritative. Consideration of the extensiveness of the lay referral structure has relevance to the channeling and reinforcement of lay culture and to the flowing-in of "outside" communications.

These variables may be combined so as to yield four types of lay referral system, of which only two need be discussed here—first, a system in which the prospective clients participate primarily in an indigenous lay culture and in which there is a highly extended lay referral structure and, second, a system in which the prospective clients participate in a culture of maximum congruence with that of the profession in which there is a severely truncated referral structure or none at all.

The indigenous, extended system is an extreme instance in which the clientele of a community may be expected to show a high degree of resistance to using medical services. Insofar as the idea of diagnostic authority is based on an assumed hereditary or divine "gift" or intrinsically personal knowledge of one's "own" health, necessary for effective treatment, professional authority is unlikely to be recognized at all. And, insofar as the cultural definitions of illness contradict those of professional culture, the referral process will not often lead to the professional practitioner. In turn, with an extended lay referral structure, lay definitions are supported by a variety of lay consultants, when the sick man looks about for help. Obviously, here the folk practitioner will be used by most, the professional practitioner being called for minor illnesses only, or, in illness considered critical, called only by the socially isolated deviate, and by the sick man desperately snatching at straws.

The opposite extreme of the indigenous extended system is found when the lay culture and the professional culture are much alike and when the lay referral system is truncated or there is none at all. Here, the prospective client is pretty much on his own, guided more or less by cultural understandings and his own experience, with few lay consultants to support or discourage his search for help. Since his knowledge and understandings are much like the physician's, he may take a great deal of time trying to treat himself but nonetheless will go directly from self-treatment to a physician.

Of these extreme cases, the former is exemplified by the behavior of primitive people and the latter by the behavior of physicians or nurses when taken ill. (Paradoxically, health professionals are notoriously uncooperative patients, given to diagnosing and treating themselves.) Between these two extremes, in the United States at least, members of the lower class participate in lay referral systems resembling the indigenous case and members of the professional class tend toward the other pole, with the remaining classes taking their places in the middle ranges of the continuum.

As Goode has noted, "Client choices are a form of social control. They determine the survival of a profession or a specialty, as well as the career success of particular professionals" (1957:198). The concept of lay referral system, thus, provides a basis not only for organizing knowledge about the patient's behavior but also for understanding conditions under which he, a layman, to some extent controls professional practice. Indeed, the lay referral system illuminates the ways in which the client's choice is qualified and channeled and how the physician's sex, race, and ethnic background affect his success—though it is often said that professions rest upon achieved status (Parsons, 1949:189, 193, 197). We can see now why a practitioner may never get any clients and why, on the other hand, he may get clients but then lose them; for the lay referral system not only channels the client's choice but also sustains it or, later on, leads him to change his mind. Interviews with urban patients reveal that the first visit to a practitioner is often tentative, a tryout. Whether the physician's prescription will be followed or not and whether the patient will come back seem to rest at least partly on his retrospective assessment of the professional consultation. The client may form an opinion by himself, or, as is often the case, he may compare notes with others—indeed, he passes through the referral structure not only on his way to the physician but also on his way back, discussing the doctor's behavior, diagnosis, and prescription with his fellows, with the possible consequence that he may never go back.

One might assume that all but the most thick-skinned practitioner soon become aware of lay evaluations, whether through repeated requests of their patients for vitamins or wonder drugs or through repeated disappearances or protests following the employment of scientifically acceptable prescriptions such as calomel or bleeding. Whether their motive be to heal the patient or to survive, professionally, they will feel pressure to accept or manipulate lay expectations, whether by administering placebos[6] or by giving up unpopular drugs.[7]

In a relatively organized community, channels of influence and authority that exist independently of the profession may guide the patient toward or away from the physician and may more or less control not only the latter's success but, to some extent, also his professional technique and manner;[8] in short, the lay referral system is a major contingency of medical practice. Practice in an indigenous extended system must adjust itself to the system in order to exist: when involving patients who are themselves professionals, it may make fewer adjustments.

The above discussion of the lay referral system should be taken to show that, in being *relatively* free, the medical profession should not be mistaken for being *absolutely* free from control by patients. Indeed, we may classify various kinds of professional practice on the basis of relative freedom from client control. But, to do so, we must examine sources of professional freedom that lie not in a complaisant clientele but in the nature of professional organization itself.

6. The placebo might be used as an index of control by the client of the terms of practice. On rationalizing sleight of hand as the placebo see Evans-Pritchard, 1937.

7. "This helplessness of regular physicians, coupled with popular distaste for bleeding and vile medicines, goes far to explain the success enjoyed by large groups of regular practitioners [in the nineteenth century]. . . . A not uncommon shingle advertisement in those early years was: Dr. John Doe; No Calomel" (Bonner, 1957:12). When doctors began to do less dosing in the late eighteenth and early nineteenth centuries, the public went out and bought its own medicine (Shryock, 1947:248ff.).

8. Cf. Dittrick (1952) and Friedenwald and Morrison (1940) on the devices used in China and in Europe to avoid offending the patient's sense of modesty.

Enough has been written about the privileged position that the organized power of the state grants the practitioners. (Indeed, this support by power located outside the community is often crucial to practice in underdeveloped countries where the prospective patients do not have a high opinion of modern physicians.) At the same time, political support sets severe limitations on competition,[9] both by prosecuting irregular "folk" or "quack" practice and by allowing restriction of the number of professional practitioners, two measures which greatly contribute to the stability and independence of the professional role.

Beyond these measures, however, we must note an additional important source of strength: Insofar as there are two "traditions" and two structures in a community, the lay referral system is one, and what we might call the "professional referral system" is the other. The professional referral system is a structure or network of relationships with colleagues that often extends beyond the local community and tends to converge upon professionally controlled organizations such as hospitals and medical schools. Professional prestige and power radiate out from the latter and diminish with distance from them. The authoritative source of professional culture—that is, medical knowledge—also lies in these organizations, partly created by them and partly flowing to them from the outside.

The farther this professional referral system is penetrated, the more free it is of any particular local community of patients. A layman seeking help finds that, the farther within it he goes, the fewer choices he can make and the less he can control what is done to him. Indeed, it is not unknown for the "client" to be a petitioner, asking to be chosen: the organizations and practitioners who stand well within the professional referral system may or may not "take the case," according to their judgment of its interest.

This fundamental symmetry, in which the client chooses his professional services when they are in the lay referral system and in which the physician chooses the patient to whom to give his services

9. To cite a dramatic instance of earlier competition: two tenth-century physicians who were competing for the favor of a king ended by poisoning each other at the king's dinner table. The one who knew the antidotes obtained the king's patronage (MacKinney, 1934). The veracity of this is questioned by Kristeller, 1945, but as the historian Louis Gottschalk once said, "Se non è vero è ben trovato." For modern times, Hall's observations on the "individualistic career" are relevant.

when he is in the professional referral system, demonstrates additional circumstances of the seeking of help. When he first feels ill, the patient thinks he is competent to judge whether he is actually ill and what general class of illness it is. On this basis he treats himself. Failure of his initial prescriptions leads him into the lay referral structure, and the failure of other lay prescriptions leads him to the physician. Upon this preliminary career of failures the practical authority of the physician rests, though it must be remembered that the client may still think he knows what is wrong with him.

This movement through the lay referral system is predicated upon the client's conception of what he needs. The practitioner standing at the apex of the lay referral system is the last consultant chosen on the basis of those lay conceptions.[10] When that chosen practitioner cannot himself handle the problem, it becomes *his* function, not that of the patient or his lay consultants, to refer to another practitioner. At this point the professional referral system is entered. Choice, and therefore positive control, is now taken out of the hands of the client and comes to rest in the hands of the practitioner, and the use of professional services is no longer predicated on the client's lay understandings—indeed, the client may be given services for which he did not ask, whose rationale is beyond him. Obviously, the patient by now is relatively helpless, divorced from his lay supports.

From the point of view of the physician, position in the process of referrals is also of importance. If he is the first practitioner seen in the lay referral structure, and if he sends no cases further on, he is subjected only to the lay evaluation of his patients as they pass back through the hands of their lay consultants after they leave him. If he refers a case to another practitioner, however, his professional behavior becomes subject to the evaluation of the consultant. In turn, when the patient leaves the consultant, he often passes back to the referring practitioner, so in this sense the professional consultant is subjected to the evaluation of the referring physician. Thus the physician who subsists on patients referred by colleagues is almost always subject to evaluation and control by his colleagues, while the practitioner who attracts patients him-

---

10. The actual specialty of the practitioner's standing in the lay referral system varies: certainly the general practitioner is almost always within it. Often pediatricians, gynecologists, internists, and ophthalmologists are to be found within it, particularly in communities of the professional classes. Pathologists, anesthesiologists, and radiologists are unlikely ever to be within it.

self and need not refer them to others is subject primarily to evaluation and control at the hands of his patients.

These observations suggest two extreme types of practice, differing in the relation of practice to the lay and to the professional referral systems. At one extreme is a practice that can operate independently of colleagues, its existence predicated on attracting its own lay clientele (Freidson, 1959). In order to do so, this "independent practice" must offer services for which those in a lay referral system themselves feel the need. In reality, of course, it will be conditioned both by the existence of competitors and by the particular lay system in which it finds itself, but on the whole, one should expect it to be incapable of succeeding unless conducted in close accord with lay expectations. To survive without colleagues, it must be located within a lay referral system and, as such, is *least* able to resist control by clients and *most* able to resist control by colleagues.

At the other extreme is postulated a "dependent practice" that does not in and by itself attract its own clientele but, instead, serves the needs of other practices, individual or organizational. The lay clientele with whom the practice must sometimes deal does not choose the service involved: a professional colleague or organization decides that a client needs the services of a professional in a dependent practice and transmits the client to him. In many cases only the colleague or organization is told the results of the consultation. Obviously, by definition, dependent practice could not exist in a lay referral system. To survive without self-selected clients, one must be in a professional referral system where clients are so helpless that they may be merely transmitted. As such, dependent practice is *most* able to resist control by clients and *least* able to resist control by colleagues.

The logical extreme of independent practice does not seem fully applicable to any professional practice, if only because a professional practitioners is trained outside the lay community before he enters it to practice and because his license to practice ultimately depends upon his colleagues "outside" and may be revoked. The "quack" seems to fit this logical extreme, for not only does he not require outside certification but, as Hughes (1958:98) defined him, he is one "who continues through time to please his customers but not his colleagues." He, like the folk practitioner, is a consultant relatively high in the structure of lay referrals, with no connection with an outside professional referral system.

Close to this extreme in the United States is the independent neighborhood or village practice (usually general in nature) that Hall calls "individualistic" (1949:249–52), with, at best, loose cooperative ties to colleagues and to loosely organized points in the professional referral system. All else being equal in this situation of minimal observability by colleagues and maximum dependence on the lay referral system, we should expect to find the least sensitivity to formal professional standards[11] and the greatest sensitivity to the local lay standards.[12] This differential sensitivity should show up best where the lay referral system is indigenous and extended.

Moving toward the position of dependent practice is what Hall called the "colleague practice," in close connection with a well-organized "inner fraternity" of colleagues and rigidly organized service institutions.[13] This practice tends to revolve around specialties, which in itself makes for location outside particular neighborhoods or villages and therefore reduces the possibility of organized control by the clients.

Finally, the closest to the extreme of dependent practice is a type that overlaps somewhat with the "colleague practice" but that seems sufficiently significant to consider separately. It might be called "organizational practice." Found in hospitals, clinics, and other professional bureaucracies (McElrath, 1958; Goss, 1959), it involves maximal restriction on the client's choice of individuals or services: clients are referred by other practitioners to the organization, or, if they are seeking help on their own, they exercise choice only in selecting the organization itself, functionaries of which then screen them and refer them to a practitioner. Here, practice is dependent upon organizational auspices and equipment. The client's efforts at control are most likely to take the form of evasion. The events of the referral process being systematically recorded and scrutinized, and ordered by hierarchical supervision, the practitioner is highly vulnerable to his colleagues' evaluations: we should expect him to be most sensitive to professional standards and controls and least sensitive to the expectations of his patient.

11. This, rather than medical education, might be an important determinant of the findings in Peterson et al., 1956.

12. As examples of the effect of clients' prejudices on success and location, see Williams, 1946, and Lieberson, 1958. For the effect of the type of legal practice on participation in community affairs, see Wardwell and Wood, 1956, and Wood, 1956.

13. See Hall, 1949; see also Solomon, 1952, chaps. 6 and 7, on physicians connected with Group I hospitals. In "colleague practice" it seems that the colleagues' racial or ethnic prejudice, not the clients', determines success.

This paper has stressed two notions—that variation in the culture and organization of patients and in the location of medical practice in the community is decisive in the introducing and sustaining of practice and in the technical and interpersonal modes of procedure in established practice. These closely interrelated notions were derived by conceiving of practice in relation to organized lay communities as well as to organized professional systems and by following the prospective patient through the two referral systems. The outcome emphasized was the relative extent to which control lay in the client's or in the practitioner's hands.

Like any analysis in which one must hold much of reality in abeyance, this has produced a certain amount of exaggeration. Where practice is already established, as opposed to where it is struggling to establish itself, much of what goes on is routine; conflict between the patient and the physician is rarely open but is masked by evasion and depends upon the practitioner's justified assumption that incompatible clientele will stay away or can be discouraged easily. Within this routine, such breaks and irritations as do exist are, of course, strategic areas to study, but the very routine, with the stable set of selected patients it implies, when compared from place to place, practice to practice, should reveal the compromises necessary to establish and maintain practice in the face of varying lay systems and varying positions in the lay and professional systems. Thus, the abstractly conceived professional role as described by such writers as Parsons may be qualified— indeed, sometimes, compromised—by the cultural and structural conditions in which it must be played.

REFERENCES

Ben-David, J.
  1958.   The professional role of the physician in bureaucratized medicine: A study in role conflict. *Human Relations* 11:255–74.
Bonner, T. N.
  1957.   *Medicine in Chicago, 1850–1950.* Madison, Wis.: American History Research Center.
Carr-Saunders, A. M., and P. A. Wilson.
  1933.   *The professions.* Oxford: Clarendon Press.
Clausen, J. A., and M. R. Yarrow.
  1955.   Paths to the mental hospital. *Journal of Social Issues* 11:25–32.
Dittrick, H.
  1952.   Chinese medical dolls. *Bulletin of the History of Medicine* 26:422–29.

Evans-Pritchard, E. E.
  1937.   *Witchcraft, oracles and magic among the Azande.* Oxford: Clarendon Press.
Foster, G. M.
  1958.   Problems in intercultural health programs. Social Science Research Council Pamphlets, no. 12. New York: Social Science Research Council.
Freidson, E.
  1959.   Specialties without roots: The utilization of new services. *Human Organization* 18:112–16.
Friedenwald, J., and S. Morrison.
  1940.   The history of the enema with some notes on related procedures. *Bulletin of the History of Medicine* 8:68–114, 239–76.
Goffman, E.
  1959.   The moral career of the mental patient. *Psychiatry* 22: 123 –42.
Goode, W. J.
  1957.   Community within a community: The professions. *American Sociological Review* 22:194–200.
Goss, M. E. W.
  1959.   Physicians in bureaucracy: A case study of professional pressures on organizational roles. Ph.D. diss., Columbia University.
Hall, O.
  1946.   The informal organization of the medical profession. *Canadian Journal of Economics and Political Science* 12:30–41.
———.
  1948.   The stages of the medical career. *American Journal of Sociology* 53:327–36.
———.
  1949.   Types of medical careers. *American Journal of Sociology* 55:243–53.
Hughes, E. C.
  1958.   *Men and their work.* New York: Free Press.
Hyde, D. R., et al.
  1954.   The American Medical Association: Power, purpose and politics in organized medicine. *Yale Law Journal* 63:938–1022.
Koos, E. L.
  1954.   *The health of regionville.* New York: Columbia University Press.
Kristeller, P. O.
  1945.   The school of Salerno. *Bulletin of the History of Medicine* 17:143–44.
Lieberson, S.
  1958.   Ethnic groups and the practice of medicine. *American Sociological Review* 23:542–49
MacKinney, L. C.
  1934.   Tenth-century medicine as seen in the *Historia* of Richer of Rheims. *Bulletin of the History of Medicine* 2:367–8.

44   DOCTOR–PATIENT RELATIONS

McElrath, D. C.
1958.   Prepaid group medical practice: A comparative analysis of organizations and perspectives. Ph.D. diss., Yale University.
Menzel, H., and E. Katz.
1955–   Social relations and innovation in the medical profession. *Public*
56.   *Opinion Quarterly* 19:337–52.
Menzel, H., E. Katz, and J. Coleman.
1957.   The diffusion of an innovation among physicians. *Sociometry* 20:253–70.
———.
1959.   Dimensions of being "modern" in medical practice. *Journal of Chronic Diseases* 9:20–40.
Merton, R. K.
1957.   Some preliminaries to a sociology of medical education. In *The student physician,* ed. R. K. Merton, G. G. Reader, and P. L. Kendall, pp. 73–79. Cambridge: Harvard University Press.
Parsons, T.
1949.   The professions and social structure. In T. Parsons, *Essays in sociological theory pure and applied,* pp. 185–99. New York: Free Press.
———.
1954.   *The social system.* New York: Free Press.
Paul, B. D., ed.
1955.   *Health, culture and community.* New York: Russell Sage Foundation.
Peterson, O. L., L. P. Andrews, R. S. Spain, and B. G. Greenberg.
1956.   An analytical study of North Carolina general practice, 1953–1954. *Journal of Medical Education* 31 (Part 2): 1–165.
Redfield, R.
1955.   *The little community.* Chicago: University of Chicago Press.
———.
1956.   *Peasant society and culture.* Chicago: University of Chicago Press.
Saunders, L. W.
1954.   *Cultural differences and medical care.* New York: Russell Sage Foundation.
Saunders, L. W., and G. H. Hewes.
1953.   Folk medicine and medical practice. *Journal of Medical Education* 28:43–46.
Shryock, R. H.
1947.   *The development of modern medicine.* New York: Alfred A. Knopf.
Simmons, O. G.
1958.   Social status and public health. Social Science Research Council Pamphlets, no. 13. New York: Social Science Research Council.

Solomon, D.
1952.   Career contingencies of Chicago physicians. Ph.D. diss., University of Chicago.
Wardwell, W. I., and A. L. Wood.
1956.   The extraprofessional role of the lawyer. *American Journal of Sociology* 61:304–07.
Wood, A. L.
1956.   Informal relations in the practice of criminal law. *American Journal of Sociology* 62:48–55.
Williams, J. J.
1946.   Patients and prejudice: Attitudes toward women physicians. *American Journal of Sociology* 51:283–87.
Yarrow, M. R., C. G. Schwartz, H. S. Murphy, L. C. Deasy.
1955.   The psychological meaning of mental illness in the family. *Journal of Social Issues* 11:12–24.

Prepaid Health Care and the New "Demanding" Patient

The future dimensions of medical practice in the United States are beginning to emerge now, both through the steady increase in prepaid insurance coverage for ambulatory care and through the pressure on physicians to work together in organizations. But what will be the impact of those changes on the people involved and on their relationships with each other? What will the doctor-patient relationship be like? There can be little doubt that prepaid medical care insurance plans will, by changing the economic relationship between doctor and patient, also change many ways in which they interact. And there can also be little doubt that when physicians routinely work in organizations where they are cooperating rather than competing with colleagues, other elements of their relationships with patients and colleagues will change.

Obvious as it is that change will occur, we have rather little information relevant to anticipating its human consequences. We have fairly good estimates of the economic consequences of those changes in the organization of medical care, and we have hopeful evidence on how the medical quality of care might be affected, but between the input and output measures there is only a black box: we have little information on how the human beings in medical practice produce the results that are measured, on the quality of their experience in practice, and on the

© 1973 by the Milbank Memorial Fund. Reprinted from the *Milbank Memorial Fund Quarterly/Health and Society* 51 (Fall 1973) by permission.

characteristic ways they try to manage their problems at work. Without knowing something about that, it is rather difficult to anticipate how doctor-patient relationships will change and what problems will be embedded in them.

This paper provides information about how the participants in a medical care program that anticipated present-day trends responded to each other and to the economic and social structure of practice. The data upon which I shall draw come from an eighteen-month field study of the physicians who worked in a large, prepaid group practice. Most of the primary practitioners (internists and pediatricians) worked on a full-time basis in the medical group, and most of the consultants worked part-time, but all fifty-five of them were on salary, officially employees of the institution. Their medical group contracted with an insurance organization to provide virtually complete care to insured patients without imposing on them any out-of-pocket charges. In studying the physicians of the medical group, a very large amount of observational, documentary, and direct evidence was collected in the course of examining files, attending all staff meetings, listening to luncheon-table conversations, and carrying out a series of intensive interviews with all the physicians in the group. The research obtained a systematic and comprehensive view of how the group physicians worked and what their problems were. Here, however, only a summary of findings bearing on a single issue is possible.

THE ADMINISTRATIVE STRUCTURE OF THE GROUP

To understand practice in the medical group, it is necessary to understand the framework in which it was carried out. The group did not have an elaborate administrative structure, since it lacked clear gradations of rank and authority and had rather few written, formal rules. It was not organized like a traditional bureaucratic organization. The few rules that were bureaucratically enforced all dealt in one way or another with the *terms* of work—with how and what the physician was to be paid, and the amount of time he was to work in return for that pay. Ultimately, the terms of work were less a function of the medical group administration than of the health insurance organization with which the medical group entered into a contract. The absolute income available for paying the doctors derived primarily from the insurance contract, which specified a given sum per year per insured person or family, plus additional sums by a complicated formula not important for present purposes. The administration of the medical group could decide how to divide up the contract income among the physicians but had to work within the absolute limits of that income.

By the same token, critical aspects of the *conditions* of work stemmed more from the terms of the service contract than from the choice and action of the group administration. The most important complaint of the physicians about the conditions of work in the medical group was of "overload"—having to provide more services in a given period of time than was considered appropriate. Such overload was a direct function of the prepaid service contract, which freed the subscriber from having to pay a separate fee for each service he wished, and encouraged many physicians to manage patient demands by increasing referrals and reappointments.

It was around these externally formulated contractual arrangements that we found the administration of the medical group establishing and enforcing the firmest bureaucratic rules, perhaps because it had no other choice than to do so in order to satisfy its contract to provide services. The prepaid service-contract arrangement could be conceived of as purely economic in character—simply a rational way of *paying* for health care, which did not influence health care itself. But it was much more than that, since it organized demand and supply, the processes by which health care takes place. In fact, it was closely connected with many of the problems of practice in the group. This is not to say that it created those problems in and of itself. Rather, it gave rise to new possibilities for problematic behavior on the part of both patient and physician and prevented the use by both of traditional solutions. To understand its relationship to the problems of practice in the medical group, to the way the physicians made sense of their experience, and to the ways they attempted to cope with it, let us first examine the way the physicians responded to the differences they perceived between prepaid service-contract group practice and private, fee-for-service solo practice.

ENTREPRENEURIAL AND CONTRACT GROUP PRACTICE

All of the physicians interviewed, including those who had left the group and were solo practitioners at the time of being interviewed, had at one time or another worked on a salary in the medical group. Thus, they reported on circumstances in which they could not themselves charge the patient a fee for the services they rendered. Their income was independent of the services they gave, just as the cost to the patient was independent of the services he received. The patient demanded and the physician supplied services on the basis of a prepayment contract that established a right for the patient and an obligation for the physician. Furthermore, the group was organized on a closed-panel basis, so that in order to obtain services by the terms of his contract, without out-of-pocket cost, the patient had to seek service only from the physicians working at the medical group, and no others.

Virtually all of the physicians interviewed had also had occasion to work on the traditional basis of solo, fee-for-service "private" practice. In that mode of organizing work and the marketplace, the physician makes a living by attracting patients and providing them with services paid for by a fee for each service. The physician's income is directly related to the fee charged and the number of services provided. He has no contractual relationship with patients. He must attract them by a variety of devices—accessibility, reputation, specialty, referral relations with colleagues—and maintain a sufficiently steady stream of new or returning patients to assure a stable if not lucrative practice. In theory, the patient is free to leave him for another physician, and relations with colleagues offering the same services are at least nominally competitive.

How did the physicians interpret these different arrangements and what did they emphasize in their experience with each? In the interviews, the prepaid group physician was often represented as helpless and exploited, with words like "trapped," "slave," and "servitor" used to describe his position. Since the contract was for all "necessary" services, however, it was hardly accurate to say that the physicians had to provide every service the patient demanded. They could have refused. But at bottom the formal contract itself was not really the issue. Rather, the physicians were responding to the absence of a mechanism to which they were accustomed, a mechanism which, by attesting to the value of the physician's services in the eyes of the patient and by testing the strength of the patient's sense of need, precluded the necessity of actually refusing. The physicians were responding to the absence of the out-of-pocket fee that is a prerequisite for service in private practice.

The fee was seen as a useful barrier between patient and doctor, a toll which forced the *patient* to discriminate between the trivial and the important before he sought care. The assumption was that if the patient had to pay a fee for each service, he would ask only for "necessary" services, or, if he were too irrational or ignorant to discriminate accurately, he would at the very least restrict his demands to those occasions when he was really greatly worried. The fee served as a mechanical barrier that freed the physician of having to refuse service and of having to persuade the patient that his grounds for doing so were reasonable. Since a fee operates as a barrier in advance of any request for service, it reduces interaction between physician and patient. In the prepaid plan, the physicians were not prepared for the greater interaction that the absence of a fee encouraged.

In addition to the service contract, there was also the closed-panel organization of the medical group. The physicians themselves were aware that some patients often felt trapped, since, in order to receive the benefits of their contract, they had to use the services only of a physician employed by the medical group. If the patient wanted to be treated by a particular individual in the group, he might nonetheless have to accept another because of the former's full panel or appointment schedule. And when patients were referred to consultants, they were supposed to be referred to a specialty, not to an individual specialist. Some of the physicians themselves found this situation unsatisfactory because they were not personally chosen by patients but were seen by patients because they happened to have appointment time free or openings on their panel, not because of their individual reputation or attractiveness.

Finally, there was the issue of group practice itself, of the constitution of a cooperative collegium rather than, as in entrepreneurial practice, an aggregate of nominally competing practitioners. In the latter case, the physician may be "scared that somebody would . . . take his patient away" or that the patient may "walk out the door and you may never see him again." Nevertheless, if he can afford it, the physician in fee-for-service solo practice can choose to refuse to give the patient what he asks for, and can even discourage him from returning. But in the group practice, the physicians did not generally have the option of dropping a patient with whom they had difficulty. The reason was not to be found in any potential economic loss, as in entrepreneurial practice, but rather in the closed-panel practice within which colleagues were cooperating rather than competing. When physicians form a closed-panel group, they cannot simply act as individuals, "drop" a patient who is troublesome, and allow him to go to a colleague, for if each of the group dropped his own problem patients, while he would indeed get rid of the ones he had, he would get in return those his colleagues had dropped, as his colleagues would get his. And so the pressure was to "live" with such patients and try to manage them as best one could—something for which the physician with ideological roots in private practice was poorly prepared.

From the view presented by the physicians, it seemed that the medical group involved them in a situation in which traditional safety valves had been tied down and the pressure increased. The service contract was thought to increase patient demand for services, while at the same time it prevented the physician from coping with that demand by the traditional method of raising prices. The closed-panel arrangement restricted the patients' demands to those physicians working cooperatively in the medical group, so the physicians could not cope with the pressure by the traditional method of encouraging the troublesome patient to go elsewhere for service. Confrontation between patient and physician was increased, and both participants explored new methods for resolving them. Indeed, the insurance scheme itself provided the resources for some of those new methods of reducing the pressure on demand and supply.

PARADIGMATIC PROBLEMS AND SOLUTIONS

The basic interpersonal paradigm of a problematic doctor-patient relationship may be seen as a conflict between perspectives and a struggle for control or a negotiation over the provision of services. From his perspective the patient believes he needs a particular service; from his, the physician does not believe every service the patient wishes is necessary or appropriate. The content of this conflict between perspectives is composed of conceptions of knowledge, or expertise, the physician asserting that he knows best and the patient insisting that he is his own arbiter of need.

The conflict, however, takes place in a social and economic marketplace, which provides resources that may be used to reinforce the one or the other position. In the case of medicine in the United States, that marketplace has in the past been organized on a fee-for-service basis, practitioners being entrepreneurs competing with each other for the fees of prospective patients. The fee the patient is willing and able to pay, in conjunction with the physician's economic security, constitute elements that are of strategic importance to private practice. If the physician's practice is well enough established, he can refuse service he does not want to give or does not believe necessary to give, even though he loses a fee and possibly a patient. On the other hand, if he desires to gain the fee and reduce the chance of losing the patient, he may give the patient the service he requests even if he believes it to be unnecessary. Like a merchant, he is concerned with pleasing his patients by giving them what they want, suspending his own notions of what is necessary and good for them in favor of his gain in income should he desire such gain.

The patient, on the other hand, has his fee as a resource (if he is lucky), and the freedom to turn away from the practitioner who does not provide him with the service he wants and pay it instead to the physician who does. He may take his trade elsewhere, but before he does he may introduce pressure by implying that if he does not get what he wants he will find someone else. In essence, the patient can play "customer" to the physician's merchant.

In contrast to these marketplace roles, there are those more often ascribed to doctor and patient by sociologists—that of expert consultant and layman. The layman is defined as someone who has a problem or difficulty he wishes resolved but who does not have the special knowledge and skill needed to do so. He seeks out someone who has the necessary knowledge and skill and cooperates with him so that his difficulty can be managed if not resolved. In dealing with the expert, the layman is supposed to suspend his own judgment and instead follow the advice of the expert. When there are differences of opinion of such character that the patient cannot bring himself to cooperate, the *generic* response of the expert is to attempt to gain the patient's cooperation by persuading him, on the basis of evidence which the expert produces, that it would be in his interest to cooperate and follow the recommended course. To *order* him to comply or to gain compliance by some other form of coercion or pressure is a contradiction of the essence of expertise and its "authority." Analytically, expertise gains its authority by its persuasive demonstration of special knowledge and skill relevant to particular problems requiring solution. It is the antithesis of the authority of office.

As a profession, however, medicine represents not only a full-time occupation possessed of expertise that participates in a marketplace where it sells its labor for a profit, but more particularly an occupation that has gained a specially protected position in the marketplace and a set of formal prerogatives that grant it some degree of official authority. For example, the mere possession of a legal license to practice allows the physician to officially certify death or disability and to authorize pharmacists to dispense a variety of powerful and dangerous drugs. Here, albeit in rudimentary form, we find yet a third facet by which to characterize a third kind of doctor-patient relationship— that of the bureaucratic official and client. The latter seeks a given service from the former, who has exclusive control over access to services. The client seeks to establish his need and his right, while the official seeks to establish his eligibility before providing service or access to goods or services. In theory, both are bound by a set of rules that defines the rights and duties of the participants, and each makes reference to the rules in making and evaluating claims. In a rational-legal form of administration, both have a right of appeal to some higher authority who is empowered to mediate and resolve their differences.

In the predominant form of practice in present-day United States, the physician is more likely to be playing the role of merchant and expert than the role of official, though the latter is real enough and too important to be as ignored as it has been by sociologists and physicians alike. It is, after all, his status as an official that gives the physician a protected marketplace in which to be a merchant. Nonetheless, to be a true official virtually precludes being a merchant, so that only in special instances in the United States can we find medical practice that offers the possibility of taking the role of official on an everyday rather than an occasional basis.

The medical group we studied was just such a special instance, for it eliminated the fee and discouraged the profit motive, while setting up its physicians as official gatekeepers to services specified in a contract with patients, through an insurance agency with supervisory powers of its own. The contractual network specified the basic set of systematic rules and established the official position of the physician. Under the rules, the physician served as an official gatekeeper to and authorizer of a whole array of services—not only his own but also those of consultants who, even though "covered" in the contract, would not see a patient without an official referral, and those of laboratories, which do not provide "covered" tests without an official group physician's signature. In other reports of this study I show how the physicians were led to use their official powers to cope with problems of work and how they exercised their role of expert. I also show how some railed against a situation that prevented them from using the more familiar techniques of the merchant to resolve their problems.

Here, however, I wish to point out that in the medical group the physician was not the only participant to whom a new role was made available. The situation, which left open the option of official and closed the option of merchant for physicians, also left open the option of bureaucratic client and closed the option of shopper or customer for patients. And when the patients acted as bureaucratic clients they posed different problems to the physician than they did when they acted as a customer, or as a patient: they asserted their rights in light of the rules of the contract. This untraditional possibility for patient behavior was one that upset the physicians a great deal and served as the focus for much of their dissatisfaction. Most of their problems of work stemmed ultimately from their relationships with patients and tended to be characterized in terms of the patient, so that it is important to understand the way the physicians saw their patients. Typically, work problems stemmed from patients who "make demands"; "the demanding patient" was seen as the root of those difficulties.

THREE TYPES OF "DEMANDING PATIENT"

It is very easy to get the impression from this analysis that the work-lives of the group physicians were constantly fraught with pressure and conflict. Such an impression stems partially from the strategy of analysis I have chosen, a strategy which focuses on work problems rather than on the settled, everyday routines that stretch out on either side of occasional crises. Without remembering that most medical work is routine rather than crisis, one could not understand how physicians manage to get through their days. Indeed, the kinds of medical complaints and symptoms that are most often brought into the office were such that the daily routine posed a serious problem of boredom to the practitioners. Furthermore, most patients were not troublesome. As members of the stable blue- and white-collar classes, most knew the rules of the game, respected the physicians, and were more inclined than not to come in with medically acceptable (even if "trivial") complaints.

Nonetheless, the fact of routine, even boredom, would be difficult to discern in the physicians' own conversations. They did not talk to each other, or to the interviewers, about their routines; they talked about their crises. They did not talk about slow days but about those when the work pressure was overwhelming. They rarely talked about "good" patients unless they received some unusual letter of thanks, card, or gift of which they were proud; they talked incessantly about troublesome or demanding patients. They almost never talked about routine diagnoses and their management but talked often about the anomaly, the interesting case, or one of their "goofs." So the analytical strategy for reporting this study is not arbitrary, since it reflects the physicians' own preoccupations. It was by the problematic that they symbolized their work and it was in terms of the problematic that they evaluated their practice. Even though all agreed that "demanding patients" were statistically few in number, many who left the medical group ascribed their departure to their inability to bear even those few patients.

Most important for present purposes was the fact that, upon analysis of the physicians' discussion of "demanding patients," it was discovered that the most important kind of demanding patient was one they had not encountered in fee-for-service practice. The patients posed demands that the physicians were unaccustomed to meeting, for the demands stemmed from the contractual framework of practice in the medical group and were generic to the role of the bureaucratic client rather than the customer or layman. Perhaps this was why they seemed so outrageous and insulting, for such demands treated the physicians as if they were officials rather than "free professionals." The distinction between that kind of demandingness and others was more often implicit than explicit in the physicians' talk when they were asked to characterize demanding patients. The tendency, however, was to distinguish one kind of demanding patient as dictatorial and another as essentially the opposite—eternally supplicatory.

The supplicant would be familiar to the informed reader as the ambulatory practice version of the "crock" met in complaints by medical students and the house staff in the clinics of teaching hospitals. The crock was the person who played the respectful patient role but presented complaints for which the physician had no antibiotic, vaccine, chemical agent, or technique for surgical repair. All the physician could provide for such complaints was what he considered palliative treatment rather than cure. He neither learned anything interesting by seeing some biologically unusual condition nor felt he accomplished successful therapy. And he worried that he might overlook something real.

Clearly, this kind of demanding patient was irritating because he had to be babied rather than treated instrumentally and because the doctor had to devote himself to treating people whom he considers to be well or simply anxious. Furthermore, he confronted the doctor with failure: he "can never be reassured. You know you are not getting anywhere with him and you just have to listen to him, the same chronic minor complaints and the same business." "I'm just not satisfied with my results, and the patient just keeps coming back, worse than ever."

In light of the distinctions I made earlier, it should be clear that this kind of demanding person was not playing either the role of bureaucratic client or that of customer. The role of the helpless layman was adopted, which did not contradict the role the physician wished to play. The problem was that the nature of the complaints was such that the medical worker could not play his role in a satisfying way—he could not really help, and his advice that there was no serious medical problem was refused.

The other kind of demanding patient was quite different, however, for he did not ceaselessly *beg* for help so much as *demand* services on the basis of his economic and contractual rights. Such rights do not, of course, exist in fee-for-service solo practice, but the analogue in such practice would be the demanding customer. Such a person is more likely to shop around from one physician to another rather than stick to one and demand his service. Given the structure of fee-for-service solo practice, we should expect in it rather less confrontation with demanding customers, though the physicians did tell stories about some who openly threatened to take their business elsewhere if they did not get what they wanted. Rare as such confrontation was, when it did occur, it was described with the same shock and outrage as was observed in the physicians' stories about demanding contract patients.

In speaking of the "power of the contract" one physician implied correctly that some patients, playing the role of bureaucratic client, threatened to and on occasion actually employed the device of an official complaint. They could complain either to the administration of the medical group or to an office established by the insuring organization to receive and investigate complaints. After all, if one has a contract, one also has the right to appeal decisions about its benefits. And naturally, the more familiar and effective with bureaucratic procedures the patients were, the more they were able to make trouble. The seventeen physicians who generalized about the social characteristic of demanding patients yielded in sum a caricature of the demanding patient as a female schoolteacher, well educated enough to be capable of articulate and critical questioning and letter writing, of high enough social status to be sensitive to slight and to expect satisfaction, and experienced with bureaucratic procedures. In the physicians' eyes, they were also neurotically motivated to be demanding.

Also specially nurtured in the framework of the prepaid group practice—contrary to the ideal of bureaucracy but faithful to its reality—was the use by the bureaucratic client of "pull" or political influence to reinforce his demands and gain more than nominal contract benefits. Analogous to political influence in the free medical marketplace is the possession of wealth or prestige, making one a desirable customer who may refer his friends to the physician. Another form of "pull" lies in having connections with an especially influential and prestigious medical colleague. Both types of patients gain special handling in solo practice. In the medical group, however, "pull" was more related to influence in those segments of the community engaged in negotiating insurance contracts. There were occasional instances when a demanding patient was also an important member of a trade union or had friends in high political places. Managing such patients was particularly difficult for the administration, since it was unable to protect its own staff in the face of such political influence.

MANAGING DEMANDING PATIENTS IN THE FUTURE

I have assumed that a prepaid service-contract medical group has important characteristics that will become more common in the future and therefore allow us to make plausible and informed anticipations of the problems of medical practice in the future. On the basis of extensive interviews with physicians who worked in such a medical group, I suggested that a new kind of problem of management was posed to them by the social and economic structure of their practice. Ostensibly, the problem was the familiar and traditional one of the demanding patient. Looking more closely at the usage of that phrase, however, led to the conclusion that there was more than one kind of demanding patient. Indeed, on the basis of the physicians' discussions of their problems, I suggested that there were three types of demanding patient, each posing a different problem of management and a different challenge to medical self-esteem.

Virtually unmet in the medical group (but mentioned by the physicians) were those who acted like demanding customers by insisting on either obtaining the services they wished or taking their business (and fees) elsewhere. Such a strategy is of course generic to entrepreneurial practice, and most effective with weakly established practitioners in a highly competitive medical market. The second type of demanding patient was the traditional "crock," what a spokesman for Kaiser-Permanente once called "the worried well." Such a patient persisted in seeking consultation for complaints that the physicians felt were trivial and essentially incurable. They were a more serious problem in the medical group than they were reported to be in fee-for-service solo practice because their demands could not be reduced by the imposition of a fee barrier or by suggesting that they go elsewhere for service. The third type of demanding patient was new and particularly disturbing to the physicians—the patient who demanded services that he felt he had a right to under the terms of his prepaid service contract and who had recourse to complaining about the deprivation of his rights to the bureaucratic system of appeal and review.

In the future, with prepaid group practice far more common, we should expect new problems in the doctor-patient relationship as that new kind of demanding patient is met with by more physicians. Insurance coverage in the future may be such as to maintain some kind of fee barrier (as in prepaid plans which now impose small charges for house calls), but the barrier will be less than that to which physicians were accustomed in fee-for-service practice and will be less effective in discouraging demandingness. In addition, since he will be working cooperatively with colleagues in group practice, the physician will be less able to simply "drop" his demanding patients. Unable to use money or evasion to cope with his relationship to problem patients, the physician will have to use other methods. What options are open to him?

Just as the structure of fee-for-service solo practice produces the possibility of using mechanical financial solutions, so does the structure of prepaid service-contract practice also produce the possibility of using mechanical solutions. The mechanical solutions observed in the medical group studied lay in providing all services covered by the contract that were not inconvenient to the practitioner—office visits, referrals, and laboratory tests. (The house call was not convenient and was resisted strongly.) But whereas the former solutions were traditional and so regarded as "natural" and "reasonable," the use of the latter was regarded as "giving in," and treated with resentment and concern. Both are, analytically, equally mechanical, an equally passive reflex to the organization of the system of care.

The consequences of passive response to the new conditions by which patient demand will be structured are already clear. In the face of rising services and costs, strong administrative, financial, and peer-review pressures will force the physician to limit his "giving in" and restrict the supply of demanded services. But how exactly can the physician limit services, and what kind of interaction will go on between him and his patient under such circumstances? I cannot provide empirical evidence from my study because in the medical group there was rather little organized pressure to limit services. The physicians could "give in" when they chose to. But the logic of my analysis would lead me to expect that when there is pressure to limit service to demanding patients in a structure like that of the medical group, the structure taken by itself provides the opportunity for doing so on the bureaucratic grounds of the official authority of the physician as a gatekeeper to benefits. He can simply refuse the patient, standing on the official position that the structure provides him.

But it need not be that way. While the prepaid service-contract group practice virtually precluded the adoption by physician and patient of a merchant-customer relationship and allowed the adoption of an official-client relationship that was precluded in private solo practice, it did not *force* the practitioners to manage their problems that way. Some chose to adopt the interactional strategy inherent in medical practice no matter what the historical framework in which it takes place—the strategy of the expert consultant who relies neither on his position in the marketplace nor on his official position in a bureaucratic system but on his knowledge and skill. Some physicians were persuaded that if they invested extra attention and energy in educating their patients and developing a relationship of trust they would ultimately have fewer management problems. To cope with suspicion on the part of the patient they initially provided services on demand in order to show that they recognized the legitimacy of the patient's contractual rights and that they were not motivated to withhold services from them. At the same time, however, they tried to explain to the demanding patient the grounds for their judgment that the services were medically unnecessary. They undertook, in other words, to persuade and demonstrate, and they avoided mechanical solutions to the problem of demandingness. The social, moral, and technical quality of the medical care of the future will depend on whether medical practice will be organized in such a way as to encourage such a positive mode of responding to patient demands, or whether it will, like traditional practice, be merely a fiscally and technically functional structure that does not take cognizance of the human qualities of those it traps.

PART TWO

The Organization of Colleague Relations

The Organization and Control of Medical Work

In the first section of this book I was concerned with the most enduring and ubiquitous element of health care—the relationship between someone seeking help and a consultant, someone believed to be an expert who can provide help. My discussion concentrated on analytic variables connected with the characteristics of the individuals involved in that relationship, some stemming from their position in the world outside the place of consultation and some peculiar to the roles they play in the course of consultation. But while it cannot be denied that differences in social status, disability, and expertise influence the content as well as the balance of the interaction between doctor and patient, fuller understanding requires taking into account additional factors.

In conceptualizing referral systems in chapter 3, I began to explore some of those factors. Still others were introduced in chapter 4, where I discussed the consequences for the doctor-patient relationship of a particular method of organizing the practice of physicians and their economic relations with patients. It imposed constraints influencing the content and character of interaction that are at least partly independent of the characteristics of the individuals themselves. The focus of this and the succeeding five chapters is on the formal organization of practice arrangements and on the contractual relations between doctors and patients, between doctors and their colleagues, and between doctors and "third parties" who negotiate the provision of medical care on behalf of the patient. The central issue is *control:* the way the social organization of practice influences medical work for better or for worse.

The organizational, contractual, and economic elements involved in practice arrangements should each be dealt with separately, for each is sufficiently different to have potentially different effects, and each can vary independently of the other. If payment is made by a third party rather than by patients themselves, then another actor is introduced into the equation; variations in the characteristics, aims, activities, and resources of that third party exert an influence on the interaction between doctor and patient even though they are alone in the consultation room. If, in turn, there is a contractual arrangement that obliges the physician to provide certain kinds and amounts of care, that too will patently have some effect on both the relationship and on the substance of the physician's performance. And of course the method and amount of payment may be cited as another variable of importance. But rather less attention has been paid to the social organization of the practice itself.

CONTRACT AND ORGANIZATION

As will be indicated in chapter 6, one can conceive of a range in the social organization of practice that encompasses a completely individual or "solo" practice, a network of physicians who practice alone but refer patients to each other, a loose association of physicians sharing physical facilities and support services, a small practice organization whose physicians share both expenses and income and cooperate in treating patients, and large practice organizations with a formal administrative structure within which a number of doctors work in a fairly comprehensive division of labor.

That typology seems as applicable to medical practice today as it did yesterday. The changes of the past decade or two have been in the legal, economic, and administrative environment of medical work, which has encouraged an increase in some types of organization and a decline in others, but no really new forms of organization. Those changes have also added new forms of contractual relations, but they vary independently of social organization.

Much of the analysis of health care practice today has devoted itself exclusively to contractual relations and modes of paying the doctor while ignoring that other, independent variable of the social organization of practice. This is nowhere more evident than in the pervasive use of the ambiguous label Health Maintenance Organization (HMO) to designate what is in fact several analytically and empirically different forms of organization that have little in common but a prepaid health service contract. Physicians can be considered part of an HMO when they work alone in their own offices, when they are partners who own and manage a practice organization, or when they are employees of a practice organization. They can be paid on a fee-for-service basis, a capitation basis, or a salaried basis and still be part of an HMO. So long as they have contracted to provide care to insured patients for a set annual sum, they are part of an HMO. Variations in the extent and degree of the physicians' interaction with each other, in the degree to which they exercise control over organizational policy, and in other elements of social organization are insignificant, the contract setting the economic terms of medical work being the key to expected efficiencies.

This virtually exclusive preoccupation with contractual relations assumes that the only really important source of influence over the physician's behavior lies in the source and method of payment and the nature of the contract governing it. It is true that when the fortunes of physicians are tied together by a common contractual scheme, the expectation is that they will make an effort to influence each other's behavior, but the vast majority of physicians do not work under such contractual arrangements. Most payment policies ignore the implications of the social organization of practice and its potential for influencing the doctor's decisions. They are established on the implicit assumption that physicians make their utilization, treatment, and billing decisions purely as individuals, not only calculating their own self-interest but doing so wholly alone, without being influenced by others. The social organization implicit in those assumptions is solo practice.

SOLO PRACTICE

Solo practitioners have long been considered to be a declining breed. And indeed, there has been a statistical trend away from such practice. It is possible that the trend is slowing, if not reversing, if only because efforts to reduce costly hospitalization have encouraged physicians and surgeons to provide services on an ambulatory basis that were previously provided in the hospital. This has probably encouraged some physicians to do more of their work outside the hospital, in their own offices. While the capital cost of outfitting ambulatory care practices with the personnel and equipment necessary for such services is too great for most individuals to bear, this is not the case for all. Until (as appears inevitable) new review and reimbursement policies designed to control the rapidly increasing cost of ambulatory care are instituted, it is premature to write off solo practice as an empirically significant form today.

What is important about solo practice as a mode of organizing medical work? Sociologically, the most important element distinguishing solo practice from more collective forms is its lack of direct observability and accountability to other physicians. In essence, those who practice alone are not subject to the day-to-day influence of anyone but the patients they see in the lay referral system. Particularly in primary care, the influence of the physicians they refer to is at best attenuated and only occasional. Thus, the performance of doctors practicing alone outside of the hospital can be shaped almost wholly by their personal character and their training, in interaction with their patients and the reimbursement policies of health insurance programs.

Physicians in such practices come closest to being able to conform to the assumption of individualistic economic calculation and rationality, but because they are more dependent than those in other kinds of practice on the satisfaction of their patients and because they do not work within the confines of an organization, they are more likely to have to engage in negotiation and compromise than are their colleagues in other kinds of practice.

GROUP PRACTICE AND THE HMO

Solo practice remains important both as an empirical form of organization and a symbolic ideal of independence. When all is said and done, however, other forms of organization are considerably more important for social policy. Perhaps the most common forms are what I call in chapter 6 the association and the small two- or three-person partnership. Physicians in those practices may very well make up the majority of those participating in the prepaid service plans known as HMOs: they are joined together with others in a financial scheme whereby they agree to accept from an insurer a fixed annual sum of money (known as capitation) for each insured patient in return for which they agree to provide all contractually specified services deemed necessary for that patient. The capitation fees form a pool of funds out of which participating physicians can be paid fees for each service they provide. Should participating physicians exhaust the pool, however, they must tap their own income to balance the books.

Obviously, under such circumstances, even though the physicians may practice alone or with two or three others in their own private offices, they are bound together in a joint enterprise. Each physician's billing reduces the pool on which the income of all depends. And while each individual's medical performance may not be directly observable to the other, at the very least claims records are, and they are subject to comparison with those of the other participants. Such a scheme deliberately creates the economic incentive for participating physicians (or their administrative representative) to identify those individuals who make the greatest claims on the common pool by billing for more than the average number of services or billing for expensive services, and to attempt to discourage them from doing so. Such attempts have been reported in the health industry news media, but we have no systematic and detailed information on how these constraints are generated and organized and how they affect colleague and patient relations and medical work itself.

Chapters 7, 8, 9, and 10 address a different kind of HMO, however—a type that has long been considered by some to be the ideal form of practice. I refer to prepaid *group* practice. In a group practice HMO, as in other HMOs, physicians representing a broad range of specialties work on a prepaid service basis, their work financed by capitation payments and their obligation being to provide all services specified by the contract without further payment by insurer or patient. However, unlike those in solo practice and in associations, those in group practice literally work together under the same roof with shared resources. They also see each others' patients—those in one specialty may see colleagues' patients when they are on emergency call or covering for those on vacation, and patients are referred back and forth among the various specialists in the group. Together they can generate a comprehensive patient record that can avoid much of the fragmentation of information and treatment that American medicine is often accused of.

The conditions of group practice are thought to maximize the degree to which physician performance is routinely subject to the direct observation of colleagues. This is a prerequisite for a truly collegial or peer-review method of assuring the professional quality of medical work. But if each person's work is observable to only a few in the group, only they, not the group as a whole, can evaluate it. And if those who are in a position to evaluate it are not inclined to discuss their judgment with others, including those they judge, they cannot influence the quality of their colleagues' medical work. A critical question for appraising variations in the social organization of prepaid group practice, therefore, is the extent to which they maximize the observability of medical performance to all members of the staff and institutionalize accountability and control.

Group practice can be organized in a number of different ways, at least some of which influence the extent to which the performance of individuals can be observable to others as well as the degree to which control over performance can be exercised. As chapter 7 shows, the division of labor between specialties limits the extent to which all specialties can in fact collaborate in seeing the same patients and observe each other's performance. No doubt some of that division of labor is subject to change so that more mutual observability may be possible, but the very nature of specialization limits observability. Merely working together under the same roof is not enough for maximizing observability. The only way that barriers to information and evaluation can be overcome is to institutionalize review by the use of such devices as case conferences involving all members of the division of medical labor.

However, while observability is a necessary condition for the exercise of collegial control of performance, it is not sufficient. As chapter 8 will show in its case study of one prepaid service contract medical group, the attitudes and values of practitioners can be such as to suppress critical judgment of the performance of colleagues. Furthermore, they can also discourage communicating critical judgments to other colleagues or attempting to correct a colleague's inadequate work. Without attitudes that support the critical evaluation and correction of the work of colleagues, institutionalized forms of peer review are meaningless.

Finally, there is the question of the administrative structure of group practice—the constitution of its governing and policymaking authority and the position of investors, consumers, and practitioners in the structure. As chapter 9 will show, there can be great variation in such organization, from highly bureaucratic and monocratic forms to very loosely organized individualistic forms. The study reported in the succeeding chapters was made before HMOs were widely established, so that prepaid service contracts were restricted to a limited number of what were then atypical groups. Were a study to be done today of group practice HMOs, the common denominators of prepaid service contracts, government regulations, and the requirements of private insurers would likely make for a more narrow range, but there is still significant variation in the organization of such groups today that is well worth close examination.

A number of commentators have been concerned with the development of organized practices that are owned by lay investors— unions, nonprofit organizations, and the like—rather than by physicians themselves. Like those concerned about the decline of self-employment in medicine, however, they assume that a particular formal status has direct and invariable bearing on the way work is organized and performed, that ownership by lay investors, for example, will inevitably force physicians into favoring commercial over professional practices. It does not take much thought to reject that assumption, however, for owners have many options to choose from in attempting to gain their ends from their enterprises. Among the possibilities are the exercise of control directly over the staff, the delegation of authority to a lay or a physician manager who is directly responsible to them, or the delegation of authority to a governing board representing the staff.

There is little reason to believe that only one form of organization results from ownership, even by lay investors. The same may be said for employment. When employed, physicians can be helpless creatures of those governing the practice, but it is also possible that they are organized to have a strong voice in policy determination. While ownership and employment status (not to speak of consumer representation in the nominal ownership and governing structure) are not meaningless features of organization, it is difficult to infer a great deal from them in themselves. It is how they are realized in the concrete operation of the organization that is critical.

Finally, it is necessary to reiterate the point that I made in commenting on the prerequisites for an adequate system of collegial control of medical performance. The formal presence of observability and institutionalized review is not enough. Those who can observe, evaluate, and exercise collegial control must have the attitudes and values appropriate to initiating and carrying out those activities. In addition, they must have attitudes and values that are compatible with cooperative work in general and formal contractual relationships. If, for example, physicians are rugged individualists, they are likely to chafe under both bureaucratic and collegial controls and either seek out methods of circumventing them or leave the practice altogether. And if physicians are comfortable in a consultative role that is so authoritarian as to preclude negotiating with patients who are demanding a service under the terms of their contract, they can only be demoralized if not also troublesome participants. Chapter 10 provides some hints of the organizational factors connected with physician dissatisfaction and the behavior connected with it.

QUALITY AND METHODS OF CONTROL

In my discussion of both solo and more organized forms of practice I have focused on interpersonal sources that influence how medical work gets done and how medical decisions are made. I posed the basic issue as the control of medical performance. This emphasis is essential for justifying the privileged position of physicians in the economy and the expenditure of enormous personal and public resources on health care. If there is no assurance that medical work is being done well, there is little or no justification for the expenditure of those resources. Such assurance requires control of the doctor's performance. The central issue for social policy is how that control should be organized and exercised.

There can be no doubt that some degree of self-control by physicians is a critical prerequisite. And indeed, it does exist. The vast majority of physicians want to do a good job and do not consciously base their medical decisions solely on what benefits them economically. Furthermore, we may assume that their professional training has equipped them with the knowledge and skill necessary for doing good work. Essential as these factors are for establishing a sound foundation for good medical work, however, they are not enough. Intentions can be forgotten or rationalized in the face of the immediate pressures and incentives of practice. And without continuous personal effort and exposure to colleagues familiar with new bodies of knowledge and skill, one's past training becomes in time inadequate as a basis for competent decisions.

During medicine's golden age, the organized profession claimed that its selection of recruits into medicine, its medical education programs, and the normal circumstances of practice in and out of hospital did in fact assure good work from most of its members. It claimed further that its own disciplinary committees controlled those few who were grievously negligent or incompetent. But there has been increasing skepticism about the adequacy of the profession's methods of controlling the quality of medical work. The profession is being required to exercise greater formal control over the performance of its members, and in many states the disciplinary activities of licensing boards have been intensified. In addition, a massive administrative framework was set into place after the initiation of Medicare and Medicaid in order to process claims for reimbursement. This framework, in conjunction with special, legislatively established review institutions and supplemented by the claims review procedures of private insurers quickly became the most pervasive source of the control of physician performance.

Within that framework a number of different methods have been used. They can be divided into two basic types. There is first what might be called a *bureaucratic* or mechanical method of control. It relies on secondhand reports rather than on the direct observation of performance. More particularly, it relies on reports (and implicit or explicit financial claims) made on standardized forms easily reviewed and processed by computer or clerk. Those reports are approved or disapproved on the basis of formal, often quantitative standards, and if they are not approved formal economic and administrative sanctions are initiated. This method of control is best fitted to deal with what is measurable and quantifiable.

The second method might be called *collegial* or discretionary. It relies as much as possible on direct observation of performance supplemented by reports of performance (such as the medical chart) that are designed to record salient factors connected with work decisions. Performance is evaluated by those who do the work. The quantitative and qualitative standards established by medical authorities are employed, but they are qualified by reference to common experience with the idiosyncratic characteristics of individual patients, the characteristics of the particular patient population served by the practice, and such contingencies of practice as the availability of personnel, special services, and the like. Formal standards for evaluation may be used, but they are subject to suspension by discretionary, situationally qualified judgment. Both interpersonal sanctions like informal or formal censure and economic or administrative sanctions are employed. Being intrin-sically discretionary, it is a method that focuses on qualities.

Both of these methods are in use today, but I think it is accurate to say that since the primary concern of policies initiated by state and private insurers has been to control cost, the bureaucratic method has been dominant. It is true that in seeking to control cost by, for example, refusing payment claimed for a purportedly unnecessary service, quali-ty is also in some sense being controlled. Nonetheless, in most current policies control of the quality of care is primarily a contingency of the control of cost. And the control of cost takes place through the review of claims for payment submitted by physicians and health care organi-zations. The administrative procedures employed in the review of claims and the system's reliance on bureaucratic forms for information about performance represent the bureaucratic method of control.

I shall discuss the significance of this emphasis on indirect and mechanical methods of control at greater length in chapter 15. In the context of this chapter, however, it is appropriate to note that the possibility for the use of the collegial method of control exists when physicians participate in a practice where they and their medical charts are directly observable by their colleagues and when their colleagues are concerned with observing, evaluating, and controlling each other's per-formance. Group practice, of course, is one way of creating the circum-stances for such activity, at least when it is organized and financed in such a way as to be considered a collective enterprise by its staff. More attenuated but nonetheless not insignificant circumstances are devel-oped by joining solo practices and associations together through the creation of a common interest in a particular contractual scheme.

THE LIMITATIONS OF ADMINISTRATIVE DATA

What is important about organizing the medical work of individuals into practices in which they can control each other is that under those circumstances it is possible to control performance directly rather than indirectly and to do so flexibly rather than mechanically. This means that efforts at control can be grounded in the valid data of the actual circumstances and activities surrounding medical work and, what is more, deal with performance qualitatively. When patients' problems and needs fall outside the normal range or standard category and the physician's decisions must take those unique circumstances into account, they can be evaluated flexibly and intelligently. *Quality* can be the issue in a double sense.

The oldest and most pervasive administrative device being used today in an attempt to influence the doctor's performance is the review of doctor or patient claims for reimbursement. Those who submit fraudulent claims may be prosecuted or stricken from the rolls of those eligible for reimbursement. Those who claim reimbursement for purportedly unnecessary services may be discouraged from repeating the claim by being refused payment. Another device manipulates the method and amount of payment to the doctor and the amount of reimbursement or coverage to the patient, thereby creating or eliminating financial incentives. Less common, and restricted primarily to hospital care, has been formal, bureaucratic review of utilization and treatment recommendations, employing accepted medical standards as well as statistical norms or profiles established by collating the practices of a defined population of physicians.

All those devices are mechanical and bureaucratic, requiring the construction of an increasingly elaborate and expensive administrative structure for review. There is good reason to be wary of the growth of such a structure. For one thing, we may assume that those who head and staff it will develop an ideological as well as a personal vested interest in expanding it well past its true usefulness. For another, we may assume that its very logic of operation will reward conformity to statistical standards even when what is being dealt with actually falls outside the norm. Finally, and most importantly, it relies on indirect and partial measures of performance, which are seriously limited and which may in fact be unreliable and even invalid. It runs the risk of controlling how forms are filled out rather than performance itself.

The actual performance of physicians goes on inside the institutions in which care is given and is at best only reflected by the data conveyed to the bureaucratic system outside of it. The bureaucratic review system cannot determine how and why medical records and claim forms are produced and so cannot determine their validity. The categories on those forms are not filled in passively, merely reflecting medical decisions. They are chosen, and they often reflect active manipulation of bureaucratic categories rather than a passive record of what goes on. For example, the health industry media discuss such things as "DRG creep," whereby physicians choose the most advantageous diagnostic group into which they assign their patients' ills—a choice made quite as often out of concern for the patient's well-being as for their own. The actual performance of physicians is the ultimate reality of practice and the primary source of reliable and valid knowledge. The record of performance, on the other hand, can easily be invented or manipulated in order to avoid administrative attention and subvert its aims.

We have urgent need of direct study of those who produce the record and fill out the claim forms. We are not now in a position to answer the question of how we can get a better and less expensive health care system in part because we know little about what actually goes on inside health care institutions. In determining policy we rely primarily on simple administrative data involving the number and types of services from which only the crudest inferences can be made. Those inferences, in turn, are grounded both in extremely simple assumptions about what motivates doctors and patients and on unreliable, often self-serving accounts by practitioners and administrators of what *does* take place within health care settings. There is very little systematically collected data on how physicians actually do their work in their consulting rooms and what influences their performance.

THE QUESTION OF DESIRABLE MODES OF CONTROL

Everyone must agree that when those actually providing care are conscientious, competent, and sensitive to the social, economic, technical, and ethical requirements of their patients, the need for an external review system is likely to be modest. A critical question for policy, therefore, is how those characteristics can be encouraged. Certainly the kind of people selected for medical training and the spirit and substance of their training have something to do with their subsequent performance. But their experience in practice is critical to controlling performance after training. If a system of control is impersonal and remote, predicated primarily on economic incentives directed to individuals and adversarial in operation, it is likely to stimulate physicians to maximize their economic benefits. This can be done by nominal conformity to formal requirements while manipulating, even subverting them. It may be that cost will nonetheless be held down to a tolerable level, but given the remoteness of the system and the indirect character of the data it relies on for its operation, deficiencies in the human quality of care will escape it, as will elements of the technical quality of care that are directed to the idiosyncratic needs of individual patients. Surely it is desirable that in addition to cost, both the human and technical qualities of care should be controlled.

I assume that controlling physician performance through collegial interaction can overcome the deficiencies of the bureaucratic method. It can do so because it rests on different grounds. It can be based on direct, interpersonal influence, on the interaction between practitioner and patient and between practitioners themselves. By operating at the place where consultation and treatment goes on, it can exploit a far richer and more powerful repertory of incentives than can a bureaucratic system. Furthermore, being based on direct rather than indirect experience, it is less likely to be misled by formalism and abstraction in appraising performance. Most importantly, it is capable of evaluating and controlling the discretionary decisions that are essential for treating patients as fully individual human beings rather than administrative categories or industrial objects. Surely it is the more desirable method of the two. The question for policy is to determine the organizational form of practice that best supports this method.

The Organization of
Medical Practice

Work in most of the established professions is carried on publicly—in the court, the church, and the lecture hall—as often as in the
office. The doctor's work, however, is characteristically conducted in
the privacy of the consulting room, and his personal services are usually
rendered to individuals rather than to congregations or classes. Perhaps
because of these characteristics, medicine is more likely than other
established professions to be seen as involving a relationship between
two individuals—the practitioner and the patient. But this view is not
entirely correct; medicine is practiced within an organized framework
that influences both doctor and patient. Indeed, the framework of practice in the United States seems to be moving toward more elaborate
forms that may be expected to change the doctor-patient relationship.

THE CONSOLIDATION OF PROFESSIONAL
AUTHORITY

Only recently has the physician obtained widespread professional authority. Until the nineteenth century, he had too little prestige, sure

knowledge, or technique to sustain the authority he sought. As L. J. Henderson put it, not until around 1910 or 1912 could a random patient with a random disease consulting a randomly chosen doctor stand better than a 50-50 chance of benefiting from the encounter. At least until the latter half of the nineteenth century, the physician was used by a rather small proportion of the population, and in the United States he was fighting—often unsuccessfully—for licensing laws (Shryock, 1947).

The physician generally had neither de jure nor de facto control over the practice of healing. Even his "science" was unpopular, as the various healing movements and the thriving patent medicine business of that century testify. Without a truly impressive foundation and without reliable training standards, how could medicine justify its desire for occupational monopoly? Certainly not by therapeutic success, nor by ethics, nor by reference to superior education. In prosecuting Jacoba Felicia de Almania in medieval times, the medical faculty of the University of Paris had to content itself with the claim—which now appears ludicrous—that she should not practice because she was not instructed in learned theory. She never made promises, she asked for a fee only in the event of success, she cured cases when physicians failed to, but she was too "ignorant" to practice (Kibre, 1953).

By the end of the nineteenth century, however, the physician's monopoly over healing was fairly well established (cf. Berlant, 1975). Unlike the lawyer's and the clergyman's, his prestige was rising in the public eye. By the time medical education in the United States was reformed, the physician was in the virtually unprecedented position of being the symbol of healing to people in all social classes. While a few early medical specialties were in direct competition with folk specialties, the general medical practitioner acquired wholesale the clientele of a variety of folk specialists. The nostalgic image of the old-fashioned family doctor who was all things to all people is based upon that fleeting period when folk practice had declined but medical specialization was still incipient.

THE FRAGMENTATION OF MEDICAL RESPONSIBILITY

During earlier times, physicians could learn most of what they needed to know during their training period. If they were wise and creative, they could enhance their sparse formal education by continually reflecting on their accumulated clinical experience. Furthermore, significant advances in medical knowledge were few. Equipped with a small shelf of basic technical books, early physicians could conceivably work in total isolation from colleagues as efficiently as the knowledge of their age would permit, occasionally watching the work of an itinerant surgeon or dentist or glancing through one of the few medical journals of the time. By and large, they could handle as well as the next person any ailment presented to them. But by the time general practitioners had reached their peak of authority in the public eye, the proliferating new medical specialties began to chip away at their effective jurisdiction.

Specialization as such was hardly new. The Hippocratic oath itself implied a specialty involving lithotomy and, as Nittis (1939) argued, perhaps castrating slaves for the eunuch market. Indeed, in the eighteenth and nineteenth centuries there were perhaps as many "specialties" among folk practitioners as now exist among physicians: witness the specialist bone-setters, blood-stoppers, baruchers, wart-doctors, and others cited by Jones (1949). What was new was the refinement of knowledge and technique underlying specialization, and its growth within the jurisdiction of a single profession.

In addition to specialists, there arose diagnostic and therapeutic tools that, unlike the instruments in the hallowed black bag, were too expensive for any individual to own and use at his own convenience and, even if he could afford them, too complex for him to operate alone. The hospital became a locus for such capital equipment and for new specialists like radiologists and pathologists. The physician came to depend upon the hospital and the new specialties for access to new medical technology (cf. Stevens, 1971).

Clearly, with the rise of modern medicine it became difficult to practice alone and positively unrealistic for one person to assay the whole range of human ills. Over the past sixty years, general practice has declined and practice limited to particular organs, specific illnesses, or special procedures has increased markedly. In 1923, for example, only eleven percent of all physicians were engaged in limited or specialized practice, as compared to much more than seventy percent today.

The general practitioner's displacement by the specialist renders continuity and comprehensiveness of care difficult if not impossible. First, members of the same family are less and less likely to be able to go to one physician—for general problems, children go to a pediatrician and the adults to internists; for anything uncommon, both children and adults go to other specialists. This fragments the patient: when the various parts of the individual have been examined by the specialists, how are those parts to be put together again? They are not likely to be, unless someone has continuing responsibility for the patient through all his consultations with specialists. Often the parts need not be put together (sentimentalists notwithstanding), but in those fairly common disorders that seem beyond the germ theory, it does seem necessary to see and treat the patient as a whole. The idea of comprehensive care expresses the prevailing uneasiness in medical educational and policy circles about the lack of continuous, well-rounded communication between patients and their doctors.

When more than one doctor is handling a case, each must communicate with the other if the case is to be handled efficiently and well. Because the hospital has become a place where many physicians are brought together around the same bed, it can facilitate communication and coordination. Conceivably, the hospital outpatient department may also provide a milieu for such communication. But in the United States, as elsewhere, the bulk of patient care is provided outside the hospital. It is precisely in extrahospital practice that the greatest problems of coordination and communication seem likely to occur as the general practitioner has disappeared. These problems are reflected in the various ways medical practice is organized.

SOLO PRACTICE: MYTH AND REALITY

The stereotypical mode of medical practice in the United States is "solo practice"—a person working by himself in an office that he equips with his own capital, treating patients who have chosen him as their personal physician and for whom he assumes responsibility. He usually has no formal connection with colleagues.

The term *solo practice* is as often ideological as descriptive. One of its ideological connotations is the central theme of independence—the notion of professional autonomy. For such autonomy to really exist, the practitioner must work alone and have no long-term obligation to his clients; he must be able to sever his relationship to his patient at any time and vice versa. A fee-for-service market arrangement rather than a contractual arrangement is thus likely to encourage solo practice.

However, a truly autonomous fee-for-service solo arrangement is inherently unstable. It is eventually bound to fall under the control of patients, colleagues, or some "third party" (cf. Johnson, 1972). In a system of truly free competition the physician may count on the loyalty neither of his patients (with whom he has no contract) nor of his colleagues (with whom he has no ties and who are competing with him for patients). If his colleagues are competitors, he is not likely to solicit their advice or trade information with them, and he certainly will not refer his patients to them for consultations. Thus, he remains isolated from his colleagues and relatively free of their control, but at the same time he is very vulnerable to control by his clients: he must give them what they want, or someone else will attract them away. Obviously, conscientious practice under such conditions is frustrating and difficult: even though the practitioner is self-employed, he is hardly autonomous. To survive, even marginally, the true solo practitioner in a competitive milieu had to swallow his pride (see Freidson, 1961, for historical examples in medicine; see Carlin, 1962, for the solo lawyer).

Banding together against the tyranny of the client, however, results in tyranny of the colleague. Autonomy can then exist only under very special circumstances. It seems plausible that sufficiently restricting the supply of physicians (and other potential competitors) to less than is demanded avoids control by the client. If, in addition, no large initial capital investment and no consultation or institutions like hospitals are necessary for a practice, then control by colleagues can be avoided and total autonomy approached. Yet, even such autonomy rests upon collegial solidarity, for only that protects the monopoly upon which such autonomy depends.

In many areas of the United States today, the supply of physicians is sufficiently limited to avoid control by the client; but, increasingly, control by colleagues cannot be avoided, for consultation, hospitals, and capital equipment are essential to modern practice. Present-day practice is thus not solo in actuality. It embraces a large variety of organized relationships, most of which currently involve more control by colleagues than by clients, and an increasing number of which involve control by financial third parties.

SOURCES OF COOPERATIVE ARRANGEMENTS AMONG PRACTITIONERS

How do cooperative arrangements among physicians develop? To see how, let us start with an ostensibly solo, fee-for-service practice and a reasonably restricted supply of physicians. Even such a practice is only partially secure, because younger practitioners are continually entering a system that does not include the predictable retirement of the older. In answer to this threat of competition, one keeps his patients to himself; but this means a deadly grind—perpetual availability for service. To take a weekend off or a vacation, or to be sick, one's practice must be covered by colleagues who can be relied on not to "steal" patients: a cooperative arrangement is necessary.

Specialization makes the need for such organization even more pressing. Patients who must see more than one physician might become particularly attracted to any one of them. Yet, to try to avoid referrals is patently unsatisfactory, since the conscientious practitioner knows that at one time or another his patients need help he cannot give. He can send some, but not all, patients to a clinic or an outpatient department, whose staffs presumably will not "steal" them. Or he can enter a fairly definite reciprocal arrangement: the general practitioner habitually refers his patients to a few specialists whom he can trust to act ethically by eventually returning his patient to him and who, in turn, will refer patients needing general care to him.

But in the United States the general practitioner is no longer in a strong enough position to be the key "feeder" to a network of specialists. The patient is more sophisticated, and accessible specialists more numerous. Often the patient seeks his own specialists. Indeed, the general practitioner's place has been taken by "limited" or specialized generalists like the internist and the pediatrician, and in urban and suburban settings, nonprofessional referrals are often the major source of patients for the average ophthalmologist, otorhinolaryngologist, and orthopedist, as well as the obstetrician-gynecologist, allergist, and dermatologist. Nonetheless, fairly well-integrated arrangements develop among physicians, both to gain and regulate access to patients and to coordinate patient care.

THE COLLEAGUE NETWORK

The "colleague network" described by Hall may be used as the prototype of a common informal but well-integrated cooperative arrangement organizing relations among physicians in solo practice.

> Insofar as the doctors of a given community are established and possess relatively loyal clienteles, they form a system. This system can effectively exclude the intruding newcomer. On the one hand they have control of the hospital system through occupying the dominant posts therein. On the other, they tend to develop, in the course of time, through association, a sort of informal organization. Rights to position, status, and power become recognized and upheld; mechanisms of legitimate succession and patterns of recruitment become established.
>
> The provision of medical facilities in a given community, insofar as a system or an order has been established, depends heavily on such an organization. As a matter of fact, . . . institutions and clienteles are intimately related to the working of the informal organization. The allocation of positions in the institutions, the pace at which one receives promotions, the extent to which one has patients referred to him, all hinge on the workings of the informal organization. . . .
>
> Sponsorship is not necessarily a one-sided process. It permits the newcomer to share in the established system of practising medicine, but it also imposes responsibilities upon him. It obligates him to fulfill the minor positions in the institutional system. Where he needs expert advice or assistance it obligates him to turn to his sponsor. And if he is designated as successor to an established member of the profession he necessarily takes over the duties and obligations involved there. Hence the protégé is essential to the continued functioning of the established inner fraternity of the profession. (Hall, 1946)

Hall's study was done over forty years ago, when medical practice was more simply and monolithically organized. Although such a network may exist today in localities having a variety of hospitals and other hierarchically ordered medical institutions, it is much less likely to be so definite and articulated in small cities where hospitals are virtual open community institutions. Even in large cities, local governmental and low-prestige proprietary institutions provide fairly free access to physicians irrespective of their location in colleague networks. For this reason, it is safe to assume that the looser form of colleague network portrayed in the sociometric studies of Coleman, Katz, and Menzel (1966) is more common in the United States.

ELEMENTARY FORMS OF COOPERATIVE PRACTICE

Because it is entirely informal, the colleague network is the most elementary type of cooperative practice. It is also uncomfortably vulnerable to collapse: under the solo practice system, patients and hospitals are not always completely monopolized; unable to completely control the treatment environment, the colleague network may lack the reliable patronage necessary to gain the cooperation of hungry young practitioners. Furthermore, the essential good faith among colleagues may break down into petty jealousies and antipathies.

The large solo practice in the United States has developed formal techniques of self-protection. The successful physician may send his overflow to a young physician in whom he takes a sponsor's interest, but he also may—and often does—instead hire the younger person to work in his office, handle the routine cases, and make the grueling house and emergency calls. This both lightens his burden and reduces the danger of losing patients. This technique is particularly effective when it is very expensive or otherwise difficult to set up a new practice (as where practices must be bought or where competition is unusually severe), or when the person hired is not able to practice on his own (statutory restrictions on independent practice by such new primary care occupations as the physician's associate and the nurse practitioner make them optimal candidates for both extending and protecting large solo practices).

When the assistant is ready to break away and become a competitor, however, the hiring physician is very vulnerable: each young practitioner who leaves may take some patients with him. One protection is a legal document whereby the younger person agrees not to set up an independent practice in the same community. Another protection (which does not rule out the first) is to take the young doctor into partnership, sharing expenses and profits by some prearranged schedule and thereby giving him a direct stake in the maintenance and growth of the practice.

The commonest type of formal cooperative arrangement among peers is not the partnership, however, but what might be called the *association*—an arrangement whereby physicians have their own patients, from whom they collect their own fees, but share the expense of maintaining such common facilities as offices, equipment, assisting personnel, and the like. In addition, when one physician is absent the other(s) may cover for him. In various forms, this rudimentary type of formal cooperation is widespread in the United States, particularly in city "professional arts buildings" with fairly elaborate suites and in "medical centers" owned by the resident physicians (Katz, 1966).

From the association it is a short (though by no means simple) step to the small, legal *partnership*—sharing profits as well as expenses. But the pooling of fees (or "billings") is likely to be a constant bone of contention, since the practices of partners, though overlapping, are not identical—particularly when different specialties are involved; one specialist may feel he brings in more money than the other and so deserves a larger proportion of the profits.

But if such problems can be overcome, the partnership is more reliable and predictable than simpler forms of cooperation. In a colleague network, by arranging trustworthy mutual coverage, doctors can enjoy their leisure hours despite the unpredictability of their patients' demands. In the simple association this virtue is carried over: moreover, the sharing of overhead costs reduces each doctor's expenses and permits more laboratory and diagnostic equipment. The partnership adds to these virtues increased long-term financial security: the younger practitioner may see many more patients and earn much more income than he would have as an isolated practitioner attempting to build up his own practice; and the older practitioner may have a higher income at a time when patients may be leaving him or when he himself would be forced, by his decreasing energy, to relinquish them. Moreover, when more than one specialty is involved, each can make referrals to the other, with mutual advantage. Fee-splitting, of dubious ethics in informal cooperative arrangements, is ethical in the partnership. The partnership gives some protection against the competition of other practitioners, and it also facilitates communication among practitioners.

Finally, a new form of cooperation that is neither association

nor partnership has been created in response to the financial induce-
ments of the federal Health Maintenance Organization legislation: the
medical *foundation.* There, physicians in a community, practicing separately in their own offices, join to offer their patients prepaid medical
care and to share in the pool of insurance funds made available by
granting such coverage (Egdahl, 1973). Cooperation between them
seems only nominal, however.

GROUP PRACTICE

Each of these forms of cooperation requires access to a fairly large
number of patients. Cooperative practice must be comparatively large-
scale, ordering expenses, referrals, consultations, and profits into a
system that meets the needs of a larger number of people than one
physician alone can handle. The more formal the arrangement, the
more systematized and rationalized it becomes. At a certain point in
growth, a qualitative change in the form of cooperative practice is likely
to occur.

   Group practice very often designates a form of association
beyond the qualitative scope of the simple partnership, but definitions
have not been very helpful in distinguishing the two. Like *solo practice,* the term is corrupted by its ideological overtones; rather than
autonomy and independence, cooperation and interdependence are
emphasized. Nonetheless, if the term is to have much analytical value,
it must denote a range of scale. Unfortunately, the commonest definitions would cover three- to five-person partnerships, and indeed, by
that criterion, the vast majority of "group practices" is no larger
(McNamara and Todd, 1970). This semantic confusion of group practice with a growing office partnership seems to be responsible for
much of the talk about the rapid growth of "group practice" as a
genuinely new and significantly different form of organization.

   If numbers are used to define group practice, a *minimum* of
five full-time physicians—not all of them providing primary care—
would seem to be of analytical significance, though ten are far more
likely to be so. Five physicians can serve an ordinary population of
anywhere from 5,000 to 20,000 depending on the proportion of primary care providers, the financial arrangements with the patients, and
the general style of practice. As the number of patients and doctors
increases, it seems likely that some of the technical characteristics of

bureaucracy will emerge: hierarchical organization, extensive division of labor, systematic written rules and procedures, and the like. Indeed, in the survey reported in chapter 9 that took ten full-time physicians as the minimum number, such a correlation between size and bureaucratization was found. There were, however, enormous variations in formal organization.

THE GROWING ROLE OF THE THIRD PARTY

Large-scale group practice is not widespread in the United States, nor is it likely to become the norm in this century. Those in existence seem to have grown out of two quite different sources. One is the traditional entrepreneurial basis of professional practice; like a successful business, the successful practice may expand by hiring or by taking into partnership many other practitioners. Some of the most famous clinics in the United States grew that way. The other source is the increasingly important role being played by agencies that assume financial responsibility for the health care of a population—"third parties." In the past, governments have sought to provide medical care for their citizens, as have employers for their employees and consumer groups for their members (Sand, 1952). In some instances, the doctor was contracted to provide care to a population for a flat salary. In others, he was paid a retainer by a city to stay in the locality and make himself available, free nonetheless to charge each patient a fee. Many physicians in rural, "underdoctored" areas in the United States are in a position similar to that of the "public physician" of ancient Greece (Cohn-Haft, 1956)—attracted to a town by its promises of guaranteed income, housing, and well-equipped medical facilities.

Third-party payment in the United States has increased enormously in scale and scope. Until the mid-1960s, the most important third parties were the giant corporations and the trade unions that negotiated and contracted private insurance coverage for some of the health care costs incurred by employees and their families. With the Medicare and Medicaid programs, however, the federal government came to play a critical role.

The role of the third party is important in two ways. First, the third party might be seen to offset an imbalance. As we have noted, as the modern medical profession developed, the practitioner came under greater control by colleagues than by clients. If practitioners become unresponsive to their clients' needs, a third party could countervail for the client's welfare, and, unlike the individual client, has both organized power and access to expert guidance in determining a valuable policy. Thus, it can be better equipped than any individual client to counterbalance the practitioner's material interests without detracting from the technical quality of practice. Does it actually work that way? This question leads to the second point about the significance of the third party—its influence over the nature of medical practice.

A third party can simply arrange some scheme for paying the doctor for his services or—less commonly—can go so far as to set up practice units of its own (Seham, 1969). The arrangement that least influences the organization of practice continues the solo, fee-for-service tradition; the doctor claims from the third party a standard fee for each service he renders a client. All that need be added to practice is some paperwork, a somewhat less flexible fee schedule than is otherwise possible, and perhaps greater delay in payment. In return for those inconveniences the physician's practice gains a more regular and secure economic foundation, for there need be no concern as to the patient's ability or inclination to pay his bills. This is the method of payment that most third parties in Western Europe and North America have chosen, no doubt for reasons of political feasibility. Until recently, there was little inclination to do more than pay the patients' bills: governmental third parties made little effort to change the character of practice itself. But as costs have risen dramatically, legislation was passed in the United States to encourage the growth of prepaid group practice under the assumption that it could provide better-than-average care at less cost. Does the organization of practice influence the quality of care?

FORM OF PRACTICE AND THE TECHNICAL QUALITY OF CARE

The foremost question about medical practice is its consequences—the technical quality of the service it provides. It is unfortunately the question about which there is least information. However, the opinion is fairly widespread that a physician cannot practice the best possible medicine without easy access to modern diagnostic and therapeutic facilities. It is reasonable to assume that the solo practitioner who lacks access to such facilities outside hospitals is least likely to do the best for his patient. Formal cooperative arrangements, whether simple or complex, are more likely to provide the capital for extensive equipment. Furthermore, the isolation of the practicing physician from his colleagues is also believed to affect the quality of his care. It is now believed that a physician must continuously keep abreast of advances in knowledge, relying less on "education" by drug manufacturers and their representatives and more on discussions with colleagues.

As we have seen, however, solo practice is not necessarily isolated. Considerable informal but nonetheless real and important interaction can take place within loose networks of practitioners. It is only the *possibility* of relative isolation that marks solo practice off from "group practice" (whether it be a three- to five-person partnership or a large-scale medical group), in which there is higher probability that the physician will interact with colleagues.

Furthermore, care by a variety of specialists is held to be necessary these days. While solo practice does not preclude the use of specialists, group practice presumably facilitates more frequent consultation and exchange of professional information. When a number of physicians of varied specialties work together within the same organization, it is easy to refer patients and perhaps easier to communicate and coordinate information about them. Coleman, Katz, and Menzel (1966) have demonstrated the importance of colleague relations to one facet of care—prescribing drugs. It is plausible that other features of practice are equally affected by the interaction of colleagues. For example, it is thought that physicians working together are likely to observe each other's work, which may constitute a supervisory function. And the use of a common medical record system, with the continuous accumulation of information in records, may also serve supervisory functions, for while the record may not be subject to routine inspection, it may always be examined if some doubt arises about an individual's work.

In theory, then, formal rather than informal cooperative arrangements provide better medical care. However, there are only scattered bits of evidence to support the theory, and that evidence is ambiguous. Apart from outcome studies like the classic reported by Densen et al. (1960) (in which methods of paying the doctor inevitably get confounded with the social organization of practice), studies of physicians seem to indicate that wide variations in performance manage to survive within even a single formal organization. Very little is known about the processes of interaction among physicians (Greenlick, 1972), but close examination of salaried physicians in a large prepaid group practice (Freidson, 1976) indicated that while the organized circumstances of practice *permit* mutual education, supervision, and stimulation, the norms of etiquette among the physicians can neutralize those possibilities to allow each to do more or less what he pleases, almost as if he were in an isolated solo practice. Obviously, much more empirical information is needed before it can be argued that group practice as an organizational form *creates* rather than merely *permits* better technical care.

FORM OF PRACTICE AND THE HUMAN QUALITY OF CARE

Medical care is more than the application of technique and the production of some measurable physical outcome. It involves service to human beings, and it cannot be evaluated adequately except by reference to what it does to benefit those human beings—benefit not only their bodies but also their very humanity (cf. Illich, 1976). In addition to the technical quality of care, therefore, it is essential to assess its human quality and the way the organization of medical practice bears on it. The most superficial index of such quality lies in the satisfactions and dissatisfactions of its participants—primarily the patients and the physicians.

By and large, there is no widespread dissatisfaction with medical care as such in the United States. Concern has been expressed about its cost and about such matters as being kept waiting to see the doctor or obtaining evening and weekend service. But there is no evidence that anything resembling a majority of the American population (or that of any other industrial country) finds its health care to be unsatisfactory. There is some evidence, however, that a greater proportion of patients whose everyday care is provided by solo, fee-for-service practitioners tend to be somewhat more satisfied with their care than patients served by physicians in prepaid medical groups. The latter patients were prone to complain of a lack of personal interest, insufficient explanation of their condition by the doctor, waiting in the office, and difficulty in obtaining housecalls. In a study by this author, patients contrasted their experience with these two types of practice; they tended to feel that the solo, fee-for-service doctor took more "personal interest" in them, but that medical care of a technically higher quality could be obtained from the medical group (Freidson, 1961). Subsequent studies, reviewed by Mechanic and Tessler (1976), give general support to these findings. For the physician, as for the patient, large-scale group practice seems to have its problems. Just as, to patients, the symbol of satisfying care is the old-time family doctor of a golden past they never actually experienced, so, to doctors, the symbol of satisfying working conditions is a solo practice of a happier day that in fact (as has already been noted) could rarely be both financially secure and autonomous. Physicians are from a primarily middle-class background and tend more than many others to expect to be independent in their work (Freidson, 1970; Baird, 1975). The form of practice in which they believe they can be independent is the successful solo, fee-for-service, specialty practice, and they tend to evaluate their experience with other kinds of practice against that ideal (and idealized) form. Furthermore, physicians tend to subscribe to norms of propriety that are appropriate to their ideal mode of practice but positively dysfunctional for other modes (Freidson, 1976:245–46). This must be borne in mind when noting that, while Mechanic (1975) found no major differences between nongroup and group physicians in overall satisfaction, those in large, prepaid group practices did seem to have more complaints about their workload and the triviality of the problems patients brought to them. Whatever the facts of workload and patient problems, independent, fee-for-service practitioners seemed more satisfied. The latter—the vast majority of American physicians—are concerned more with the political and economic forces now encroaching on the convenience and simplicity of their desired practice arrangements (Colombotos et al., 1975). What is the direction of those forces?

THE FUTURE ORGANIZATION OF MEDICAL PRACTICE

Future organization of medical practice will be determined by many factors, not the least of which is political. Assuming no revolutionary change in the form of government of the United States for the remainder of this century, but nonetheless steadily more involvement of the state in financing and evaluating health care, it seems fair to say that the organization of medical practice will become more complex and less individualized. Just as the small, independent entrepreneur is becoming restricted to a marginal niche in trade, so is he becoming in medicine.

Not only has the practitioner become dependent on colleagues whom he must consult and on technologies to which he must have regular access, but he has tended as well toward dependence on the assistance of other workers—not only the hospital's elaborate, supportive division of labor, but also that growing corps of nurses, aides, and assistants in ambulatory practice. Finally, the trend has been toward dependence on the state for one's income.

There is no reason to believe that these trends will stop; while some may slow and level off in the future, all are likely to continue. Their net effect on the organization of practice will certainly be to remove from it the last resemblances to an individual "private" enterprise in a free market, and they will certainly encourage more and more physicians to join more elaborate forms of cooperation than they have been accustomed to. Yet, the majority of U.S. physicians are not likely to become salaried employees of large, bureaucratically organized institutions (Oppenheimer, 1973). While developments within the hospital seem to presage such a status, they seem unlikely to continue much longer. Indeed, since the cost of hospitalization has already climbed almost catastrophically, policy is likely to do all it can to discourage hospitalization in favor of ambulatory care. While large teaching hospitals are likely to expand their ambulatory care facilities, manned by salaried but transient physicians-in-training, perhaps supervised by a small full-time, salaried staff, few American hospitals are likely to do so because they would thus threaten the community physicians on whom they depend for their patients. The majority of the physicians who serve the ambulatory public are likely therefore to remain in their "private" offices and, given the nature of the political process, will continue to be paid on the piecework (or fee-for-service) basis that they prefer.

But while ostensibly solo, fee-for-service practice is likely to remain the norm in ambulatory care, its administrative and collegial context will be changed markedly—and this can change the quality of practice. It seems certain, for example, that the physician will have to report more and more standardized information to collect fees from the third party—whether government or government-subsidized private insurance companies. This is the paradoxical outcome of his very insistence on piecework rates, which presuppose more record keeping than does a flat salary. And since fee-for-service tends to be an expensive method of payment (Glaser, 1970), its financing by government may breed a political reaction, with attempts to reduce costs by close scrutiny of service claims for their propriety and "medical necessity." In this limited but significant sense bearing on "red tape," practice will indeed be bureaucratized, but it will remain an individual rather than a large-scale corporate enterprise, and the physician will remain a nominally "self-employed" worker. He will become increasingly integrated into limited cooperative arrangements like medical foundations and partnerships, taking advantage of their financial and bookkeeping benefits, but he is likely to insist on nominal financial and clinical individualism. Whether or not he will preserve that individualism past the end of this century depends in large part on whether he maintains a reasonable relationship with patients, who are becoming more and more concerned with their rights as human beings, and whether the third party accepts both his billings and his clinical decisions.

REFERENCES

Baird, L. L.
1975.   The characteristics of medical students and their views of the first year. *Journal of Medical Education* 50:1092–99.
Berlant, J. L.
1975.   *Profession and monopoly.* Berkeley: University of California Press.
Carlin, J. E.
1962.   *Lawyers on their own.* New Brunswick, N.J.: Rutgers University Press.
Cohn-Haft, L.
1956.   *The public physician of ancient Greece.* Northampton, Mass.: Smith College Studies in History, no. 42.
Coleman, J., E. Katz, and H. Menzel.
1966.   *Medical Innovation: A diffusion study.* Indianapolis: Bobbs-Merrill.
Colombotos, J., C. Kirchner, and M. Millman.
1975.   Physicians view national health insurance: A national study. *Medical Care* 13:369–96.
Densen, P., E. W. Jones, E. Balamuth, and S. Shapiro.
1960.   Prepaid medical care and hospital utilization in a dual choice situation. *American Journal of Public Health* 50:1710–26.
Egdahl, R.
1973.   Foundations for medical care. *New England Journal of Medicine* 288:491–98.
Freidson, E.
1961.   *Patients' views of medical practice.* New York: Russell Sage Foundation.

———.
1970.   *Profession of medicine: A study in the sociology of applied knowledge.* New York: Harper & Row.

———.
1976.   *Doctoring together: A study of professional social control.* New York: Elsevier.

Freidson, E., and J. Mann.
1971.   Organizational dimensions of large-scale group medical practice. *American Journal of Public Health* 61:786–95.

Glaser, W. A.
1970.   *Paying the doctor: Systems of remuneration and their effects.* Baltimore: Johns Hopkins University Press.

Greenlick, M. R.
1972.   The impact of prepaid group practice on American medical care: A critical evaluation. *Annals of the American Academy of Political and Social Science* 399:100–13.

Hall, O.
1946.   The informal organization of the medical profession. *Canadian Journal of Economics and Political Science* 12:30–41.

Illich, I.
1976.   *Medical nemesis.* New York: Pantheon.

Johnson, T.
1972.   *Professions and power.* London: Macmillan.

Jones, L. C.
1949.   Practitioners of folk medicine. *Bulletin of the History of Medicine* 23:480–93.

Katz, G.
1966.   Pilot study of medical practices in medical arts buildings. *Public Health Reports* 81:1025–30.

Kibre, P.
1953.   The faculty of medicine at Paris, charlatanism, and unlicensed medical practices in the later Middle Ages. *Bulletin of the History of Medicine* 27:1–20.

McNamara, M., and C. Todd.
1970.   A survey of group practice in the United States. *American Journal of Public Health* 60:1303–13.

Mechanic, D.
1975.   The organization of medical practice and practice organizations among physicians in prepaid and non-prepaid primary care settings. *Medical Care* 13:189–204.

Mechanic, D., and R. Tessler.
1976.   Consumer responses in varied practice settings. In D. Mechanic, *The growth of bureaucratic medicine,* pp. 119–58. New York: Wiley Interscience.

Nittis, S.

1939.   The Hippocratic oath in reference to lithotomy. *Bulletin of the History of Medicine* 6:719–28.

Oppenheimer, M.

1973.   The proletarianization of the professional. In *Professionalization and social change*, ed. P. Halmos, pp. 213–27. *Sociological Review* Monograph no. 20.

Sand, R.

1952.   *The advance to social medicine.* New York: John de Graff.

Seham, M.

1969   An American doctor looks at eleven foreign health systems. *Social Science and Medicine* 3:65–81.

Shryock, R. H.

1947.   *The development of modern medicine.* New York: Alfred A. Knopf.

Stevens, R.

1971.   *American medicine and the public interest.* New Haven: Yale University Press.

Knowledge and Judgment in Professional Evaluations

Co-author: Buford Rhea

Professionals have the special privilege of freedom from the control of outsiders (Hughes, 1958; Caplow, 1954). Their privilege is justified by three claims. First, their work entails such a high degree of skill and knowledge that only fellow professionals can make accurate assessments of professional performance. Second, a high degree of self-lessness and responsibility characterizes professionals, so they can be trusted to work conscientiously. Third, in those rare instances in which individual professionals do not perform with sufficient skill or conscientiousness, their colleagues may be trusted to undertake the proper regulatory action. These claims support the professional's attempt to avoid submission to conventional bureaucratic controls when he works in an organization.

The claims of special knowledge and conscientiousness could be made by any number of occupations, the only question being one of degree. The most distinctive claim is that the profession may be trusted to perform regulatory functions that, for most occupations, are commonly left to clients, employers, administrative superiors, or the state. There are, however, very few systematic empirical studies on how professions regulate themselves. Even the most ordinary descriptive infor-

© 1965 by the Graduate School of Business and Public Administration, Cornell University, William D. Carmichael, Dean. Reprinted from "Knowledge and Judgment in Professional Evaluations" by Eliot Freidson and Buford Rhea, in *Administrative Science Quarterly* 10 (June 1965), by permission of *Administrative Science Quarterly*.

mation is lacking (Goss, 1961; Pelz, 1956). It is not clear what mechanisms are involved in the self-regulation that does take place, the forms regulation takes, or its efficiency. It is not even clear whether the work of professionals is organized so as to be amenable to some refined regulatory process. It is the purpose of this paper to contribute some information on the subject, not on regulation as such (see below, chapter 8), but on the *prerequisites* for effective regulation, that is, the distribution of information about performance and the consistency of assessments of that information. The assumption is that if each professional does not know what the other does in the course of his work, and if each evaluates the other in a different way, mutual regulation by professionals will be considerably less effective than regulation by bureaucratic administration.

The results reported here come from an empirical study of professionals working in a complex organization that leaves them fairly free of administrative controls and that is predicated on the conventional assumption that professionals will regulate themselves. In the clinic studied, it was found that both the specialty of the physician and the administrative organization of work structured each physician's access to the amount and type of information that he could gather about the performance of his colleagues, so that his evaluation of them varied accordingly. The restrictions on the distribution of information and differences in assessment appear to impose distinct limitations on the kind of regulation that can take place.

SETTING

The data presented here come from a case study, and so are not generalizable without peril. First, although processes discerned among physicians must be considered quite germane to the formulation of a concept of professional regulation, medical work is not easily comparable to the work of the scientist or engineer. Unlike the work of the scientist or engineer, a physician's work is organized around the face-to-face treatment of individual persons. Second, the data deal with physicians in a clinic rather than in individual practice. In this sense, work goes on within a formally organized framework. Clinic practice is not typical; but it does represent a form said to encourage the highest professional standards (see chapter 6), and unlike individual practice allows fairly clear specification of the role of administrative organization in work.

Third, the clinic is an organization serving ambulatory patients, each physician working in the privacy of his consulting room. It is thus not comparable to the hospital, where the patient and his treatment are always potentially if not actually on display to colleagues and lower-order workers. Consequently, the type and degree of information available about the performance of colleagues—prerequisite to evaluation and regulation—are likely to be significantly different in the hospital from the information available in a clinic or any other ambulatory practice, where medicine is practiced privately.

The clinic studied is a large, urban, hospital-affiliated medical group composed of fifty-four physicians. All are salaried and employed by a nonprofit community agency. Less than half of them are employed full time, the remainder working in the clinic part time and maintaining private practices elsewhere. All have the privilege of working at the same hospital, where most of the patients are taken when hospitalization is necessary. All of the clinic physicians have better-than-average professional qualifications, and the clinic itself has a very high professional reputation. Other elements of clinic organization are mentioned in the course of presenting the data, but here it is sufficient to indicate that the clinic is not typical of most and to emphasize that its deviation is toward standards that are highly valued by the profession. The case study should therefore reflect optimal rather than merely average conditions of work and experience.

DATA

The data upon which this analysis is based are taken from a larger study of the relationship between professionalism and formal organization in medical practice.[1] During the first phase of this study the clinic was studied in great detail. The doctors were interviewed several times, and during the last interviews each was asked to evaluate each of his colleagues on various aspects of his practice, including his technical competence. During the interview the meaning and source of the evaluations were probed and recorded on magnetic tape.

Of the fifty-four doctors in the clinic, five did not give ratings because of their absence or because of scheduling difficulties. Of the

1. For a description of the total study, which includes a survey of physicians in thirty-eight clinics, see chapter 10 below.

remainder, only three refused to evaluate their colleagues by rating them, though an additional seven did so with reluctance and with what seemed to be less than perfect candor. The remaining thirty-nine doctors apparently gave honest ratings, though a number had difficulty bringing themselves to use the "below average" rating freely.

The forty-six cooperating clinic physicians were asked to rate each colleague as "average," "above average," or "below average." Since an absolute standard was undesirable, because all physicians in the clinic had better-than-average qualifications for practice, the raters were instructed to take the clinic as the average, not the profession, and rate accordingly. And since lack of knowledge was as much of interest as knowledge, the raters were instructed to use a question mark when they felt they lacked sufficient information to make an evaluation.[2]

Several simple measures were derived for these data. First, numerical weights were assigned to each of the substantive ratings: 1 to "below average," 2 to "average," and 3 to "above average." This made it possible to calculate numerical mean scores, which could be used to characterize either individuals or groups, raters or rated. Second, the proportion of question marks in the total set of ratings was used as a measure of the amount of information available. The percentage of possible ratings a rater could actually make became his "index of knowledge"—that is, the more question marks a rater used in the ratings he gave others, the lower his index of knowledge. In turn, the percentage of possible ratings that a physician *received* from others was taken to be his "index of observability." Taken together, these measures made it possible to document fairly clearly the way both the division of labor and the administrative organization of the clinic practice patterned the knowledge each physician had about his colleagues, and they explained differences in the way each evaluated the others.

PATTERNING OF INFORMATION

One prerequisite to making an evaluation is information of some kind, whether gossip or detailed observation. Before examining the evalua-

2. When someone claimed total ignorance about the performance of all colleagues and could not be persuaded to give any rating other than a question mark, it was concluded that he was in effect refusing to rate, so his question marks were not counted. In some cases, it was suspected that question marks were being used to evade decisions, but as long as some substantive ratings were made, question marks were also counted.

tions themselves, therefore, it seems desirable to determine how well-informed the various physicians were. It appears that the division of labor structured the flow of information and therefore patterned the information available for professional evaluation.

The grossest distinction in the division of labor in medicine is that between generalist and consultant, between the physician who refers patients and the physicians to whom they are referred (see chapter 3). In the clinic studied, fourteen specialists were represented. The largest department, internal medicine, was composed of twenty internists, all of whom functioned in the clinic as "family doctors" who treated adults. Six pediatricians composed another generalist department, devoted to the general care of children. All but one of the remaining departments were clearly consulting specialties devoted to particular organs, pathologies, or procedures. The exception, obstetrics-gynecology, occupies an ambiguous position: as obstetrics, it is closely related to the generalist departments, assuming primary responsibility for treating a particular type of person for almost anything that bothers her and for referring her out when necessary, but as gynecology, it is a consulting specialty, receiving all special problems connected with female organs. Although obstetrics-gynecology is a typological inconvenience, it is an analytically interesting deviant case.

As a specialist, a physician's ability to obtain information about his colleagues depends on the relationship of his specialty to theirs. In general, the observability of members of a specialty to others and their knowledgeability about members of other specialties are a function of the flow of referrals, patients, and their records. Thus, observability and knowledge are greatest between generalists and consultants, and least between parallel specialties—that is, specialties that do not refer to each other. Table 7.1 demonstrates the pattern.

Some interesting exceptions indicate why the differences in table 7.1 are not greater than they are. Pediatrics and radiology, for example, know little about each other, though one is a referring and the other a consulting service. This is because children rarely need radiological services, so there is little contact between the two specialties. And some of the consulting specialties, such as orthopedics and surgery, actually do share patients and thus know each other better than might be expected. Were these atypical instances eliminated, table 7.1 would contain even more emphatic evidence of the structuring of knowledge by the division of labor in medicine.

TABLE 7.1   Knowledge of Competence, by Specialty

Specialties Rated	Specialties Rating*	
	Consulting Specialties	Referring Specialties
Consulting specialties	40†	74†
Referring specialties	74†	65†

Note: Obstetrics-gynecology is excluded from tabulation.
* Ratings of one's own service are excluded.
† Index of knowledge is the percent of ratings actually made, out of total number of ratings possible.

Table 7.2 indicates graphically some of the special ways in which knowledge is structured. Following *rating* specialties down their columns makes it possible to see the specialties about which each has a comparatively low index of knowledge. Following *rated* specialties across their rows makes it possible to see the number of specialties to which they are relatively little known and thus their level of observability. Surgery, for example, knows relatively little about two other specialties and is known relatively little by one specialty. Obstetrics-gynecology knows relatively little about three other specialties and is relatively little known by four. The main outlines of the patterning of knowledge and observability by the division of labor are clear, though in a few cases somewhat confused by such idiosyncratic elements as the number and the length of tenure of physicians in a specialty. Dermatology, neurology, and radiology, for example, are all one-man departments in which the physicians have had long tenure; their observability score is consequently higher than one would expect.

Thus far, the exploration of the way the division of labor patterns access to information about performance has dealt with ratings of *competence,* that is, technical performance. Important as competence is, also important is the physician's relations with patients, the speed with which he works, the extent to which he visits patients in their homes, and the extent to which he is inclined to refer his patients to consultants. Before the physicians of the clinic were asked for ratings of colleagues by competence, they were asked to rate the generalists[3] by

3. Only generalists and particularly the internists are visible to virtually everyone. This is why similar attempts were not made to rate nontechnical areas of performance for consultants.

TABLE 7.2 Knowledge of Competence among the Different Specialties

Specialty of the Rated	Allergy	Internal Med.	Ob.-Gyn.	Ophthalmology	Orthopedics	Pediatrics	Psychiatry	Surgery	Urology	Observability Score of Rated Specialties
				Specialty of Raters*						
Allergy	X	X	O†	O	O	X	O	O	X	51
Dermatology	X	X	X	O	X	X	O	X	X	76
Ear-nose-throat	X	X	X	X	X	X	O	X	X	81
Internal medicine	X	X	X	X	X	X	X	X	X	85
Neurology	X	X	X	X	X	X	X	X	X	86
Ob-gyn.	O	X	X	O	O	X	O	X	X	58
Ophthalmology	O	X	O	X	O	O	O	O	O	37
Orthopedics	O	X	O	O	X	X	O	X	O	60
Pediatrics	X	X	X	O	X	X	X	X	O	66
Physical med.	O	X	X	O	X	O	X	X	X	69
Psychiatry	X	X	X	O	X	X	X	X	O	59
Radiology	X	X	X	X	X	O	O	X	X	74
Surgery	O	X	X	X	X	X	X	X	X	83
Urology	X	X	X	X	X	X	O	X	X	84
Index of knowledge of rating specialties	63	82	60	62	68	68	54	78	62	

Note: Read down the column vertically to see the knowledge (X) and lack of knowledge (O) that the specialties at the top of the table have about the specialties in the left-hand column. Read horizontally across the row of a particular specialty to see how many rating specialties have little (O) or much (X) knowledge of it.

* Ratings by specialties represented by only one rater are omitted to avoid excessive individual bias.

† O indicates where the index of knowledge for ratings was 49 or less. A cutting point of 49 was used to minimize the influence of individual raters on the score of specialties represented by only two people.

the relative number of house calls they made, their popularity with patients, their tendency to finish scheduled office hours on time, and their tendency to refer their cases out to consultants rather than handling them themselves. Since pediatrics and internal medicine are largely parallel in the division of labor, and pediatrics is a considerably smaller service, the focus here is solely on the internists.

Among the internists rating their fellow internists, the index of knowledge is identical for three areas of performance: it is 91 in ratings of competence, patient popularity, and tendency to make house calls. For finishing hours on time, however, the index of knowledge is 61, and in the case of referral habits it is 33. The consultants, on the other hand, demonstrate a different pattern of knowledge in rating the internists. Their index of knowledge about the competence of internists was rather high—86. However, consultant knowledge about internists' house calls was 31; about popularity with patients, 55; and about finishing hours on time, null. Consultant ratings about referral habits proved unusable because of mistaken variation in the instructions given in the course of fieldwork, but it seemed probable that the index in that case would be relatively high.

These differences in knowledge include a number of instructive contradictions. First, it should be noted that house calls are not very observable, even by fellow internists: they are made off the premises, sometimes from the physician's home and often during the night. However, the administrators of the clinic tabulate and post house calls, thus making the data available to all. The availability of data on house calls can thus explain why something as unobservable as house calls can result in such a high index of knowledge for the internists; but it raises the question of why the consultants' index was so low. When consultants were asked why they expressed ignorance about house calls when posted information was available, they said that they had not noticed such listings or that since they had no interest in whether internists made house calls, they paid no attention to the listings. The internists, however, talked about house calls continually; they felt that if one physician sloughed off his house calls, the others would be called upon to make them. This led to attention to all available information about such performance.

But the same can be said for office hours, for if a physician leaves early, patients coming in late (but before the official end of hours) will have to be seen by one of the internists still in the clinic. Furthermore, keeping office hours is something one can determine; the internists all have offices in the same building and on the same floor, and offices are not divided into private waiting-room areas or suites. The behavior was of interest, it was observable; yet the index of knowledge was relatively low. Obviously, some other variable intruded to reduce observations or comparing notes with others on the observations that were made.

The other differences require little comment. Referral habits by fellow internists are most difficult to observe, and one physician's referral habits have little import for another's work load; therefore lack of knowledge is to be expected. Consultants were expected to have a higher index of knowledge because they were able to observe referrals considerably better and, since referrals increased their work load, to observe them with greater interest. Finally, the relatively high index of knowledge for patient popularity may be seen as testimony to the central place of the patient in the flow of work, being "shared" by many, as well as evidence of the role of the patient as a carrier of information.

INFLUENCES ON ASSESSMENTS

The extent to which information moves through the group of physicians allows assessment of performance to take place. It seems clear that in the clinic studied the critical element in the movement of information is the flow of work. Information about performance traveled between physicians who were cooperating in the division of labor; comparatively little information flowed between physicians who were not sharing work. Furthermore, there is the suggestion that not all available information was used and that the information bearing on the work relationship seemed better attended to and retained.

These limitations on the amount and type of information available to any single physician in the clinic constitute obvious qualifications on the kinds of assessment that could be made. There seem to be other qualifications on assessments, however, that are imposed by the perspective from which the assessment is made. Some perspectives were a function of the individual's own background; others, more interesting for this study, were a function of those elements of the individual's position in the clinic that led him to observe and be interested in some aspects of colleague performance and not in others.

Personal Characteristics

First a few findings are presented that reflect the fact that people with different characteristics have different habits of assessing their colleagues. Table 7.3, presenting the average ratings of competence made by internists and consultants, indicates that internists give characteristically lower competence ratings to everyone than do consultants but that the competence of consultants is nonetheless rated relatively higher by both groups. This reflects first of all the hierarchical prestige relations between generalist and consultant. However, it also reflects other variables.

The numbers are too small to allow controlling all the elements that may explain differences, but both absolute age and the length of time one has been in the group play a part in the influences.[4] Table 7.4 presents the way physicians rate each others' competence when age and length of tenure are controlled. The younger doctors consistently give lower ratings to their colleagues than do the older, the young doctors with short tenure giving even lower ratings than those with long tenure. Age is thus an important determinant of how one will *rate* his colleagues, the younger person being more critical than the older. However, tenure seems to be the more important determinant of how one will *be rated* by his colleagues: "new" associates are rated lower than old-timers, regardless of age.

TABLE 7.3   Average Ratings of Competence by Internists and Consultants

	Raters	
Rated	*Internists* (N = 20)	*Consultants* (N = 18)
Internists	2.25	2.38
Consultants	2.34	2.54

Note: A score of 1 represents a lower than average rating; 2, average; 3, higher than average.

4. Seventy-five percent of the internists are in the younger age group, compared to 40 percent of the consultants. Seniority does not distinguish the two markedly, however, since 50 percent of the internists and 46 percent of the consultants are in the shorter tenure group.

ABLE 7.4 Average Ratings of Competence, by Age and Tenure

	Raters				
ated	*Young, Short Tenure (N = 17, 625 Ratings)*	*Young, Long Tenure (N = 8, 342 Ratings)*	*Old, Short Tenure (N = 3, 103 Ratings)*	*Old, Long Tenure (N = 18, 574 Ratings)*	*Average Rating Obtained From Others*
oung, short tenure	2.19	2.22	2.39	2.44	2.28
oung, long tenure	2.31	2.43	2.59	2.67	2.49
ld, short tenure	2.17	2.15	2.00	2.54	2.39
ld, long tenure	2.02	2.45	2.64	2.61	2.45
verage rating given to others	2.24	2.35	2.52	2.57	

Note: A score of 1 represents a lower than average rating; 2, average; 3, higher than average.

The significance of length of service to one's rating by others probably reflects the fact that it takes a certain amount of time to develop a positive rather than neutral evaluation (familiarity breeding respect) and the fact that over a period of time, at least some of those not rated highly are likely to drop out or be dropped out of the clinic, leaving the higher-rated physicians to form the long-tenured group.

Division of Labor

Besides personal differences, one's specialty may lead him to experience different aspects of a colleague's practice than does a physician in a different specialty, which may produce a different evaluation. A concrete example of how structured experience screens information and influences assessments is to be found in the relations among pediatricians, internists, and obstetricians-gynecologists.

Internists and pediatricians assessed the competence of those in obstetrics-gynecology quite differently. Pediatricians thought them better than most specialists, rating obstetrics-gynecology an average of 2.67, as compared to an average rating of 2.46 for all other specialties and 2.43 for itself. Internal medicine, on the other hand, gave the obstetrics-gynecology physicians one of its lowest ratings—2.15, compared to its average rating of 2.29 for all other specialties. In fact, if two ratings given by one member of an otherwise unknowledgeable department were ignored, the lowest ratings given to the physicians in obstetrics-gynecology were given by internal medicine. On the other hand, if six other similarly questionable ratings (out of a total of 124) were eliminated, obstetrics-gynecology received its highest rating from pediatrics.

This difference in evaluation is easily explained. In this clinic, pediatricians saw primarily the healthy product of the obstetricians' work, without being able to follow the problems leading to that product. Internists, however, shared their gynecological problems with the gynecologist and so had occasion to share in their problems. One pediatrician explained the situation very well:

> We don't see the newborns in the hospital, and that's why we don't have much to do with the obstetricians. In private practice, if an obstetrician runs into problems, he is supposed to bring the pediatrician into the nursery, and since we don't do this here, we can't say whether he should not have used this or whether he should have done a Caesarian section earlier or shouldn't have done the section and should have let her be in labor longer. We have nothing to do with that. By the time the baby comes home, it is all right. Whatever came before, well, we don't know. We get a healthy baby.

Something of the same pattern holds between internal medicine and pediatrics. Internal medicine, with qualifications to be discussed, does not share patients with the parallel specialty of pediatrics. Instead, it receives patients who graduate from pediatrics at a certain age and who are fairly healthy. It is therefore understandable that internal medicine gives one of its highest ratings to physicians in pediatrics—giving an average of 2.41, against an average of 2.29 for all others and 2.22 for physicians in internal medicine itself. So it should be clear from this that in addition to limiting access to any information at all in some cases, the division of labor in medicine exposes different specialties to different kinds of information, thus structuring differentially the assessments of those who have sufficient information to form judgments.

Administrative Organization

The relation between pediatrics and obstetrics in the clinic studied is not common elsewhere. It stems from some of the formal administrative structure of the clinic and constitutes one example of how administrative arrangements as well as the purely functional division of labor can influence assessments.

Another such example is found in the relation between pediatrics and internal medicine. During the day, pediatricians treat children up to the age of ten. At night, however, pediatricians are on emergency call only for children up to the age of four, the internists on duty being responsible for seeing children between four and ten years of age. This arrangement provides opportunity for pediatrics and internal medicine to observe each other's work, even though ordinarily they are parallel specialties. During the night, internists on call see some of the sick patients of pediatrics, and the next day pediatricians see how the internists have handled their patients.

In general, there would seem to be equal opportunity for observation, though if anything, the weight of opportunity should rest with the internists because they not only see the sicker children but also receive the children who graduate from pediatrics to them, bringing along the written record of past pediatric performance. Yet internal medicine, ordinarily one of the most knowledgeable services in the clinic, with a general index of knowledge of 82, ventures ratings of the competence of pediatricians in only 56 percent of all possible cases. Pediatrics, on the other hand, knows internal medicine as well as it knows the consulting specialties, being able to rate those in internal medicine 68 percent of the time compared to 69 percent for all consulting specialties. Even after eliminating the ratings of the two pediatricians who were new to the clinic (and therefore less knowledgeable), the index of knowledge of pediatricians for internal medicine is 62, still higher than the index of knowledge of internal medicine for pediatrics.

The most reasonable explanation for this difference seems to be that though internists have as much and probably more opportunity to observe the work of pediatricians than pediatricians have to observe them, the internists simply do not pay much attention to what they observe. One internist put it this way: "There really isn't too much contact between [internists] and pediatricians, in part because the prime responsibility is not shared. Although the [internist] may see the patient of the pediatrician, it would only be during the night, and the [internist] probably wouldn't be too interested in the case." If the assumption of at least equal opportunity to observe each other is correct, then this relationship between pediatrics and internal medicine illustrates two rather important points. First, the location of primary responsibility, that is, whose patient someone is, operates as a powerful intervening determinant of the degree to which attention will be paid to the information available for assessing performance. Second, when administrative arrangements alter the pattern commonly associated with that responsibility, as was the case when pediatricians were excused from visiting the nursery and from making their own night calls on their older patients, the pattern of knowledge and assessment is also altered.

Finally, it might be pointed out that fairly extreme differences in assessment can arise in this system without very much awareness on the part of the participants. Within specialties there seems to be general agreement in assessments, though numbers are so small in most instances that we can only state this as an opinion; extreme contradictions in assessing individuals—that is, some rating a physician above average and others rating him below average—occur rarely when raters are rating a physician in their own specialty. Such contradiction, however, is not uncommon between raters rating a physician in their own specialty and raters in another specialty rating the same physician. In one case involving a large enough number of raters to approach reliability, for example, colleagues in a physician's specialty gave him a mean competence rating of 1.38, more than two-thirds rating him *below* average. Those in other specialties, however, gave him a mean rating of 2.12, less than one-eighth rating him below average and more than two-fifths rating him above average. This and several similar cases were known of before ratings were solicited, but in spite of careful probing in the course of obtaining ratings, there was little evidence that physicians outside the specialty involved were aware that those inside held opinions so divergent from theirs. In this clinic, apparently, gossip about competence was not very open nor did it extend outside the specialty group in which it arose. This means that *communication among colleagues is too limited to compensate for the structural barriers to first-hand knowledge.*

THE PROBLEM OF PROFESSIONAL REGULATION

The material presented here indicates that in an organized group of physicians, members do not have equal access to information about the activities of their colleagues, that their assessments of available information vary with their perspectives, and that all with access to information do not pay the same kind of attention to it. In the particular instance studied, the prerequisites for regulation do not seem to be well enough developed to allow an extensive and coherent process of professional regulation. Such limitation may seem to result from the way the division of labor structures access to and assessment of firsthand information about performance, and therefore it may be seen as merely reflecting the increasing specialization of medicine. While specialization limits and structures firsthand information, however, it has little to do with the *exchange* of such information. The results indicate that there was little communication and discussion of each other's performance among the physicians of the clinic. In the course of interviews, the doctors indicated that it is virtually unprofessional (if not socially dangerous) to pass on and exchange such information to any but very close colleagues. If this is true, *professionalism itself*, rather than the existence of specialization, *may be considered the chief barrier* to the distribution of information about performance.

What is the significance of this fragmentation of information and evaluation? We have only anecdotal data bearing on this question, and a sense of the logic of consequences, but it appears that its major consequence is that regulation is most likely to occur on a slow, individual-to-individual, trial-and-error basis, that is, each physician must learn about his colleagues largely by his own experience. Where the performance of another is not satisfactory to him, he adopts whatever regulatory device he thinks necessary. The patient whose treatment conveys information about unsatisfactory performance may be discomfited somewhat, but the physician tries to see to it that no subsequent patients of his will be discomfited. Meanwhile, other physicians and their patients will have to go through the same experience before they too adopt some regulatory measure, since little information is available to spare each individual physician and his patients from having to learn from experience. Obviously, it takes time before a widespread opinion and tactic of control can spread through the clinic, and this results in multiplication of patient discomfort.

It should be observed that this system of regulation resulting from barriers to information may be slow, superficially inefficient, and somewhat wasteful of patients; but it is not necessarily undesirable or inefficient in the long view. If well-trained physicians may be generally counted on to perform adequately, then the waste will be slight. And if, as the clinic physicians claim, truly gross or mortally dangerous forms of misconduct would be immediately communicated throughout the clinic and quickly dealt with, then the waste is comparatively trivial. The professional is inclined to see that waste as part of a margin of error necessary to sustain his willingness to undertake what he claims is complex, uncertain, and risky work, a consequence of protecting him from others' possibly overhasty and arbitrary judgments of his difficult-to-assess work. But the ultimate evaluation of such waste should be contingent upon gathering much more objective and systematic information about the organization of professional behavior than we have now, and it is clear that the profession's claim of self-regulation cannot be accepted without close scrutiny of the facts.

REFERENCES

Caplow, T.
1954.   *The sociology of work.* Minneapolis: University of Minnesota Press.
Goss, M. E. W.
1961.   Influence and authority among physicians in an out-patient clinic. *American Sociological Review* 26:39–50.
Hughes, E. C.
1958.   *Men and their work.* New York: Free Press.
Pelz, D. C.
1956.   Some social factors related to performance in a research organization. *Administrative Science Quarterly* 1:310–25.

Processes of Control in a Company of Equals

Co-author: Buford Rhea

Recently there has been an increasing amount of attention paid to professionals and scientists working in formal organizations (cf. Parsons, 1947; Wardwell, 1955; Ben-David, 1958; Solomon, 1957; Goss, 1961; Kornhauser, 1962). Much of the discussion revolves around the issue of control—namely, whether or not conventional bureaucratic methods are appropriate or practical for controlling the work of scientists and professionals. The consensus seems to be that those workers require a kind of autonomy that is antithetical to Weber's model of rational-legal bureaucracy, indeed, that the value of their work is actually reduced when done "by the book" or otherwise subjected to the detailed directives of an administrative hierarchy. The proper way for such individuals to work is as members of a self-regulating "company of equals."

What exactly is a company of equals? Following Parsons, Barber has described the pattern as

a social group in which each permanent member . . . is rough-ly equal in authority, self-directing and self-disciplined, pursuing the goal [of his work] under the guidance of the . . . morality he has learned from his colleagues and which he shares with them. The sources of purpose and authority are in his own conscience and in his respect for the moral judgments of his peers. If his own conscience is not strong enough, the disapproval of others will control him or will lead to his exclusion from the brotherhood. (Barber, 1962:195)

Patently, this is a very unorthodox way of organizing complex and responsible work, and it is described too briefly. It is rather difficult to accept the assignment of such heavy weight to individual conscience and self-direction. Colleague pressures do constitute an external source of control in the definition, but how, if a deviant is permanent and equal in authority to others, can pressure by others influence him?

Furthermore, there is the problem of the relation of the company of equals to administrative arrangements. As Barber indicates, the company of equals is an ideal rather than an empirical phenomenon. Discussing the university, he indicates that hierarchical organization and formal control by "the administration" must necessarily be added to the company of equals pattern in order that departments be coordinated and the outside environment dealt with (1962:197–98). But by and large, this, along with the dirty work of "housekeeping," seems to be all the necessity conceded to bureaucratic administration in professional or scientific settings: the critical task of controlling work can be left in the hands of the workers.

Most writers regard the infringement of bureaucratic devices on professional work as a problem, in some sense threatening (Kornhauser, 1962). However, since so little is known of how the company of equals actually works, it is by no means self-evident that bureaucratic devices are in fact so dangerous to professional work. Perhaps bureaucratic infringement is a consequence of the inadequacies of professional methods of controlling work. So we might ask, is the company of equals really self-regulating, and if so, how? Are its methods of control adequate to its goals? What are its characteristic difficulties? With one important exception (Goss, 1961), little empirical material has as yet been published that can suggest how these questions might be answered. In this paper we will describe the processes of control in one "company of equals," hoping thereby to indicate some of the analytical problems raised by the idea. For reasons of both space and strategy, we will restrict ourselves to a description of internal processes, arbitrarily excluding reference to the external environment that figures in any organization.

THE CLINIC

We have been engaged in an intensive study of a clinic[1] staffed with highly qualified physicians and owned by a nonprofit agency. The prime workers, the physicians, are not merely technical specialists, as are also secretaries and plumbers, but unquestionably "professionals" in the sense that, for example, Wilensky's union experts (1956) and Blau's civil servants (1955) are not, but would like to be. In very few if any other occupations are the sense of individual responsibility and autonomy and an objective position of prestige and strength so well developed for the support of a company of equals pattern.

Furthermore, the organization is staffed by exceptionally qualified physicians, all of whom are either board-certified or eligible, by virtue of their training, to take board examinations. In this sense they are "more professional" than the average run of doctors. And while it is a fairly large clinic of about fifty doctors (all on salary, not partners), equipped with a fully developed administrative staff, numerous clerks, and paramedical personnel, it is considerably less bureaucratic than, for example, a college (though considerably more than most clinics).

Over the past eighteen months we have examined the files of the organization, both confidential and routine, official and unofficial; we have attended all of its meetings, including those of the executive body; we have interviewed all the doctors, most of them three or four times; we have interviewed a sample of thirty doctors who are no longer employed by the clinic; and of course we have interviewed the administrators. The result has been a large accumulation of data ranging from verbatim interview transcripts to notes on luncheon gossip and including sociometric ratings, minutes of meetings, and extracts from records. The present report is based on such data.

Hierarchy

Like the university, the clinic follows the principle of hierarchy, albeit unusually simply. The medical director is responsible for the conduct of the organization in general, including that of the physicians, and the administrator is responsible for everyday operations, particularly but not exclusively for the conduct of the paramedical and clerical

1. The organization calls itself a "medical group." On the varieties of medical practice and the problems of conceptualization, see chap. 6, "The Organization of Medical Practice."

staff. The latter is organized into offices and departments, with clear lines of authority, but while the physicians are divided into various medical specialty departments, there is little division into vertical ranks. There are titular chiefs of some departments, but it is not at all clear what their duties and prerogatives are, not even to them. Aside from this, there is no system of graded ranks analogous to those found at universities, and while seniority is an important source of influence, it is not a locus of hierarchical authority.

Clearly, the concrete elements of Barber's definition are present in the clinic. The workers have had the long period of training characteristic of professionals; they have tenure and so may be regarded as "permanent"; and formal subordination and superordination among colleagues are almost nonexistent. We feel justified, then, in designating the colleague group as a company of equals, bearing in mind that, as elsewhere, administrative authority does temper colleague behavior. We will spend the remainder of this paper analyzing the role of both the administration and the colleague group in the control of work.

Rules

In most models of bureaucracy subordinates are said to be so placed by virtue of the obedience they must render to superiors and their obligation to conform to various rules and regulations. This is also partially the case for the clinic.

In the first place, the physician has "contractual" obligations, such as the number of hours he must spend in his office seeing patients, which are spelled out in some detail and which he accepts as conditions of his employment. All physicians recognize (even if unwillingly) the legitimacy of these administratively determined "punishment-centered" regulations.[2] In addition to them, there are intramural rules whose purpose it is to ensure the coordination of effort required when a number of physicians must practice together—for example, whether it is the obstetrician or the generalist[3] who is to be responsible for provid-

2. We refer to the analysis in Gouldner, 1954. It will be clear later, however, that "punishment-centered" rules are not so unambiguously present in our clinic as they are in the gypsum plant.
3. In this clinic there are no general practitioners. Pediatricians and internists provide everyday family services, referring to consultants what they cannot manage. We refer to the pediatricians and internists here as "generalists."

ing initial emergency medical care for spontaneous abortions. These rules may be worked out by the physicians themselves, may be suggested by the administration, or may be agreed upon in joint administration-physician discussion, but in all cases they are seen as mutually agreeable expedients to solve unavoidable and obvious problems. These are clearly "representative rules." Finally, there are some rules that should but in fact do not affect the physicians—"mock rules" in Gouldner's phraseology. Some of these rules come from external sources, and if they conflict with medical or organizational efficiency and there is small chance of detection, both administration and collegium may tacitly agree to ignore them.

The variety of rules thus far parallel those found by Gouldner in the gypsum plant he studied, and they are doubtless common to most formal organizations. However, we must note that none of the rules bearing on the purely technical core of medical practice—examination, diagnosis, prescription, and treatment—may be classified as punishment-centered in Gouldner's sense. The few concrete rules that do specify elements of that core are either representative or mock in character. By and large, the most important rule bearing on the purely technical core of medical practice is more a policy statement than a regulation—it asserts that the highest possible medical standards will be maintained regardless of cost. Like many another organization in which unusually skilled work is performed, the clinic does not specify in detail the actual technical procedures to be used, but it does attempt to specify that procedures generally approved by the professional community should be used. This places determination of what is proper first of all in the hands of the workers themselves, and second, no less importantly, in the hands of any representative of the extraclinic professional community who may be called in to evaluate the work being performed inside. This "rule" effectively prevents the development of the conflict in *technical* affairs between bureaucratic office and the expert of which Parsons made so much in his discussion of the two (Parsons, 1947). What conflict we observed in technical affairs was between professional opinions—for example, between that of the clinic doctors and that of professional consultants from outside the clinic.

Mention of technical affairs brings up the need to distinguish the areas of work over which control may be exercised. The technical core of medical practice is one major area. The other is the degree to which effort is exercised and the way effort is organized. It is in the latter area, having no necessary relationship to technical expertise, that conflict is most likely to occur between administration and physician and among physicians. For example, the organizational need for calculability and coordination in the provision of services leads to administrative pressures on the doctor for punctuality; organizational responsibility for the patient leads to the creation of administrative channels for patient complaints. Neither the need for punctuality nor that for responsibility for the patient is questioned by most physicians. But being accountable to the organization for one's time and for one's difficulties with patients is seen as undignified, as being treated like a factory worker or a clerk. Conflict between administration and collegium, and even between colleagues in such areas as these, is persistent in the clinic and is based on quite different rules and norms than is the conflict that may occur about technical procedures.

ADMINISTRATIVE COLLECTION OF SUPERVISORY INFORMATION

Obviously, rules would be meaningless if one never knew when they were broken. How can conformity to the rules we outlined be ascertained by the administration when the physician does so much of his work in the privacy of his office?

First, certain gross aspects of a physician's organization of effort are noted in routine ways. Receptionists are supposed to notify the administration in the event that a physician changes his hours, does not allow her to make an appointment for an open time period, or is habitually late. Similarly, when a physician rushes through his patients to finish early or books patients earlier than he can actually see them to make sure they are "stacked up" and ready for him whenever he is ready, these and like behaviors are visible to all who would take the trouble to look. Judicious tapping of the paramedical grapevine and inspection of appointment books constitute fairly regular devices for checking on the organization of physicians' efforts. But this is the *only* regular and continuous administrative check on performance, and it yields information primarily about punctuality and speed of work, nothing about technical performance.

The patient is directly in contact with the physician during his work, and the clinic is organized to provide regular channels for patient complaints, to the administration. But the patients' opinions are something few physicians will accept as valid indication of technical performance, and while some complaints do stimulate investigation, instances are fairly rare and provide only random bits of evidence.

Interestingly enough, an accurate source of information about all physicians exists, but it is used only after it is suspected that something might be wrong. The medical record for each patient is, in its wealth of detailed information, a bureaucratic delight. But although the information is continuously recorded (in part because of the legal liabilities of the work) it is not scrutinized by anyone on a routine basis. The medical chart is a working tool rather than a supervisory device, becoming a supervisory device only when interest in the case has been triggered by some event suggesting the necessity of investigation—a patient complaint, a law suit, an accidental observation, and the like. It is thus only latently supervisory, used after the fact to reconstruct past performance in damning or exonerating detail.

COLLEAGUE COLLECTION OF SUPERVISORY INFORMATION

The question is how, without routine review of the charts, information about a doctor's technical performance can be gathered at all. While the patient's complaint does provide the administration with clues to the spirit of performance, it is in the long run the collegium that must provide information on actual performance before action may be taken. Indeed, consonant with the idea of a company of equals, it is assumed in the clinic that the collegium performs everyday supervision. Such supervision could be collective, that is, a function of the company of equals as a whole, if each man's work were observable by all others or, if only observable by some, observations were uniformly communicated to the others. Neither circumstance exists, either in the realm of the organization of effort or the realm of technical performance.[4]

4. Note that the following comments refer to the direct or indirect observability of work, not inferences about an individual's work from his shop talk. Our comments are based on a segment of our study in which we had all the physicians in the clinic rate each other. Some rating criteria required the opportunity to observe specific facets of the doctor's performance—such as house call habits, punctuality, and referral practices. Other rating criteria—such as medical competence—required more general observation. Detailed findings are reported in chap. 7, "Knowledge and Judgment in Professional Evaluations."

Information about a physician's organization of effort is observable to the collegium on such a fragmented, selective basis that it is probably impossible for any individual to have a rounded and informed view of any other. For example, in the case of generalists, Doctor X on the emergency service in the evening is in a position to observe that he is receiving requests for house calls from patients who were refused house calls during the day by their own doctor, Y. But it is considerably less likely that Doctor X could ever observe that Doctor Y comes in late for his office hours and leaves early. It is even less likely that he could observe that Doctor Y refers his patients out to consultants on the slightest pretext. In turn, while a consultant is in a very good position to learn of Y's referral habits and possibly his mode of ordering laboratory tests, he is unlikely to know anything about Y's mode of managing his time and avoiding house calls.

Similar selectivity and fragmentation exists in the observability of *technical* performance. Aside from gossip or the opportunity to guess how competent a colleague is from the way he discusses his cases over coffee, opportunity to observe the work of colleagues varies a great deal. Part of the variation of opportunity is due to the organization of the clinic and part to the medical division of labor.

Within specialties such as surgery that involve on-the-job teamwork in a theater, both work and its results are in the nature of the case observable, and the characteristics of colleagues come to be known rather quickly to all those within the specialty itself. Within other specialties, where work is done more privately and individually, observation is more problematic. In them, a person's quality comes to be known more slowly and more indirectly. Among generalists, some opportunity to see the work of the other is provided by the system of regularly rotating night and weekend emergency coverage, so each time someone is on duty he has the opportunity to see a few of his colleagues' patients and perhaps their medical records. Over a period of time this may provide a fair sampling of a colleague's handiwork so that, all else equal, old-timers are likely to know a good deal about each other, while new associates will be little known to and know little about others. A factor in addition to time is of course popularity: unpopular doctors lose patients to popular doctors, and patients carry both records and tales.

Ordinarily, however, more patients are shared *between* specialties than within them, so that a frequently consulted specialist, especially if he is the only representative of the specialty, may be able to make a very comprehensive assessment of the internists who refer to him, whereas internists who consult each other only infrequently and even then quite selectively, may have less observational knowledge of each other than of the physicians they refer to. Certain departmental affinities bias the flow of information: pediatrics refers more to orthopedics (for turned feet) and otolaryngology (tonsils) than to urology and gynecology; urology and gynecology deal with contiguous tissue and so have occasion to see each other's patients; orthopedics and physiatry use different approaches to many of the same complaints. Some of these affinities are blocked by the clinic requirement that the generalist must be the one to refer patients; for if the specialist must return the patient to the generalist when he picks up a symptom relevant to another specialty, he is thereby denied contact with the man whose field it is. Obviously, that requirement gives the generalist the most widespread contact with all specialties.

TRANSMISSION OF SUPERVISORY INFORMATION

It should be clear that neither the administration nor the collegium observes both the doctor's organization of effort and the technical quality of that effort. Furthermore, what is observed is segmentary and rather specialized, each class of data insulated from the others: the administration collects information about office hours that is not very accessible to the collegium; the consultant collects information about the generalist that is not readily observable to other generalists; generalists collect information about each other that is not very observable to the consultants. Obviously, the colleague group cannot behave as a collectivity or company as long as these bits of information are scattered discretely through its ranks. They must all share the same information. This can occur when an individual practices such persistent and thoroughgoing deviance that in one way or another it will become apparent to everyone in the company; it is more likely to occur when those bits of information are communicated each to the other and shared.

By and large, while sharing of observations does occur, it is slow and limited. While colleagues do gossip about each other, they are generally not inclined to communicate their observations bit by bit, as they collect them. There is no continuous revelation spreading information among peers. Rather, each individual usually stores up his own observations, saying little or nothing about them until he can no longer contain his indignation or until he discovers from others' hints that they too have had the same experience with the same individual. If his observations are few and he has no strong opinion about them, he may never communicate them to others. Given the accidental character of many disclosures, and given the necessity for them to accumulate before they are shared, a considerable period of time can elapse before any widespread opinion about someone emerges.[5] And obviously, the time will vary with the strategic visibility of the specialty.

In unusual cases, a sufficiently large number of observations has been stored in the memories of a sufficient number of physicians to allow a coalescence of opinion. Arriving at a certain critical mass of discontent with an individual seems to be necessary before most physicians will begin complaining about him to each other and the administration. One physician may make a rather neutral but probing remark to a second about a third, whereupon the second may have his story to contribute, and so forth. This collective definition, though, is formed only among groups of physicians who have the opportunity to discuss such matters, and as a result there may be identifiable pockets of quite different opinion about the same man within the clinic. Opinions coalesce by specialties as well as by cliques: internists, for example, who are in close contact with obstetricians for both obstetrical and gynecological problems, may have a totally different impression of the doctors in that department than do the pediatricians, to whom obstetricians are merely transmitters of healthy children.

PUNISHMENT

Albeit slowly and selectively, some information about deviance does come to light. How is it handled? When physicians are asked what they would do about an offending colleague, the usual response is, "Nothing." Asked what they would do if the offense were repeated, however, they answer, "I'd talk to him." "Talking-to" is in fact the most ubiq-

---

5. We ran across instances in which people who were practicing in the clinic for up to three years were unknown to some of the more remote specialties. We ran across other instances in which grave doubts about an individual were felt by others in his department and were not even suspected by anyone else outside, so far as we could determine.

uitous sanction in the clinic, used by both colleagues and administration as virtually the only means of punishment. From the examples we have collected, talking-to seems to involve various blends of instruction, friendly persuasion of error, shaming the offender, and threatening him with retaliation.

The incidence of talking-to varies with social distance. A colleague is more likely to talk to someone in his own department than someone outside and more likely to talk to a peer or junior than a senior man. He is likely to say nothing at all to an individual outside his department or his senior, and when he gets mad enough he will complain instead to his peers or even the administration. Talkings-to are also graded according to severity. The mildest (and by far most common) talking-to is a simple man-to-man affair. If the offender does not mend his ways the offended physician may enlist the aid of other talkers, either the administrator or one or more colleagues. Eventually, if misbehavior persists and there is strong feeling about it, the offender may be talked-to by the medical director or a formal committee of colleagues.

Talking-to is of course a very common informal sanction among peers in all work groups, and this approach is also used by superiors everywhere to warn of further sanctions. What is interesting about talking-to in the clinic is that *it is the only institutionalized punishment short of dismissal.* There are no intermediate forms of direct punishment. And since formal dismissal is almost impossible, talking-to is virtually the only sanction available.

Tenure regulations require that three-quarters of the members of the clinic must vote for a doctor's dismissal before it can occur. This means that a decision by the collectivity is necessary. As we have already seen, the conditions for the formation of a collective opinion are not generally present in the system. Given the unevenness of the distribution of information in the clinic we have described, it is understandable that even a simple majority of the doctors is unlikely to be in a position to have had personal experience with an individual's deficiencies. Without such personal experience, most physicians are loath to vote for so drastic a step as expulsion on the basis of the complaints of the few colleagues or the patients who have experienced them. Only the most gross and shocking deficiency will do. The practical impossibility of dismissing a tenured doctor is thus inevitable. In fifteen years, about eighty doctors have resigned from the clinic, most of them for their own reasons, some with encouragement,[6] but no tenured physician was dismissed.

REWARDS

Talking-to is thus the only practical form of direct punishment in the clinic. Aside from this, there are only rewards to motivate the physicians. Most of those rewards are bureaucratized so as to operate automatically, independent of the physician's deportment. There is, for example, a system of automatic increments, vacation with pay, bonus increments for obtaining specialty board certification and the like. And at a certain age an individual may, if he wishes, buy out of the chore of making night and weekend emergency calls. These rewards are rights of which an offender cannot be deprived. There are, however, other rewards that are particularly important because they are not bureaucratically guaranteed and because they are characteristically indirect and discretionary. Insofar as they are not mandatory, an individual can be "punished" by being "passed over" in their assignment. Some are controlled by colleagues and some by the administration.

As we have seen, the colleague group is unlikely to expel one of its members from the clinic. Other forms of direct punishment lacking, what is done about an offending colleague when talking-to does not work? By and large, the offended individuals use the technique of personal exclusion—attempting to bar someone from working with them individually or with their own patients without attempting to bar him from working with the patients of those colleagues who have either no grievance with or no knowledge of him.[7] The offender is not referred patients, or, if referral must be made, only unimportant cases are sent to him. He is not consulted about problems in his specialty or subspecialty: his advice is not sought and he is not called in to look at an interesting or peculiar case. And finally, he is not included in the system

6. Active encouragement to resign most commonly involves making life unpleasant by frequent talkings-to and intimations of the use of devious administrative devices to "get around" formal requirements for dismissal. As in the university, tenure regulations buttressed by a conservative and ill-informed collegium create a situation that almost by the nature of the case begets covert forms of administrative harassment.

7. The more loosely organized system of solo practice has an even greater tendency to encourage a physician to segregate himself and his patients from a poorly regarded practitioner without concern for other colleagues and their patients.

of exchanging favors that is so important in professional work: if he asked someone for a favor, he would not likely be refused, but others would not ask him for favors and so refuse him the credit that would allow him to ask with impunity for another favor in the future. All these methods of exclusion are practiced by *individuals:* they are not actions of the collegium as a whole. Therefore, they do not prevent an offender from working and maintaining his work relations with the colleagues whom he has not offended. They punish him only insofar as he is sensitive to the good opinion of those individuals who exclude him.

In a somewhat different fashion does the administration employ discretionary rewards. The set of such rewards might be called a *privilege system*—special tokens, sometimes rather trivial in character, which have not been codified and bureaucratically guaranteed as rights or increments and which, taken individually, may be unique and non-recurrent, even subject to invention by the administration. In the clinic, some of the more stable privileges involve extra money, supervising the laboratory, handling official correspondence about patient complaints, serving as special consultant, and supervising a research program. Others are more symbolic in character—for example, being invited to represent the organization to a group of distinguished visitors, being chosen to travel at clinic expense, or being allowed to take a leave of absence.

The most strategic privileges play upon the physician's image of himself. They constitute recognition of what he feels is due him at his stage of career or level of attainment. For example, among physicians the middle stage of a successful career not only involves increasing income and decreasing labor but also being relieved of the necessity to perform the dirty work of the profession. The major form of dirty work for the generalist is the house call, particularly at night and on weekends. Another kind of dirty work involves treating minor, uninteresting ailments and performing routine, mechanical procedures—the common cold for the generalist, refractions for the ophthalmologist, removing warts for the surgeon—otherwise called "garbage" by those who must perform them.[8] Although reduction in garbage through appointment to a consultantship or being made chief of service is ordinarily associated with seniority, the administration still has the power to

8. Analogous garbage in the university is teaching introductory and other little-valued courses, and even teaching as such.

exercise discretion and "pass by" one in favor of another who is cooperative or who might thereby be induced to be cooperative. Thus the
grumblings about "favoritism" that surround the dispensation of all
privileges by the administration.

THE NORMATIVE FOUNDATION OF THE SYSTEM

We have seen that the elements involved in the process by which control
may be exercised in this company of equals are fairly unbureaucratic in
character. Access to information about work performance is not, by
and large, hierarchically organized. At best it is a selective function of
the division of labor, at worst a function of unsystematically random,
accidental revelations to accidental observers. This state of affairs is a
consequence of the fact that for most areas of performance, the administration does not exercise ordinary bureaucratic methods of gathering
information, leaving the matter instead in the hands of the colleague
group. And while the physicians' access to information about each
other's performance is spotty, this would not be so significant if they
were not also disinclined to share this information with each other. In
consequence, the formation of a collective colleague opinion and the
initiation of collective colleague action are made rather difficult. Indeed, deviance is controlled almost entirely on an individual rather than
collective professional basis and by administrative exercise of discretionary rewards. Furthermore, what methods of control there are are
largely normative in character.[9]

　　We have implied that technical performance goes generally
unobserved, and, even if observed, uncommunicated, and, even if communicated, uncontrolled. This is not entirely true, for professional
norms do specify the need to control incompetence and unethicality.
Some of the doctors conceded that they didn't know very much about
their colleagues, but they felt sure that if someone did something *really
serious,* like kill a patient, they would learn about it very quickly. They
felt that if a colleague were shown to be grossly and obviously incompetent or unethical there would be no question but that he would be
dismissed from the clinic. And they pointed out that the really serious
forms and consequences of work are brought to the hospital, where a

　　9. In this sense the clinic is a "normative organization." See Etzioni,
1961:40–50.

system of professional surveillance does operate (Goss, 1961). However, their idea of what is "really serious" is so extreme as to be removed from their everyday experience. What they are saying, in essence, is that butchers and moral lepers would be spotted and controlled quickly: to that extent the system works remorselessly. However, almost all forms of deviance lie somewhere between the performance of the moral leper and that of the saint. And in that middle ground the exercise of control is made more difficult by virtue of the perspectives and norms governing professional activity.

In medicine work is seen to have potentially dangerous consequences. Since those consequences are also relatively unpredictable and the law holds him responsible, the physician assumes some unusual risks in his work. By virtue of his willingness to assume responsibility under such circumstances, the physician claims autonomy. Also contributing to the claim as well as the grant of autonomy is the belief that there is often no single right way of tackling a problem, that the personal judgment of the individual who handles the case cannot be replaced by definite, abstract rules. Colleagues who do not know the case are inclined to suspend their judgment of their associate's handling of it. And a sense of vulnerability stemming from this indeterminacy leads to the feeling that one shouldn't criticize an erring colleague because "it may be my turn next," or "there, but for the grace of God, go I."

This characteristic perspective on medical work thus leads to norms that encourage granting a large measure of autonomy and privacy to physicians. It also leads to constant pressure for autonomy and privacy in the organization of effort. If one's personal judgment is that a call is an emergency, it follows that he should be free to cancel his less important appointments, keep patients waiting, even indefinitely, or push his waiting patients off on other physicians, and no one is to say nay. If one's personal judgment is that a patient in the consultation room has a trivial illness while another waiting is in a serious condition, it follows that he should be free to deal with the former perfunctorily, even brush him off if he must. In such a fashion does the way the work is organized gain a degree of freedom from scrutiny and accountability by virtue of the technical characteristics imputed to it. When one adds an extreme valuation of autonomy and dignity for their own sakes, one begins to understand the foundation supporting the system we have described.

Furthermore, the physicians expect mutual trust from their

colleagues. They do not expect others to be checking up on them and they themselves try to avoid giving the impression of checking up on their colleagues. There is even a feeling of embarrassment when one accidentally observes a colleague's apparent peccadillo, and sometimes an attempt to turn the eyes away, to act as if the observation were not made. The purely accidental observation, particularly that stemming from a division of labor that directly involves the observer or his patient, seems to constitute a legitimate observation that might, on occasion, be talked about with an offender or communicated to other colleagues. Other forms of observation, with the exception of those made by a professional committee with the recognized function of review, are likely to remain private or to be resented when they are made public. One can easily see how this avoidance of "snooping" reduces the amount of information available to the company of equals and thus increases the difficulty of corroborating and evaluating whatever few observations happen to come to hand. And so the tendency to avoid sticking one's neck out by saying nothing to anyone is reinforced.

That professional norms rather than bureaucratic rules govern the system creates several characteristics. First of all, the system of control is not characteristically either collective or hierarchical in its operation. It is inclined to operate like the economist's free market, private individuals brought into interaction at the points where their labors meet, exercising control where their personal interests are involved. Second, the system works slowly, for a system of control can work only as rapidly as the information necessary for control can accumulate and here it does not accumulate readily. The slow pace characteristically provides a certain margin for human error that professionals are inclined to think necessary.

Third and finally, the system has a characteristic vulnerability. In the nature of the case, in order to be effective the sanctions used require that all participants be fully responsive to the norms involved. The system is quite helpless in the face of an individual who does not depend upon the esteem and trust of his colleagues and who does not respond to the symbolic values of professionalism. In a very basic way the system depends upon recruiting into it properly socialized workers—workers not merely well trained but also responsive to the values of their colleagues. Confronted by someone who is not so incompetent or unethical as to be grossly and obviously dismissible, and who fails to show any pride as a professional, the administration and the colleague group are helpless. This person cannot be flattered, shamed, or insulted and so cannot be persuaded to mend his ways or resign: all that can be done is to seal him off and try to minimize whatever damage he is believed to do.

PREREQUISITES FOR A SELF-REGULATING COMPANY OF EQUALS

Is the company of equals actually self-regulating? From the instance described, we can only answer both yes and no. There are self-regulatory mechanisms, but they are limited and contingent. Of course, our data come from but a single case, so that even if much of it rings true to our experience in universities, we cannot make any secure generalizations. However, we can use this case as a basis for tentative suggestion of the functional requisites for self-regulation in a company of equals. If nothing more, the suggestion can point to problems requiring analysis.

First of all, it should be clear that one requirement for a successfully self-regulating company of equals is a mode of recruitment that gives fair assurance that the worker has been both adequately trained and socialized into the normative system by which he can be controlled. Successful completion of a professional education is an objective measure of such technical and normative socialization, but its inadequacy seems to be implied by the characteristic tendency of professionals to rely on personal testimonials and recommendations. Such a "rational," impersonal, and specifically bureaucratic device as an examination administered to job applicants is uncommon among professionals precisely because it, like the license to practice and the professional degree, does not allow assessment of the applicant's personal qualities as a normatively socialized rather than merely technically trained professional. This deficiency is quite apart from the difficulty of measuring competence by examinations. The most effective mode of recruitment at present seems to require assessment of the applicant's "professional character" by people who have known him personally, for only by such assessment can a tolerable idea be gained of his responsiveness to the normative controls on which the company of equals relies.[10]

10. It is in this light that one might take issue with the assessment of academic methods of recruitment in Caplow and McGee (1958).

A perfect method of recruitment does not seem to exist, but even if it did, it is unlikely to be able to take into account the way a person will change over time and in different settings. For this reason, it would seem necessary that observability of work be a second prerequisite. Only if some form of observability exists can deviant performance become known and subject to control. Obviously, more analytical attention to the concept of observability is required before it can be used precisely enough to specify the conditions for the most effective supervision.

Third, as we have seen in our clinic, observability is not enough either. Colleagues may observe, but they may not choose to communicate their observations to others or to the offender. And they may not choose to assert control. The critical variable here, we may suggest, is a portion of the normative system of the colleague group and the self-images underlying it. Should one try to observe his colleague's performance or turn his eyes away? Should one "pass judgment"? Should one give unsolicited advice and opinions to a colleague about his behavior? These questions imply a set of values that have no necessary relation either to technical skill or to the conscientiousness with which those skills are performed. They refer to the norms dealing with one's dignity and autonomy as a professional and with one's relation to his peers. As opposed to individual conscience, which *allows* one to be controlled by others, this set of values determines whether one will *attempt* to control others and how one will respond to others' attempts to control him.[11]

In conclusion, we may suggest that in the light of such considerations as have been discussed here, it may be possible to assess the role of the administration in the affairs of the professional more adequately than has yet been done. It is very easy to see how, under some circumstances, administrative efforts at control of work are not mere bureaucratic aggrandizement, but conscientious efforts to fill a genuine vacuum engendered by the peculiarities of the professional system of self-regulation.

---

11. This might explain why there is so much bad teaching and so much good scholarship in the American university, for the former is protected from observation and control by etiquette, and the latter forced into public scrutiny by the pressure for publication.

REFERENCES

Barber, B.
1962.   Science and the social order. New York: Collier Books.
Ben-David, J.
1958.   The professional role of the physician in bureaucratized medi-
           cine: A study in role conflict. Human Relations 11:255–74.
Blau, P. M.
1955.   The dynamics of bureaucracy. Chicago: University of Chicago
           Press.
Caplow, T., and R. J. McGee.
1958.   The academic marketplace. New York: Basic Books.
Etzioni, A.
1961.   A comparative analysis of complex organizations. New York:
           Free Press.
Goss, M. E. W.
1961.   Influence and authority among physicians in an out-patient
           clinic. American Sociological Review 26:39–50.
Gouldner, A. W.
1954.   Patterns of industrial bureaucracy. New York: Free Press.
Kornhauser, W.
1962.   Scientists in industry: Conflict and accommodation. Berkeley:
           University of California Press.
Parsons, T.
1947.   Introduction to Max Weber, The theory of social and economic
           organization, pp. 58–60. New York: Oxford University Press.
Solomon, D.
1957.   Professional persons in bureaucratic organizations. In Proceed-
           ings of Symposium on Preventive and Social Psychiatry, pp. 253–
           66.Washington, D.C.: Walter Reed Army Institute of Research.
Wardwell, W. I.
1955.   Social integration, bureaucratization, and professions. Social
           Forces 334:356–59.
Wilensky, H. L.
1956.   Intellectuals in labor unions. New York: Free Press.

N I N E

Organizational Dimensions of Large-Scale Medical Groups

Co-author: John H. Mann

Public policymakers of the present day have, with few exceptions, assumed that group practice is by the nature of the case a desirable mode of organizing medical care (US. Dept. of Health, Education, and Welfare, 1967). When all is said and done, however, the generally used conception of what is group practice is so vague and nonspecific as to serve few of the needs of analysis and evaluation that underlie the adequate formulation of public policy. The usual definition may be represented by that used in a recent American Medical Association (AMA) survey:

> Group medical practice is the application of medical services by three or more full-time physicians formally organized to provide medical care, consultation, diagnosis, and/or treatment through the joint use of equipment and personnel, and with the income from medical practice distributed in accordance with methods previously determined by members of the group. (Balfe and McNamara, 1968)

Clearly, a great deal of variation in experience and product can take place within that general definition. Assuming that what is important about any form of medical practice is the quality of care it provides, and the way it provides satisfaction both to the patient and to the physician, it follows that the source of variation of such outcomes constitutes the prime problem of analysis. And so it should be with group practice: Are all practices falling under the general definition the same in their constitution and their outcome? Are there specific types of group practice that can be delineated by constitution and outcome?

Unfortunately, aside from anecdotal material and polemics, very little systematically collected information is available about group practice to answer those questions. And what are apparently the only systematic attempts to collect information about group practice in the United States over the past two decades—those of Hunt and Goldstein (1951), Pomrinse and Goldstein (1961a, 1961b, 1961c), and, most recently, Balfe and McNamara (1968)—have generally limited themselves in reporting such elementary data as the size of the groups, whether or not they include more than one specialty, whether or not they have some prepayment scheme, how old they are, and the like. Such information is of course important for learning about the distribution of grouped physicians in the United States and how those groupings vary along elementary parameters; but it does not tell us how medical groups are constituted as organizations, how they work, and what are their operating problems.[1] In this paper we wish to report data from a study designed to redress the paucity of detailed information about group practice. In essence, we wish to report data designed to determine some of the important ways by which large-scale group practices vary in organization and operation.

SIGNIFICANCE OF THE LARGE MEDICAL GROUP

The study reported here was designed to examine only one segment of the commonly defined universe of group practice—a segment representing a distinct minority of the universe. Most medical groups are quite small, the overwhelming majority composed of three to five physicians. Such groups, however, by their very smallness, cannot be said to encourage or even allow what are thought to be the major virtues of group practice—significant economies in cost and professional time

---

1. Hunt and Goldstein (1951) reported anecdotal materials from their survey. Pomrinse and Goldstein (1961a, 1961b, 1961c) used an elaborate questionnaire but reported only the most schematic results.

and significant elaboration of the professional division of labor to allow the presentation of a variety of coordinated specialist services, both of which require a relatively large scale of operation before they can occur. It follows that such small groups cannot be taken to reflect the operational problems that stem from the scale necessary to produce significant economies and specialization. Furthermore, such groups are so small that it is unlikely that such desirable modes of systematic professional supervision as chart review and medical audit will exist in them, reliance instead being on informal modes of supervision. In addition, such groups are so small that it is unlikely they could develop very strongly some of the bureaucratic characteristics of group practice that are thought to be antithetical to professional satisfaction. And, finally, as a purely practical consideration for data collection, we may note that such small groups are not likely to possess the administrative resources in the form of records and a full-time administrator that are most useful for obtaining questionnaire returns on more than the most cursory questions. For these reasons we felt that a study of the majority of large medical groups alone would be at once more feasible and analytically productive than a study of the entire universe composed mostly of quite small groupings.

Ultimately, of course, the entire universe should be studied, but the segment of large medical groups represents in most parsimonious form the issues central to the evaluation of group practice as such. They represent the possibility for significant economy of scale and specialization of well-supervised services. Whether or not such possibilities are realized is another question. The data presented here suggest that not all of the dimensions of group practice considered desirable are in fact compatible with each other.

THE DATA AND THE ANALYSIS

The data to be reported here come from a larger three-part study involving (1) an intensive case study of one large medical group, (2) a 1962 survey of large medical groups in the United States, and (3) a 1963 survey of physicians in a subsample of those medical groups.[2] In this paper we will discuss the second part of that study, analyzing the data from the survey of large medical groups. That survey involved an at-

2. Chapters 7 and 8 above report some of the data from the first portion of this study. The overall study is described in chap. 10.

tempt to administer a questionnaire by mail to business managers or administrators of all listed medical groups in the United States that were composed of no fewer than ten full-time physicians (or the equivalent in part-time physicians) involving the practice of more than one specialty and the treatment rather than merely the diagnosis and referral of patients (Pomrinse and Goldstein, 1961a; American Association of Medical Clinics, 1962). Returns were received from 156 groups, 64 percent of the known universe at the time. However, *usable* questionnaires were fewer, the analysis reported here being based on data from 125 medical groups.

The questionnaire queried group administrators primarily about the formal administrative characteristics of their groups. A number of facets were explored—the number of personnel, the presence of formal administrative offices held by physicians, contractual service relations with patients, referral patterns, relations with organizations and practices outside the group, the character of professional supervision within the group, the pattern of economic compensation to physicians and of their voice in group affairs, reports of the character of patient dissatisfactions, and the reported degree of professional satisfaction with a number of problem areas in group operation.

The question is, how are those variables related to each other? To answer that question in such a way as to get at the organization of group practice as such, holistically, requires something more than the conventional cross-tabulation of a limited number of variables. Factor analysis was chosen for use here because it allows the examination of all the variables at the same time and so is able to delineate a limited number of clusters or factors to which variables are all mutually related. In factor analysis, coefficients of correlation are computed between each variable and every other variable. All those variables that are closely correlated with each other as a cluster are assumed to have something in common. Interpretation of the meaning underlying the cluster leads to characterizing it by a name chosen by the analyst to represent what seems to be the dimension the clustered variables have in common. To determine what those clusters of variables are, the Centroid method of factor analysis was used, rotated to an orthogonal solution using the Verimax method. Two factor analyses were made, the first designed to determine what clusters of variables, or factors, exist, and the second designed to determine whether the factors themselves are interrelated.

DIMENSIONS OF MEDICAL GROUP ORGANIZATION

The first factor analysis was of the R type, conducted to determine how the information contained in the individual questionnaire items was intercorrelated, and what clusters or factors it formed. Those resultant factors may be taken to represent dimensions of medical group organization. They are presented in table 9.1, where names have been suggested for each of the factors. The "loadings" in the table may be evaluated by the reader as he would evaluate a correlation coefficient, their possible numerical value ranging from $-1.$ to $1.$ Numerical values smaller than 0.5 are not considered to be very impressive. Eight factors were obtained, the loadings and the items being presented in table 9.1.

Of the eight factors, six are fairly clear. Factor 1, which has been named Consumer Plan, seems to involve a cluster of elements revolving around medical consumer plans in which patients have service contracts through some insuring organization, union or otherwise, which influences group policy and stimulates the evaluation of the quality of care by review committees from outside the group. Putative "overutilization" being a problem in such plans in the United States, physician complaints about patient overdemandingness and excessive referrals are understandably part of the cluster. Both the desire to have qualified representatives of all specialties to serve the contracted plan and the contract character of the work, which allows segmental commitment (cf. McElrath, 1961), seem to be implied by the frequency of part-time physicians in the group. And the minimization of patient self-referral to consulting specialists also reflects the lack of a free market system dominated by individual patient choices such as can more easily occur in a fee-for-service system.

Factor 2, which has been named Formal Internal Professional Supervision, is considerably simpler, reflecting the clustering of all items bearing on formal supervision of the quality of care by the members of the group themselves. The index falling into this cluster was originally created in order to select the subsample of groups from which physicians were to be surveyed. It was weighted most heavily by such supervisory devices, but also included within it items reflecting group policy stimulating research, writing, and postgraduate education. This factor represents procedures that are considered desirable by medical policymakers but that are by no means present in all kinds of groups, as we shall see.

oadings	Item	Loadings	Item
actor 1—Consumer plan			specialists about the cases proper for each to handle in group
.82	Referral from family doctor required for patient to see a consulting specialist		
		.65	Reported problem of specialists complaining that referral of appropriate cases to them is too slow
.81*	Small percentage of full-time doctors in group		
.79*	Group professional policy influenced by insurance and other "outside" organizations		
		Factor 4—Equalitarianism	
		.71*	No problem reported of physicians complaining they do not have enough voice in determining group policy
.70	Significant proportion of patients gained by contract		
.70	Medical records reviewed by a committee from outside the group	.66*	Relatively small number of physicians in group
.65	Physicians reported to complain that patients are overdemanding	.56*	No problem reported of physicians complaining of too much supervision in group
.58	Specialists reported to complain of excessive referrals from internists, pediatricians, and general practitioners	.52*	Few formal professional rather than purely economic fringe benefits reported
		.47*	Most group physicians are partners rather than employees of group
actor 2—Formal internal professional supervision			
.85	Professional supervision of all physicians in the group rather than only those on probation	.47*	No formally designated and rewarded chiefs of specialty departments
.84	Formal professional supervision by peers through staff meetings, staff record committee, hospital rounds	*Factor 5*—Bureaucratization	
		.67	High index of bureaucratization (formal offices; physicians on salary; written rules)
.76	High index of encouragement of professional standards	.59	Written rules governing jurisdiction of specialties
.63	Professional supervision by medical director and/or department heads	.52	Written directives governing routine medical procedure such as immunization schedules
actor 3—Unsatisfactory division of labor			
.77	High index of strain among physicians	.47	Written statement of number of hours to be worked by group physicians
.68	Reported problem of controversy between		

(*continued*)

TABLE 9.1   (continued)

Loadings	Item	Loadings	Item
Factor 6—Entrepreneurialism		.60	Large proportion of group personnel is paramedical
.45	Group policy that patient have a personal physician	.58*	No problem of controversy among physicians over the division of gorup income reported
.43*	No strain reported in relations with community physicians outside the group		
.41*	No problem reported of physicians complaining that they are overloaded	.43*	Physicians in the group are mostly satisfied as reported by group administrator
.36*	Small percentage of specialists in the area belong to the group	*Factor 8*—Monopolistic elements	
		.43*	No problem reported of physicians complaining they are overloaded
.33*	Physicians paid on incentive rather than equal-shares-of-total-income arrangement	.34	Large percentage of the general practitioners in the area is in the group
.32*	Increments to physician income are dependent on the number of bills he collects	.27	Significant proportion of patients is gained by contract
Factor 7—Physician satisfaction			
.65*	Small proportion of group personnel is clerical		

*In reality a negative loading. For ease in reading, the negative loadings have been presented a positive, and the items with such loadings have been suitably revised. For example, the fir asterisked loading is actually −.81 and the item is "large percentage of full-time doctors in th group."

Factor 3, Unsatisfactory Division of Labor, is a small cluster reflecting the presence of a relatively high level of reported strain among physicians in groups. The first item is based on an index that is a simple sum of the problems checked off by the group administrator. The other items deal specifically with problems of the referral relations among specialists and between consultants and those who are supposed to refer cases to them. These clearly represent problems of a badly functioning division of labor in which specialists quarrel over the cases each should deal with, and in which they accuse generalists of holding on to cases they are not equipped to handle.

Factor 4, Equalitarianism, is a large but consistent and straightforward cluster of items that together reflect a relatively small group of partners, with few formal titles and offices and little complaint of authoritarianism or oversupervision.

Factor 5, Bureaucratization, reflects classical elements of bureaucracy as sociologists have analyzed and defined it. The first item is an index created to facilitate the selection of the subsample of medical groups from which physicians were to be surveyed. It was based largely on the presence of formal offices and of written rules governing the performance of work. The written rules themselves form the remainder of the cluster.

Factor 6, Entrepreneurialism, seems to reflect individualistic elements of group practice, though the loadings are low. Patients are linked to individual physicians whose income depends upon the amount of effort or charm he personally expends in order to attract and keep his clientele. In these circumstances, of course, the physician works as much as he chooses, which should discourage the possibility of complaints about being overloaded.

Factor 7, Physician Satisfaction, is not easy to interpret. On its face it indicates that group physicians are reported pretty much satisfied with their lot when there is little controversy about the division of income and when there is a large proportion of paramedical workers to aid them in their daily work.

Factor 8, Monopolistic Elements, has loadings of quite low value. It presents a picture in which a large percentage of the general practitioners in an area are in a group with patients by contract and complaining little of being overloaded.

These eight factors account for 47 percent of the variance of the forty-four items included in the analysis. In view of the unreliability of many of the single-item responses, the analysis seems to have been successful in accounting for much of the true variance in the matrix of intercorrelations among all variables. It is, however, of some interest to inspect some of the specific items that did *not* show up to any significant degree in the factor structure.

Two items sought indexes of the groups' relations to the physicians in the community outside them by seeking estimates of the proportions of patients referred to the group from the outside and of those the group refers outside. When we pretested the questions, administrators often protested that it was impossible for them to estimate referrals accurately: while in our survey we optimistically kept the questions in anyway, the lack of findings suggest that the data are unreliable. In any event, report on neither direction of referral has a higher correlation than .35 with any other questionnaire items.

Another set of items sought information about patients' complaints: too few administrators reported complaints to make any meaningful interpretation. Similarly, a series of items sought information about the complaints of group physicians regarding their colleagues: "discretion" or ignorance or poor question-wording may have discouraged responses by group administrators. Another item sought to gain an estimate of the degree to which social relations among group physicians exist outside of work. This item will be explored more completely in the survey of group physicians. All that may be said here is that it is not clear why it does not fall into some factor, but that it did not correlate with any other item in the matrix higher than .26. Finally, two of the ten "problems that appear in some medical groups" did not show up in the factors or have substantial relations with any other items— "friction between older and younger men," and "physicians complain of lack of opportunity to deal with interesting cases or do research." These will be reconsidered when the survey of physicians is analyzed.

In summary, it seems fair to say that the R analysis has yielded fairly coherent factors in most cases and that it has encompassed most of the true variance. The factors constitute dimensions that are of course not exhaustive of group practice as a whole but that do allow one to begin to distinguish separate elements of the organization of group practice. Factor 1 relates to formal consumer plans. Factor 2 concerns a cluster of formal professional supervisory practices. Factor 3 points to the division of labor and the completeness of specialization. Factor 4 involves a cooperative or equalitarian set of practices. Factor 5 suggests bureaucratic elements distinct from those involved in consumer plans or professional supervision. Factor 6 points to individualistic elements, Factor 7 to elements of physician satisfaction, and Factor 8 to monopolistic tendencies.

But while these factors can serve as helpful guides in analyzing what dimensions of organization exist in medical groups, they tell us nothing of how each factor is related to the other. Is what has been delineated as Factor 1 usually found together with Factor 2 in the same type of organization, and Factor 3 usually found together with Factor 4, or is there no pattern in the way those organizational dimensions are found to occur together in medical groups? If we find a tendency to cluster, we are able to use those clusters of interrelated organizations to delineate an empirical typology of medical groups as such. A second factor analysis of the data was designed to determine whether the factors representing dimensions of group organization themselves formed clusters that could be used to specify types of medical groups.

TYPES OF MEDICAL GROUPS

In order to put this issue to empirical test each medical group was given a score on each factor, using Harmon's Short Method. These scores were then subjected to a Q factor analysis by the Centroid Procedure and a Verimax orthogonal rotation. By this means particular medical groups that best represented the Q factors were identified. The R factor scores of these selected medical groups were averaged for each Q factor and all such average scores were standardized to make them directly comparable. The results of this analysis are given in table 9.2, where,

TABLE 9.2   Empirical Types of Medical Groups

Factors (Types Groups)	R Factors (Standardized)							
	1—Consumer plan	2—Formal supervision	3—Unsatisfactory division of labor	4—Equalitarianism	5—Bureaucratization	6—Entrepreneurialism	7—Physician satisfaction	8—Monopolism
—Bureaucratic organization	1.80	1.50	.43	− .89	2.18	.12	.33	.28
—Equalitarian organization	−1.03	− .83	.00	1.67	− .64	−1.87	1.13	.39
—Confederation	− .77	−2.00	.00	1.00	− .73	1.00	.87	−.11
—Individualistic collectivity	− .83	− .50	−.14	− .66	− .82	1.12	.20	−.33
—	.01	− .17	.00	.33	.00	1.25	.00	.78
—	.73	.33	.71	.66	.36	.63	−2.20	−.06
—	− .21	.00	.57	−1.78	− .36	.00	.51	−.17

unlike the values in table 9.1, the cell entries consist of average factor scores rather than factor loadings.

The data in table 9.2 suggest that there are at least four distinct types of group practice organizations, three others being rather difficult to interpret. Q Factor 1, Bureaucratic Organization, is made up of groups that have high bureaucratization scores, and high scores on consumer plan (and the bureaucratic elements it involves, including consumer service contracts) and formal professional supervision of medical work. Consistently enough, it has a low score on equalitarian attributes, a fact which, on inspection of the items in R Factor 4 in table 9.1, reinforces the plausibility of the interpretation of the pattern as a formal medical bureaucracy.

Q Factor 2, Equalitarian Organization, represents quite a different type of group, high scores on equalitarian attributes as well as those connected with general physician satisfaction. It has low scores on attributes of individualistic organization, consumer plan, formal internal professional supervision, and bureaucratization. This factor seems to delineate a small partnership in which each physician participates as an equal, even in the sharing of group income, and which is governed more by informal understandings than by formal offices, contracts, and directives. Whatever professional supervision exists is informal and not consciously organized. It might be called a democratic, cooperative, or equalitarian organization.

Q Factor 3, Confederation, shows a distinctly different pattern of organization that might, logically, be considered a mixed type despite its empirical existence as an entity. It has high scores in *both* equalitarian and individualistic attributes and on the factor expressing physician satisfaction, and it is low on all factors connected with bureaucratization. Its lowest score is on the factor representing formal professional supervision. This type of organization might be labeled a loose confederacy, in that while there is a degree of equal participation in affairs of common interest, there is also apparently enough looseness in the organization for each individual to guide many of his own affairs by himself.

Q Factor 4 seems to represent a "pure" type—that of an individualistic form of organization in which each person is more or less free to work as he chooses within a generally agreed-on loose framework. Scores are low for virtually all other factors but that of individualistic attributes, and lowest for those factors representing consumer plans and bureaucratic organization. Indeed, it may be that this factor reflects an organization only in the light of legal or tax advantages, a marriage of convenience rather than consummation, similar to the individualistic collectivity formed by small shopkeepers (cf. Bechhofer and Elliott, 1968).

The remaining factors are less clear. Q Factor 5 is more or less identical to R Factor 8, and scoring low on individualistic attributes of organization: its meaning is not apparent. Q Factor 6 seems to represent a strange form of group practice built around a consumer contract plan but organized very loosely and showing evidence of extensive dissatisfaction among group physicians. And finally, Q Factor 7 is composed primarily of a very low score on R Factor 4, equalitarianism, whatever that means.

While it is true that the clarity of the Q factors is not as great as that of the R factors, there can be little doubt that a typology of medical groups does in fact have some empirical validity. The orthogonal R factors do occur in certain typical arrangements in real medical groups, arrangements which suggest that important differences bearing on the quality of patient care and the satisfaction of practitioners are to be found among organizations that all conform to the usual definition of group practice. Indeed, they suggest that the usual definition of group practice is so general as to be well-nigh useless for analysis. In fact, when one considers that the data presented here bear on only a segment of the much larger universe denoted by the usual definition of group practice, it should be obvious that variation in the universe is likely to be even greater than what has been found here. The dimensions isolated here, however, and the patterns they form may be seen as a first step toward the empirical delineation of critical elements by which group practices may be distinguished and evaluated.

SIGNIFICANCE OF THE DIMENSIONS

One can go on at some length speculating on the meaning of the details of the empirical patterns revealed by the factor analyses, but it seems appropriate to reserve most of the analysis of those details for another paper where controlled cross-tabulation can present a more concrete view of the interrelations of the salient variables. Here, however, it seems well to emphasize the importance of one of the most marked gross findings—namely, the relation of professional supervisory practices to other elements of the organization of group practice.

One major focus of the overall study of which the survey reported here is but a part lies in the issue of professional supervision of medical performance. Such supervision lies at the heart of evaluating professions, for unlike most occupations, professions are generally left free to regulate themselves: The test of the honesty of their claims is provided by examination of how they regulate themselves. In medicine the academic norm is to undertake such supervision by means of systematic review of the medical records, case conferences, and the like. We took the presence of such procedure in medical groups to be a prime index of efforts to assure an adequate level of competent medical care. While it is patently possible that other kinds of efforts to assure competent care could exist, we can only assume greater variation in the efficiency (and honesty) of such efforts than can occur within the narrower limits of formal review procedures.[3] The latter, then, are taken to be the more critical reflections of efforts to assure an adequate level of professional performance. That a variety of such procedures carried on by members of medical groups clustered into a single factor reinforced our belief that they constitute a single, general dimension of the organization of group practice. What is the relation of that dimension to others?

What we have labeled formal internal professional supervision of the quality of work includes a wide range of procedures. In formulating our questionnaire we assumed that differently organized medical groups would have different modes of professional supervision. However, all formal modes, from hierarchical review by chiefs to peer review in a variety of contexts, fell into the same dimension—only that involving a review committee from outside the group falling into another factor. This dimension, we submit, measures empirically the extent to which group practitioners are likely to be living up to the claim of their profession that it regulates itself. *But the only type of group in which this dimension is strong is that which also includes the attributes of bureaucratization and consumer service plans.* Such supervisory practices are not to be found in association with equalitarian or individualistic dimensions of organization. Furthermore, unlike the latter cases, *there is no item included in the configuration in which formal*

---

3. For an evaluation of the informal process of supervision commonly described as "looking over each other's shoulder," see chaps. 7 and 8.

supervisory practices are embedded that reflects satisfaction on the part of the working physicians.

Superficially, there seems to be a serious paradox in the findings. Reports of physician satisfaction (and lack of physician complaint) are restricted to dimensions of medical group organization that allow physicians the autonomy and independence generally valued by the profession: they do not extend to the dimension of supervision that is also said to be valued by the profession. The latter instead is associated with organizational features that, insofar as they include formal administrative positions and offices, are hierarchical in character and, through written rules of procedure and formal contracts, bureaucratic. Both hierarchy and bureaucratic procedures are thought to be specifically antithetical to professional work. Thus, one professionally desirable dimension of work, supervision, is in the medical groups studied connected with the professionally *un*desirable bureaucratic mode of organizing or administering work rather than with the professionally desirable equalitarian or individualistic modes.

This finding permits us to say that variations among medical groups that conform to the conventional definition of group practice are so marked and have such great importance for the formulation of medical policy as to preclude the fruitfulness of discussing group practice in terms of that vague definition. The policy issues surrounding group practice are hardly touched on by the mere number of physicians involved, the number of specialties, and the sharing of physical and economic resources. Within those general limits can be found bureaucratically organized groups with formal review procedures, closely cooperative groups of peers without formal review procedures, and loose aggregates of individual practitioners. It is in the *organization* of group practice that policy issues come to the fore.

REFERENCES

American Association of Medical Clinics.
  1962.   Directory. Chicago: American Association of Medical Clinics.
Balfe, B. E., and M. E. McNamara.
  1968.   *Survey of medical groups in the U. S., 1965.* Special Statistical Series. Chicago: American Medical Association.
Bechhofer, F., and B. Elliott.
  1968.   An approach to the study of small shopkeepers and the class structure. *Archives Européenes de Sociologie* 9:196.

Goldstein, M.
1952.   Medical group practice in the United States. *Journal of the American Medical Association* 177:1049–52.
Hunt, G. H., and M. Goldstein.
1951.   Medical group practice in the United States. Public Health Service Publication no. 77. Washington, D.C.: U.S. Government Printing Office.
McElrath, Dennis.
1961.   Perspective and participation of physicians in prepaid group practice. *American Sociological Review* 26:596–607.
Pomrinse, S. D., and M. Goldstein.
1961a.   A preliminary directory of medical groups in the United States, 1959. Public Health Service Publication no. 817. Washington, D.C.: U.S. Government Printing Office.
———.
1961b.   The growth and development of medical group practice. *Journal of the American Medical Association* 177:765–70.
———.
1961c.   Group practice in the U.S. *American Journal of Public Health* 51:671–82.
U.S. Department of Health, Education, and Welfare.
1967.   Promoting the group practice of medicine. Report of the National Conference on Group Practice, October 19–21, 1967. Public Health Service Publication no. 1750. Washington, D.C.: U.S. Government Printing Office.

TEN

Physicians in Large Medical Groups

Co-author: Buford Rhea

Much is being written about physicians in the United States, but little of it is based on any systematic collection of information. This is true not only in general but also in particular: lengthy and pontifical discussions of "private practice" are largely based on severely limited personal experience and observation, and only rarely on any shreds of objective information. Like solo practice, group practice too is discussed more as a way of life than as a form of human organization whose character can be studied systematically and in detail (see chap. 6 above; Freidson, 1961–62).

The present paper is intended to be a small contribution to the large body of data that must exist before we can say we really know very much about physicians and their work. It is an early report of a study of group practice that is now in its third and last year.

The study was designed to use two quite different modes of analysis: (1) the "clinical case method," whereby one medical group was studied in great and intensive detail by means of inspecting documents, systematic observation, and focused interviews; and (2) the survey method, whereby a number of medical groups yielded standardized information that allowed quantification and ready comparison. All data have now been collected, but only gross forms of analysis have been undertaken by the time of writing. The present paper can only present the most general and distinct findings of our study, reserving some of the more complex findings for a later time, when analysis has proceeded further.

THE STUDY AND ITS DATA

Our study fell into three parts. First, from January 1961 to June 1962, an intensive investigation of one medical group was undertaken in order to obtain close familiarity with the way a medical group operates, to allow a holistic analysis of that organization in and of itself, and to formulate hypotheses amenable to statistical testing in a larger universe of medical groups. All meetings of the medical group were observed, administrative and medical records were examined, key administrative figures in the group were interviewed personally a number of times, as were the fifty-four physicians working in the group, and thirty physicians formerly with the group were interviewed once.

The basic source of information lay in these personal interviews. The general order of interview topics (which formed four separate interviews for internists and pediatricians, and three for consulting specialists) was: (1) personal background, career aspirations, and general response to group practice; (2) problems of patient management in the group, and how solution is attempted; (3) administrative problems of practice, and the physician's relation with and assessment of administrative officers, procedures, and requirements; (4) problems of referral and other relations with colleagues, as well as an assessment of colleagues. Almost all interviews were recorded on tape and subsequently transcribed.

Later, the transcribed interviews were broken into content units, abstracted, and typed onto Royal McBee Keysort cards, and cross-classified by content categories in order to facilitate fairly precise and thorough analysis of this qualitative material.

Throughout this first portion of the study, we were concerned with gathering enough reliable information to allow us to understand how the group practice, as an organization, works and what its problems of operation are. At the very outset, however, it was assumed that two basic elements would be found to conflict to some degree—the element of *bureaucratic organization* (by which is meant the ordering of a relatively complex division of labor into a hierarchical system regulated by rules rather than purely individual judgment) and the element of *professionalism* (one of the attributes of which is said to be the assumption of personal responsibility for and authority over one's work and its consequences). During the course of the intensive study, we were formulating hypotheses about the interaction of those two elements and the influence of each on the other.

Toward the conclusion of that study we began to formulate a questionnaire for determining the kind of administrative structure other medical groups had and for exploring the relation between problems of group operation and that structure. Armed with a draft, several groups in our region were visited, and the draft was pretested. In the late fall of 1962, we sent a copy of that questionnaire to all administrators or business managers of all medical groups in the United States that were listed as being multispecialty in character, and having ten or more full-time doctors. Of those 243 groups, we received replies from 156, a 64 percent return. Our intent was to obtain a sample large enough to provide us with analytical specimens of various types of medical groups, not to obtain a representative cross section of all medical groups. For this the responses we obtained were quite adequate.

The questionnaires filled out by group administrators provided us with information about the administrative organization of the medical groups, as well as information about the administrator's view of the problems of group operation and of the physicians' responses to their groups. Preliminary cross-tabulation gave us hints of what seemed to be empirically important independent variables. On that empirical basis and, more important for us, on the basis of our concepts of bureaucratic organization and professionalism, we developed two indices to be used for the classification of the medical groups.

The first index we have called bureaucratization. It is a numerical score consisting in the sum of weighted scores assigned to answers to various questions in the administrator's questionnaire. Reasoning that the essence of bureaucratic organization lies in the conjunction of hierarchical authority and written rules to govern both the exercise of authority and the division of labor, a number of questionnaire items were used to define it empirically. The existence of a medical director who devotes more than ten hours a week to administration, the existence of department chiefs whose office is sufficiently well-defined that special rewards are attached to it, and the existence of written statements about the number of office hours one is expected to have are among the indices used. All items, weighted, contributed to a score that, numerically, could run from 0 to 56 in any single medical group.

The second index we call, for want of a better term, professionalization. A more accurate but stylistically unwieldy phrase is "the bureaucratization of professional standards." Like the other, this index is a numerical sum of weighted scores assigned to a number of items. Reasoning that *organizationally* significant elements of professionalism lie in the way controls over the technical quality of work are exercised and in the kinds of professional activity stimulated and supported, the existence of such systematic supervisory procedures as chart review and of formal—that is, financial—encouragement of postgraduate education, research, and publication were among the items forming the index. Numerically, the index could run from 0 through 17.

Allowing for variation in size, a subsample of medical groups was drawn from those whose administrators originally replied. It was drawn as far as possible to represent the various combinations of high or low bureaucratization and high or low professionalization, and various degrees of size. A special questionnaire was then administered by mail to the physicians in those groups. A reasonable response rate, averaging 78 percent, was obtained from 38 groups. The total number of physicians responding from those 38 groups was 774, and it is their responses that we shall be reporting here.

The questionnaire for group physicians was designed to obtain information about a number of variables. Some are fairly routine, such as the personal background of the physician, his position in the group, and the like. Others deal directly with his response to his group practice—his satisfaction with and commitment to his group, his assessment of his relations to his patients, of the influence of the group on his personal and professional life, and of the adequacy of various group policies. Still others deal with what may be important professional values—autonomy, intellectual gratifications in work, patient relations, money, and conceptions of professional motivation. Our assumption was that by reference to the administrative organization of a medical group, mediated by the influence of personal background and values, we could explain the physician's response to his group.

It is, however, much too early to test that assumption, for our analysis has only just begun. Here, we will report only the overall characteristics of the physicians we surveyed, and the way they respond to the medical groups in which they work. After that overall picture of the 774 physicians of 38 groups, we shall present some of our earliest ideas about the way the results seem to be ordered. In reading these findings, one should be warned that they are *not* representative of the total universe of group physicians. They refer only to physicians in relatively large medical groups, and even then, only to the range of variation of such groups, not the universe as such. Furthermore, they are preliminary and tentative.

BACKGROUND

The doctors in the group practices we studied are relatively young, 37 percent of them being 39 years or less. Consonant with their age, we find that 38 percent have been in their groups for only five years or less. Finally, again consonant with our expectations for relatively young physicians, we find that almost half of the doctors responding—44 percent—came directly into their present group after their residency, having no significant experience with solo practice; 10 percent came from a small partnership, and 22 percent from practice in hospitals, the military, and the like.

By far the vast majority of the doctors in our survey—87 percent—work full-time in their groups. The majority (65 percent) are full or partial partners in their groups; of the others, 12 percent are on probation, 22 percent are on salary, and 2 percent are in miscellaneous categories.[1] Since the groups are largely partnerships, 46 percent of those responding are or were in some major executive position in their groups. Furthermore, the physicians in those groups are relatively well-trained—90 percent of the doctors who responded are either board-eligible or board-certified.

PROFESSIONAL ACTIVITY

Medical groups are not merely places in which people work. They are also supposed to be places where physicians are subjected to various stimuli presumed to improve the quality of their work. In this sense, it is important to ask about the varied types of professional activity of group doctors and about the role of their groups in that activity.

In the absence of comparative data, we cannot easily judge our

---

1. Totals may be a bit more than 100 percent in some cases due to rounding. Where totals are less than 100 percent, either rounding is involved or a small proportion of individuals failed to answer the question.

findings. We found that 52 percent of the respondents said that they regularly attended meetings of their professional specialty societies. In contrast to this, 30 percent said that they regularly attended meetings of their county medical society. In addition to attending meetings, we inquired about reading and publishing; 43 percent of the doctors reported "keeping up with" three professional journals or less and having published not more than two articles; at the other extreme, 20 percent of the physicians read on a regular basis at least four professional journals and had published at least three articles. There are variations between these extremes of relatively little and great reading and publishing but it is clear that a respectable proportion (but by no means a majority) of group physicians read and publish a fair amount.

Attendance at meetings, reading, and publishing can be quite personal individual matters, with no necessary relation to one's group practice. However, the group itself is a potential source of stimulation in professional affairs. Both knowledge and stimulation can be given by colleagues. Our respondents were asked how often, during an average month, they talk over their problem cases with group colleagues both in their own specialty and in some other specialty. A third of the doctors answered that they speak to somebody in their own specialty about a problem case at least once a day and also speak to a colleague in some other speciality at least once a day. This seems to be a fair amount of contact. Somewhat less frequent colleague contact is reported by the remainder of the respondents, but fully 27 percent report talking over cases only once or twice a week with colleagues both in their own specialty and in other specialties. A related item is the matter of friendship, which can also be a basis for professional interaction; 14 percent of the doctors claimed no close personal friends among their group colleagues, but 36 percent claimed five or more.

Finally, we may mention a question intended to determine directly the extent to which the medical group as an organization is responsible for stimulating the doctor professionally. The doctors were asked to indicate the rank order of various sources of intellectual stimulation—such as contacts with colleagues and other meetings in the medical group, contacts with colleagues, and meetings in the community outside the medical group, reading periodicals, and attending professional meetings taking place outside of the local community. By and large, the major source of stimulation to the doctors responding seems to lie in events going on outside of both the medical group and the local medical community. Just over half of the physicians ranked reading periodicals and attending professional meetings outside the community as their prime source of intellectual stimulation. The medical group itself was reported to be the main source of intellectual stimulation by 29 percent of the doctors responding, while contact with nongroup colleagues and meetings within the local community were ranked first by only 18 percent of the group physicians.

PROFESSIONAL VALUES

We have spoken of professional activity as if it were important to the physician. But do the physicians themselves feel it to be important? Do they feel any other elements of practice are important? One of the main aims of our questionnaire was to explore the various dimensions of professional values.

Intellectual values in medicine. We might call the first value intellectualism—the extent to which the physician is interested in medicine as an intellectual scientific pursuit. A series of questions dealt with this dimension.[2] Asked about the relative importance of professional stimulation from colleagues in their practice, of seeing cases which constitute a real medical challenge, and of practicing high-quality academic medicine with minimum compromise in standards, most of the doctors checked the end of the scale indicating relatively great importance. In the case of doing research, however, only 19 percent indicated that it had any relative importance to them, 54 percent expressing relative indifference.

On the whole we feel that there was a great deal of piety to the answers we obtained, for in our intensive study of one medical group and in our reading of other studies (Peterson et al. 1956) there is good evidence that by no means a majority of physicians gain their prime gratification in practice from the scientific, intellectual elements of medicine. No doubt our questions could have been better designed to elicit less pious responses. Be that as it may, we found that the answers to our questions could discriminate among the physicians if we classi-

---

2. In what follows, we will be discussing responses that took the form of checking points on a scale of intensity, the center point reflecting either no opinion or no preference. Since we will be discussing only those responses reflecting a preference, the total percentage presented here may fall short of 100.

fied them by the relative degree of importance they assigned to each of the items: assigning extreme importance to one item is correlated with assigning extreme importance to all others. The most predictive item was the question about research, belying our initial hope that we could distinguish two kinds of intellectualism, one clinical and one scientific. Using answers to the question about research for our estimate, it would seem that while most group physicians profess general intellectual interest in medicine, only 19 percent seem to assign heavy weight to the active intellectual investigation that research implies.

Entrepreneurial values. Rather distinct from and empirically uncorrelated with intellectualism is a set of different values. Taken together, they seem to portray interest in the practical demands and special rewards of solo, fee-taking practice. For this reason, we call them entrepreneurial values. One is the value of autonomy. Our questionnaire had a number of different items bearing on areas of practice in which autonomy might be an issue. First, there is the matter of freedom from professional supervision. For 44 percent of the doctors this was relatively important; for 30 percent it was relatively unimportant. Second, there is the matter of regulating one's time. To 48 percent of the doctors, being able to regulate their own time was important to them compared to 19 percent of the doctors who said that it was relatively unimportant. Third, there is the matter of managing patients "one's own way, without interference from anyone else." In all, 69 percent of the doctors said that this was relatively important to them, compared to 11 percent who said that it was relatively unimportant. Autonomy in a number of areas thus proves to be important for a near majority of our group physicians. Insofar as group practice involves of necessity the constraints of cooperation among and coordination of varied services, this valuation of autonomy may be of some significance for its success.

Those who value autonomy highly are also likely to value two other things—money and their relations with their patients. Two-thirds or more of the doctors indicated that having a fairly substantial income and a secure income are relatively important to them. Three-quarters of the doctors indicated that giving emotional support and understanding to patients was relatively important to them, and somewhat fewer—63 percent—indicated the importance to them of attracting a circle of loyal patients.

Patient relations. In addition to direct questions about the value of patient relations to group physicians, we asked a number of questions designed to determine the philosophy of patient management. Generally speaking, "intellectuals" were more likely to adopt an authoritarian attitude toward patients than were the "entrepreneurs." However, most doctors agreed with the pieties that "It is more important for patients to respect you as a doctor than to like you as a person," and "A doctor shouldn't expect patients to respect him just because he is a doctor." On the matter of being firm with patients, however, there was considerably less consensus. Given the statement, These days there is a tendency to coddle patients; doctors should be more firm with them," 47 percent of the doctors agreed to one degree or another, and 30 percent disagreed.

A number of items were intended to clarify the meaning of being firm with patients. Most of the doctors disagreed with the statement that, "If a patient won't follow the doctor's advice, the doctor should feel no obligation to try to persuade him to." In this sense, most feel at least abstract obligation to attempt to work with the patient even in the face of the patient's resistance. Most also agreed with the item, "Quite aside from any legal implications, if a patient wants to see a doctor he should be seen, even though the doctor may be short of time and it is very likely that there is nothing seriously wrong with the patient." And most even felt that "there should be some formal arrangement whereby patients can register their complaints against doctors and be assured that they will be investigated." Answers to those items suggest that the group physician is willing to go more than halfway in cooperating with patients, but where medical treatment is involved there is less agreement on how cooperative one should be. Asked their opinion of the item, "If a patient insists on some harmless medication, the doctor might as well go ahead and give it to him even though he knows it will do no good," 37 percent of the doctors agreed, and 47 percent disagreed.

Values applied to administration. If we were to take the responses to the above items at their face value, we might assume that these physicians could not possibly be happy in their medical groups. Group practice is a cooperative venture, and these men sound like rugged individualists. And like all practice, that in the group is by and large routine and often trivial, and these men sound like academics infatuated with rare, interesting cases. However, the physicians do seem fairly well committed to their groups. And we find that most of our respondents have no difficulty contradicting their abstractly expressed values in ways that are prone to be more plausible for successful group practice.

Let us look first at items bearing on the value of autonomy. To a statement that, "It's only fair, that, barring emergencies, a group should insist that doctors keep their office hours strictly so that patients and colleagues won't be inconvenienced," 87 percent of the physicians agreed and only 9 percent disagreed. *Most* prone to agree were those to whom abstractly expressed autonomy was most important! Then there was the item, "A lay administrator would be justified in reprimanding a doctor for nontechnical inadequacies in his work—not returning charts to a file, habitually coming in late for hours, failing to submit billings, and so on." We expected that the mention of a lay administrator and the use of the word *reprimand* would occasion violent disagreement, but 64 percent agreed. And to the statement, "A medical director or chief of staff would be quite within his rights to formally reprimand a physician for being impolite to his patient," 64 percent agreed. Our physicians thus seem far more willing to submit to direction in a number of areas than we would assume from their general values.

Two items bearing on medical work attracted somewhat greater differences of opinion: 54 percent of the doctors agreed with the statement, "In order to avoid conflicts between specialties, groups should establish a formal policy about responsibility for particular complaints"; 31 percent disagreed. And to the statement that "The best way to guarantee a high quality of medical care in a group, aside from recruiting good doctors, is by regular and formal supervision of professional work through such devices as chart review," 49 percent agreed and 36 percent disagreed.

Finally, our questionnaire had a series of items that at once bear on the physician's view of his own autonomy and on his view of what motivates the professional. To the item, "One of the dangers of an incentive system of payment in a group is that the doctors are likely to sacrifice quality to quantity so as to make more money," 58 percent of the doctors agreed, and 34 percent disagreed. Those who agree, we may note, concede that economic motives may outweigh professional motives in work. However, there is implicit contradiction in the fact that while the majority of the doctors agreed with the above item, they also agreed with two others that imply quite a different view of the doctor and his motivation. The first item, "If a doctor is lazy or inconsiderate, no amount of pressure from his colleagues is going to change him," gives the impression of a self-sustaining being whose interaction with others has no influence on his behavior; 68 percent of the physicians agreed with it, and 28 percent disagreed. The second even more blankly implies this image: "In the final analysis, the only thing that makes a doctor practice good medicine is his own conscience." To this, 83 percent of the doctors agreed and only 12 percent disagreed. The responses to these items have been put in a baldly pro-con fashion, without regard to discriminating *degree* of responses among the physicians. Put so oversimply, the physicians appear to have both abstract values and conceptions of self that are belied by the requirements of everyday experience. At some later date, after more refined cross-tabulations are undertaken, we hope to comment in more detail and with more certainty on this contradiction.

RESPONSES TO GROUP PRACTICE

Thus far, we have presented a thumbnail sketch of the preponderant attributes of our physicians. The majority of them are relatively young and well qualified. Most profess interest in both the intellectual and the practical sides of medical practice and a generally humane attitude toward their patients. As individualistic as they seem, most also seem willing, by and large, to impose restraints on practice in medical groups. However, the responses we have described thus far are all abstract, referring to general value and policy. How do these physicians respond to their own concrete group practices?

We may say first of all that commitment to their groups is rather extensive among our physicians. Confronted with a hypothetical question, "Would you leave your present position in the medical group if you were offered a full-time post on the faculty of a medical school, or would you leave if you were invited to enter as a full partner into a good, compatible 2- or 3-man partnership," fully 50 percent of the physicians answered that they wouldn't leave for either circumstance, income notwithstanding. If we add to this the 12 percent who said that they would leave for one only if offered a greater income and not leave for the other under any circumstances, we have a total of 62 percent rather firmly committed to their group practices.

This relatively extensive commitment implies a fairly high degree of satisfaction with group practice. This is indeed the case. Asked about their patient load, 70 percent indicated it to be neither too great nor too little. Asked to compare their patients' behavior with that of patients in solo practice, there was little hint of difficulty: more than three-quarters felt that their group patients were about as considerate or more considerate than they are in solo practice. In the case of patient gratitude, patient satisfaction, and the tendency of patients to accept the doctor's advice, the same high proportions asserted that group patients are at least as positive in their attitude as they are in solo practice. There is thus no strongly marked sense of dissatisfaction with patients on the part of these physicians in group practice.

In addition to questions about the behavior of patients in group practice, the survey included a series asking the physicians how they believed their groups have influenced their own abilities or careers. In the case of income and leisure, 55 and 62 percent, respectively, felt that their group has been responsible for some degree of improvement (or increase). More than 70 percent of the physicians felt that their group practice had been responsible for increasing the scientific quality of their work and for their keeping up with the latest medical advances. It was felt by 56 percent that their group was responsible for an increase in their specialization or subspecialization. Lesser proportions ascribed to their group's influence an increase in their "sensitivity to the psychological needs of the patient" (46 percent) and in their "professional autonomy" (36 percent), but in no item was a *negative* influence ascribed to group practice by anything resembling a majority of the physicians.

This same generally positive attitude to their practice was manifested by our group physicians in their response to a series of items evaluating group policy. In only one item—emphasis on and encouragement of research—did a majority of the physicians (58 percent) indicate that their groups left something to be desired. A high proportion—40 percent—also indicated that there were too few professional meetings, such as journal clubs, in their groups. In all other instances a clear majority of the physicians indicated satisfaction with their groups as they are. In the technical domain, what criticism there was tended to focus on too little supervision of professional work rather than too much, and too little referral among members of the group rather than too much, though criticism of the group's emphasis on specialization was divided.

The direction of all these critical responses points consistently to dissatisfaction among a significant proportion of physicians with the *professional* policies of their groups. Other areas of group policy do not seem to elicit as much dissatisfaction. About a quarter of the physicians felt that there was too little informal socializing, but 71 percent felt that the amount of socializing was about right or expressed no definite opinion. While over 60 percent had no criticism of their group's attention to patient desires and to service to the community, what criticism was made, stressed underattention more often than overattention. The same is true of the degree to which group members participate in policymaking—the minority of complaints most often stress underparticipation. And those few who felt that the supervision of hours, coverage, and the like left something to be desired most often stressed undersupervision.

On every item but one, then, where dissatisfaction did exist, it was far more likely to stress the absence or underemphasis of a policy than the presence or abuse of a policy. Those criticisms, mild as they are, point to the degree to which even these atypically large medical groups are nonetheless predominantly primitive organizations, likely to have a policy or program only where the purely logistic demands of the consulting room are involved.

PROSPECTUS ON FUTURE ANALYSIS

The material presented thus far has been summary in character, stressing the attributes of the majority. Insofar as our sample is not, strictly speaking, representative of the universe of American group practice, these "marginals" are relatively meaningless. What is considerably more important for understanding group practice is likely to be found in cross-tabulating the data. At this early stage of analysis, the few cross-tabulations we have suggest that our chances of finding useful ways of ordering and explaining our physicians' responses to relatively large-scale group practice are good.

For example, three administrative variables—the size of the group, the extent of its bureaucratization, and its financing of care on a service-contract basis—have been tabulated. Very generally speaking, the simple contrast between the doctors in the smallest groups and those in the largest parallels that between individuals in the groups scoring *low* in our bureaucratization-professionalization index and those scoring *high,* and doctors in groups giving little service on a contract basis, and those giving predominantly contract service.

In the smallest groups, as in the low-bureaucratic and non-contract groups, comparatively little interest is expressed in research. Instead, comparatively great importance is assigned patient relations and freedom from supervision. In turn, physicians in the smallest groups are more likely to believe their group patients to be more considerate than those in solo practice; physicians in the largest, high-bureaucratic and service-contract groups are more likely to believe their group patients to be less considerate than those in solo practice. Small group doctors, however, more often seem to get their gratification from patients rather than colleague relations, for they are less likely to talk over cases much with group colleagues and less likely to report their group to be a major source of intellectual stimulation. It seems no accident, therefore, that they are more likely to criticize their groups for putting too little emphasis on research and for having too few professional meetings. Unlike physicians in the largest, bureaucratized and service-contract groups, however, they are quite satisfied with the degree to which there is general professional participation in group policymaking.

These differences associated with variation in size and administrative organization begin to suggest critical differences among medical groups. They bear on the operation of the group as well as on the individual attributes of the physicians involved. Furthermore, these organizational variables seem to order more of the data than do the values held by the physicians recruited into the groups, for in our preliminary cross-tabulation of thirteen strategically chosen items covering the whole range of variables we have discussed in this paper, such an organizational variable as size discriminates eleven of the total. The personal values of the physicians, on the other hand, do not discriminate more than five of the thirteen.

It seems, then, that the originally hypothesized direction of analysis is worth following. In future analysis, we plan to explore further how useful administrative organization is as an independent variable to account for many problems of medical practice in groups.[3] On the other hand, physicians' values are hypothesized to *intervene* between the influence of administrative variables on responses to group practice, as are such other attributes as seniority, specialty, and social

3. Plans for a more detailed and systematic analysis were never carried out due to the accidental destruction of the data.

isolation in the group. The analysis we have made thus far persuades us that by following out such reasoning in detail, much of both practical and theoretical value may be learned about the group practice of medicine in particular and professional practice in general.

REFERENCES

Freidson, E.
1961–   The sociology of medicine: A trend report and bibliography.
62.   *Current Sociology* 10/11, no. 3 (entire issue).
Peterson, O. L., L. P. Andrews, R. S. Spain, and B. G. Greenberg.
1956.   An analytical study of North Carolina general practice, 1953–
         1954. *Journal of Medical Education* 31 (Part 2): 1–165.

PART THREE

The Present Status of the Profession

ELEVEN

The System Surrounding
Practitioners

The social organization of medical practice, discussed in the preceding chapters, must be distinguished from the social organization of the medical profession itself. It is a common tendency to conceive of the profession as the aggregate of individual physicians who practice medicine. Indeed, this is the way doctors, lawyers, college professors, and other professionals also conceive of their professions. They consider those who assume administrative positions or who devote themselves full-time to research to have abandoned, even betrayed, their profession. Similarly, they look upon those who are active in the politics of the profession with some suspicion, as they do upon those who work in state agencies. Only those who perform the basic work of the profession in its characteristic work settings are considered to be "the" profession.

However, those who consider themselves to be the profession could not have any reasonably secure assurance of working at their trade under the terms and conditions they expect were it not for the activities of those they are inclined to rule out as true colleagues. Their most elementary protection from competition from members of other occupations willing to work at lower cost and claiming the same or better results stems from credentials that give them the privilege of something resembling a monopoly to perform particular kinds of work. Those credentials and the educational, administrative, and legal systems that create and sustain them owe little if any of their existence and persistence to practitioners as such.

As the histories of the professions in the United States show, they gained legal or quasi-legal license and mandate through the activities of those who led professional associations and professional schools. Their activities were both administrative and political, involving the creation of organizations, curricula, licensing bodies, and the like, intensive public relations efforts, and indefatigable lobbying in the halls of state legislatures. The result of those efforts is embodied not only in the fact that professionals enjoy a special position in the labor market and in their workplaces, but also in the fact of a complex of institutions organizing professional work into a system and a set of functional roles and positions that are quite different from those of practitioners but an intrinsic and essential part of the profession nonetheless. Without those institutions and professionals serving in special, nonpracticing roles, neither the present-day substance nor organization of professional work would have been possible.

It follows that an adequate analysis of medical work—of the behavior of doctors—requires more than direct study of the work itself, of the interaction between doctor and patient and of the relations between colleagues. It also requires close study of the culture that creates the background meanings of health and illness; of the political economy that establishes, finances, and shapes the resources available to health care; of the institutions responsible for training health workers and for creating, sustaining, and organizing medical work; and of those who perform the nonpracticing but functional roles intrinsic to medical work today. It is essential to understand those broader forces in order to understand what goes on in practice. I shall sketch the character of those forces in this chapter.

THE AMERICAN CULTURE OF HEALTH

In discussing the doctor-patient relationship I referred to the ideas patients have about health and illness and the possibility that they deviate considerably from those of the doctor. Marked deviation does exist in particular ethnic groups, especially for those members who have not been brought up in the United States or who live in communities that are insulated from the media and the public schools. The bulk of the American population, however, differentiated in part by the amount of formal education they have had, may be said to share a roughly common set of concerns about health and beliefs about health, illness, and medicine itself. We might call this the American culture of health.

All people everywhere are concerned about health and illness. But I think it can be said with some accuracy that Americans are more preoccupied, even obsessed, with health and illness than many other people. Furthermore, they differ from many others by being optimistic and active rather than fatalistic and passive. Rather than considering complaints something to bear, an inevitable part of life which one might deplore but must nonetheless accept, Americans seem to be unusually inclined to seek cures even for what others might consider minor problems.

The American preoccupation with health is often said to emphasize curative and remedial rather than preventive medicine. But that is not entirely true. There is a tradition extending well back into the nineteenth century for Americans—at least middle-class Americans— to be concerned with the prevention of illness by the proper diet, fresh air, personal cleanliness, exercise, and the avoidance of alcohol and tobacco. That tradition emphasizes the preventive activity of the *individual,* with very little expected from the state. That characteristic focus on the individual as the unit of action encourages intense preoccupation with the development and use of curative and remedial techniques and restricts preventive techniques to those that must be the responsibility of individuals themselves.

There is more to it than that, however. Capitalism makes a critical contribution to the American health system's emphasis on curative treatment and repair and to the public's preoccupation with health and illness. Profit on investment capital is the engine that drives firms in capitalist nations, and profit is more likely when investment is in activities that produce discrete goods and services that can be both proprietary and sold to a mass of individuals. Investing in a communal resource like a water supply system that is not protected from politics is considerably less attractive than investing in the production and sale of individual household water filters needed to cope with a poor water supply.

But while capitalism certainly contributes to an emphasis on curative health care, it would be a mistake to consider its influence to be determinative, for the same emphasis on curative technique exists in the actual policies of state socialist countries whose official ideology emphasizes commitment to preventive and environmental health programs. In both kinds of political economy, it is cheaper in the short run and less difficult politically at all times to deal with individual complaints rather than with communities and environments. Furthermore, physicians everywhere seem to find curative medicine more interesting and challenging than preventive medicine.

In capitalist countries, however, there is great effort on the part of pharmaceutical and other health-related manufacturers to market new as well as old products and to try to increase consumption. This requires publicizing products in two quite different markets—the market for controlled goods, which only physicians and other health care providers are entitled to order, and the market for over-the-counter drugs and, increasingly, health-related devices, which are sold directly to the public. Those manufacturers mount extensive advertising campaigns, some addressed to physicians and others authorized to order restricted products and others addressed to lay consumers.

It is characteristic of such advertising, like all advertising, to exaggerate the importance of the issue it deals with as well as the virtues of the product it is marketing. Advertising, after all, is meant to attract consumers and persuade them to buy. Except when required by government regulation, the presentation of complete information about advertised products, including possible limitations or negative consequences, is avoided. When it is required, such qualifying information is displayed in the smallest acceptable print on page or screen and in the shortest, most rapid announcement or display possible. In the case of health-related products, advertising exaggerates the importance or danger of the particular signs, symptoms, and diagnosed conditions the product is said to deal with. While few unqualified claims or promises can be made about the consequences to be expected from the product, every effort is made to claim or imply the most positive, if not entirely miraculous, results. Advertising of health-related products, then, in some cases tries to lead people to perceive health problems they did not previously recognize and in all cases tries to convey the impression that there is effective relief or cure.

The stimulation by advertising of public interest in curative and repair measures is intensified by the mass media. Their profitability and survival depend on the advertising they carry. But in order to carry enough advertising at profitable rates, they must attract a large audience of readers, listeners, and viewers, for the larger their audience the more advertisers they will have and the more they will pay. So the media are involved in a double process of intensifying as well as catering to public interest in health and illness. On the one hand, they compete energetically to get new information on the illnesses of the moment and on efforts to find better ways to diagnose and treat them. They present this information in such a way as to attract the attention of consumers, namely by dramatizing and simplifying the issues, proclaiming a "miracle cure," "breakthrough," "new hope," and the like. In addition, they display the advertising of the health-related manufacturers, who imply if not actually certify that their products will bring the consumer freedom from discomfort and illness, bring a life of health and well-being.

The clinicians and researchers who are concerned with developing new techniques and extending old ones, and with isolating the apparent causes of illnesses and disabilities so as to find better methods of treating them, also play a part in this process of intensifying public concern. Indeed, they have little choice but to do so if they are to gain support for their activities. Nowadays most research requires space, personnel, equipment, and other resources demanding a level of financing that is beyond the resources of individuals. Researchers must obtain financing from government agencies, drug and medical technology companies, and private foundations and associations concerned with health issues.

Such dependence requires that they persuade others of the importance and legitimacy of their activities. In the case of gaining support from pharmaceutical and health technology companies, they must emphasize the potential for profit in the discoveries they seek. In the case of government financing, they are most successful when their research can be related to illnesses or disabilities about which there is widespread and intense public concern.

For researchers and scientists, then, as well as for profit-oriented manufacturers, distributors, and mass media, there is enormous pressure to dramatize the complaints people have, to rediscover them by medicalizing them as illnesses, to produce new methods of dealing with them and to promise much for them. This produces the climate of daily life that intensifies the American consumer's concern with personal health and optimistic search for remedies.

THE STATE AND THE PROFESSION

American society is exceptional not only in the degree of its preoccupation with health and illness but also in the character of its government.

Unlike most modern industrial societies, it is a loosely centralized federal system. And in the United States far more than in other modern industrial nations, private associations play an unusually influential role. For example, its higher educational system is a blend of private and public institutions, with private institutions often receiving public funds. By and large, the credentialing of higher educational institutions (including professional schools) is carried out by private associations, whose approval is usually a prerequisite to the ultimate legal sanction of state licensing.

The same sources of legitimization and support exist for health care institutions and occupations. The licensing of practitioners—and it is in the health sector where occupational licensing is most common—is a function of the states rather than of the federal government. There, private professional associations often play a large, perhaps determinative role in administering both state licensing and the disciplinary machinery attached to it. Health care institutions like hospitals are also licensed by the states rather than the federal government, with private sources of accreditation as important for many of their needs as public operating licenses themselves.

However, while the states are the primary source of the laws governing and regulating the practice of medicine, and while they have been generally permissive in their governance, the federal government has been assuming an increasingly influential and demanding role in health affairs. This has come about primarily through the growth of its role in financing health services. In order to be accountable for the disbursement of public funds, its agencies have developed both consistent guidelines for determining what institutions and individuals are eligible for financing and procedures for limiting costs and assuring that public funds are spent appropriately. This political necessity has led to the rapid expansion of the role of the national government in setting the terms and conditions of health care as well as in establishing standards of care that become the criteria for the review of practitioner performance. While the review of claims for payment is performed by government agents, the review of practitioner decisions is performed by private groups empowered by enabling legislation and delegated the task by government.

Given the peculiar roles of the state and private associations in the organization and operation of the health care system, it follows that an essential part of the system lies in the activities of private groups and individuals lobbying in both state and federal legislatures. The most important private groups are of course the various trade and professional associations attempting to advance the interests of those in the health industry. Much remains to be learned about the activities of individual associations as well as the shifting alliances and conflicts that sometimes join together and sometimes divide *groups* of associations in the political arena. As I note in chapter 12, what were in the past common causes for medical, educational, and hospital interests now seem to be dividing them, thereby weakening what was once the very powerful influence of the American Medical Association on legislation and its implementation by government agencies. And too little has been documented of the influence on public policy of private capital: surely large corporate employers concerned about the cost of their health benefits programs must attempt to advance their ends, as must private insurance companies, health-related manufacturers, and commercial health service enterprises.

Another critical set of forces that are shaping the broad economic and legal context of medical work is to be found in the government agencies that are now responsible for implementing legislation. They determine *how* legislation is implemented, and their changing regulations become extremely important factors in setting the conditions for payment from public and private insurers for services and commodities. Indeed, in some cases their regulations set the terms for the very survival of health-related enterprises.

Mere formal regulations do not tell us all we need to know in order to understand actual agency practice. Clearly, particular administrations have their own policy orientations. The heads of agencies who are appointed by the executive branch of government are chosen for the compatibility of their political philosophies with those of the executive branch. The heads of agencies in the recent Reagan administration, for example, have emphasized reliance on private rather than government enterprise and have stressed (somewhat selectively) reliance on control by free competition in the marketplace rather than by government regulation. Translated into policy, that emphasis led agency heads to force professions, and most particularly medicine, to forsake practices restricting overt economic competition among their members.

Still, the influence of agency heads can be exaggerated. It should be apparent that policy is not always implemented as the executive and its appointed agency heads wish. This is so because a hostile legislature can sometimes block executive policy, as can legal actions by individuals or organizations. A less obvious source of influence on implementation stems from the permanent civil servants who perform the day-to-day work of agencies. Tenured through successive administrations, their habits and aims shaped by earlier times, they may very well have their own conceptions of the proper goals and procedures for their agency. And while their power is markedly limited by legislation and administrative regulations, merely the way they carry out their duties on a day-to-day basis can have important consequences. Their backgrounds, their training, their careers in and out of government, their personal political and social philosophies, and their views of the health professions and health care itself are likely to be important factors in the way they carry out their duties.

THE LEGAL SYSTEM

The legal system in the United States must be considered somewhat separately from government. While the judiciary is committed to sustain laws formulated and approved by the legislative branch and the administrative law formulated by the executive branch, it is nonetheless a separate branch. The courts are empowered to adjudicate the legitimacy of legislation, executive orders, administrative law, and the ways they are implemented or enforced. As I note in the chapters to follow, the Supreme Court has handed down decisions that have critically altered the economic climate of professional practice.

However, the legal foundation of the health care system is firmly based on restrictive practices that are unlikely to go through any drastic changes. The most fundamental restrictions are manifested in the elaborate system of credentialism built around medical education and health care. The legal system sustains the exclusive right of accredited medical schools to give medical degrees that are in turn the prerequisite for an exclusive license to practice medicine. So, too, are health care facilities, most obviously hospitals but also other diagnostic and therapeutic institutions, all subject to restrictive licensing and regulation by federal and state agencies. Such regulation is far more complex and demanding than that imposed on ordinary commercial enterprises seeking state charters as legal entities. Indeed, remembering that commercial pharmaceutical and medical technology manufacturing enterprises also need state approval before they may market their products, one must never overlook the fact that health care in the United States is a highly regulated industry. Any attempt to represent health care as being conducted in a free marketplace, subject only to the forces of unfettered competition, is grievously misleading—a point to which I shall return in chapter 15.

Finally, I may note legal issues of a quite different sort—the adjudication of grievances between individuals and institutions in which defendants may be held liable for malpractice or negligence. The outcome of some of those civil suits and the threat of others have without doubt changed the psychological climate of medical practice and the policies of both health care institutions and the manufacturers of health-related products. Some of the awards given successful plaintiffs have been very large, and liability insurance rates have so increased as to add a considerable sum to the costs of practicing medicine. Indeed, some claim that those costs have produced a crisis in health care, and efforts are being made to reduce them by restricting the nature and amount of awards to successful plaintiffs. It has also been claimed that malpractice suits have raised the cost of health care by stimulating the practice of "defensive medicine"—performing tests and procedures that are not immediately necessary in order to be "covered" in the event of a suit.

There are major differences of opinion about both the role of civil suits and the cause of the enormous rise in the cost of liability insurance. Some dispute the claim that there has been an especially steep increase in either the number of such suits or the average amount of damages awarded successful plaintiffs. Some argue that the rise in insurance rates does not reflect the cost to insurance companies of awards to plaintiffs so much as their desire to increase their profits. All we can be sure about is the sharp rise in the cost of such insurance and the pervasive concern with the possibility of civil suits among both practitioners and health care institutions, a concern that introduces yet another source of tension in their relations with patients.

PRIVATE CAPITAL

In the past, the most important and powerful institutional actors of the health care system were the health-related professions and such institutions as hospitals and medical schools, most with nonprofit status.

Private capital and for-profit enterprise controlled by lay investors played a relatively minor role. Over the past two decades, however, there has been a great increase in commercial enterprises owned by lay investors that organize and sell such health services as home care and kidney dialysis and that operate ambulatory care centers, hospitals, and HMOs. Private capital has come to be an important feature of the system.

Perhaps the greatest concentration of private capital is to be found in insurance companies, which finance the health care of the vast majority of the American population. The manufacturers of health-related goods, however, mostly financed by private capital, have been growing rapidly in number and importance. Advances in electronic and biological/genetic technology over the past two decades have attracted the investment of large amounts of private capital in the manufacture and sale of new, highly sophisticated products for use in the diagnosis and treatment of illness and disability. As in the case of health services, the assurance of payment for those products by a limited number of heavily capitalized insurers rather than by individual consumers and institutions has produced a very attractive environment for investment. To be sure, government approval of medical products is required before they can be sold, but once approval is obtained, the potential for profit is great and probably subject to less risk than is the case for products unrelated to health.

The rise of private capital has led to a shift in the political alliances and strength of the medical profession. During the golden age of medicine, before the expansion of governmental and private health insurance, perhaps the heaviest concentration of private capital was in the manufacture of pharmaceutical products. Because physicians controlled the prescription of "ethical" drugs and many other health-related products, their good will was essential for their sale. Thus, professional associations could usually count on the powerful political and economic support of those manufacturers. Then medicine and private capital appeared to be allies. Since that time, however, private capital invested in enterprises that are not directly dependent on the good will of physicians has grown in importance and developed interests directly in conflict with those of physicians. Large corporate employers seek to reduce the cost of their employee benefit programs so as to maintain or increase their profits by negotiating reductions in what physicians charge for their services. Private health insurance companies also seek to maintain or increase their profits by the same tactic and by more aggressive review of claims for reimbursement. The economic interests of the medical profession, if not also its professional interests, seem less and less compatible with those of private capital.

THE EDUCATION AND RESEARCH SECTOR

Of the institutions shaping practitioners, the medical school is usually considered to be the most important. The rise of university-based medical schools early in this century, along with a legally sustained system of licensing based upon successful completion of a relatively standardized curriculum followed by postgraduate training in hospitals, had an enormous impact on both medical work itself and the social and economic position of the physician. It is in the course of their medical education that physicians learn their basic skills, the foundation upon which the quality of their subsequent work rests.

But the American medical school developed into much more than an institution for the training of physicians. It also undertook the task of research, of developing new knowledge and techniques for the diagnosis and treatment of illness and disability, and for the discovery of hitherto undiscerned pathologies and agents. Those who teach in medical school are also engaged in research and experimentation. Indeed, for many of the faculty in medical schools, like those in research universities, research and experimentation have become more important than teaching or conventional practice. Until recently, at least some of the financial resources required for such research in teaching hospitals were gained by the device of cost shifting—that is, factoring some of the costs of research and training into the patient's bill. This source has been constricted, however, and government support for medical education itself has declined, so that medical schools, if not also teaching hospitals, are now enduring comparatively difficult times.

Those teaching and doing research in medical schools and teaching hospitals are not the only ones adding to the knowledge, technique, and technology that underlie modern health care. Certainly one must take account of researchers developing new drugs in pharmaceutical laboratories or exploiting the practical potential of such recently created fields as genetic engineering. And one cannot neglect those who work in the research institutes of the federal government, where basic as well as applied work is undertaken. There are creative and prominent researchers in all those sites, private and public, but if we were to delineate a research establishment in health care, it would have to be located in the major medical schools and teaching hospitals. And the members of that establishment seem to share a common disdain, perhaps even contempt, for mere practitioners in the communities outside their institutions. Understandably committed to the value of their own research, they are prone to assert the greater reliability and validity of their findings over the clinical experience of the practitioner. Indeed, it might be said that they are preoccupied with creating knowledge, technology, and technique that are precise and reliable enough to displace the art of medicine by expanding its science. Their research and opinion set the standards employed by insurers and others to evaluate and control the work of practitioners.

THE NEW CADRES IN MEDICINE

Teachers and researchers in medicine perform an essential role for the profession even though many may not be counted among its practitioners. They preserve, transmit, elaborate, and advance the knowledge and technique of the profession, advancing it in part by their own discoveries and in part by gaining command over the innovations of those from outside the profession. Unlike engineers and other scientists doing research with a bearing on health care, they have medical degrees. This gives only them the right to experiment with the treatment of patients; thus, researchers with medical degrees can control the use of innovations in health care. Their activities, therefore, greatly strengthen the profession's efforts to maintain its jurisdiction over health care even in the face of the extremely rapid pace of the development of new knowledge and technology in academic and engineering disciplines. An engineer may design an artificial heart, but a physician must install it and monitor its use in a human being.

The same function of maintaining control for the profession may be seen in the activities of another, more recently developing group of physicians who specialize in administering organizations in which medical work takes place. In the past, when practice was organized simply and economic relations between patients and doctors were direct, physicians could manage their own affairs. They kept their own medical and financial records, ordered their own supplies, and hired and supervised their own modest staff. As practices grew in size and became more complex in organization, administration became a part-time rather than merely after-hours role for physicians, or it became the duty of a lay person who was responsible to a medical superior. First in hospitals and only later in group practices and clinics, full-time positions as director or manager grew up, many filled by lay people with training in business or public administration. For a time it seemed as if those lay managers and executives would become the administrative cadre of the health system.

It is too early to tell whether it will be physicians or lay people who will predominate in the executive and managerial positions in health care institutions. Certainly the number of such full-time positions has been increasing as more organized and larger forms of practice develop, and physicians are filling many of them. Their work includes performing the conventional administrative functions of mediating between the organization and the public and private insurers who pay patients' bills, allocating resources within the organization itself, and attempting to coordinate the performance of the various specialized tasks of the members of the organization. Furthermore, they must also perform a task that is rather new for physicians—namely, encouraging or sometimes even requiring physicians to conform to the standards established by agencies outside the organization. And they must somehow get practitioners to perform in ways that contain costs. The activities of this growing cadre of physician-administrators and executives are an increasingly important element shaping the character of medical work.

These are not the only new administrative positions for physicians in the present health care system, however. Others are emerging in the organizations that are developing to exercise both review and control functions. Peer Review Organizations (PROs) now exist to review physicians' decisions in order to determine whether their reimbursement claims should be honored and whether their decisions are appropriate to the case at hand. The physicians who staff those organizations are thus engaged in evaluating the technical quality of the work of practitioners. Unlike those who serve on review committees in hospitals and HMOs, however, they do not share the experience of practicing in the same setting with those they review. Present trends suggest that more physicians will come to specialize in the role of reviewing physician performance, but too little is known about them and their work to allow saying more than that, like physician-administrators, they represent an aspect of the profession that poses new problems for practitioners and their work. While both are nominal colleagues, the immediate goals of each are in conflict, even though both may share the broader goal of the profession as a whole to advance the public interest by providing reliable health care.

MAKING SENSE OF THE SYSTEM

In this chapter I have outlined the major elements of the system surrounding practitioners. Brief as it has had to be, it is not complete, but it covers the essentials. It is primarily descriptive, providing the information required for analysis but no theory or concept by which it can be organized. This omission has been deliberate, for I believe that it is preferable to begin making sense of things only after gaining a clear picture of what they are. This keeps conceptualization honest, for a theory that does not take the details of that picture into account should be rejected out of hand.

Throughout this and other chapters my exposition has been handicapped by the paucity of reliable information, the rapid rate of change, and the sheer variety of institutions. In the light of those circumstances, one must be cautious about theorizing. But caution must not degenerate into intellectual paralysis, and the easiest way to become paralyzed is to become mired in the complex and rapidly changing detail of the American health care system. One cannot make sense of it without ignoring some detail and abstracting what remains: by ignoring the individual trees, after all, one can see the forest.

However, one cannot grasp the nature of a forest without taking into account the character of its trees. To make good sense of things therefore requires the choice of a concept or theory that can characterize the whole in such a way as to take into account the important elements of all its parts. This is the methodological position implicit in chapters 12 and 13, where I reject several popular conceptions of the present status of physicians and their supposed future of deprofessionalization or proletarianization. Those conceptions characterize the forest without due regard for the trees, and they are therefore misleading. These views ignore most of the elements of the system that I discuss in this and succeeding chapters, while they read portents for the future from a few issues and events treated in isolation from others of equal if not greater importance.

Taking into account the increased role of government and private capital in the health system today, I suggest in the essays to follow that the legal and institutional position of the medical profession is firmly enough established to preclude drastic changes. Its economic position is clearly eroding, but many factors limit the extent to which that will occur. Members of the profession remain pretty much in control of the innovations in knowledge, technique, and technology that are being introduced into medical work. And members of the profession staff managerial positions in health care institutions as well as those devoted to the review and appraisal of medical performance. But practicing physicians, who fulfill the profession's primary function and constitute the majority of its members, are approaching a crossroad. They are unlikely to lose their basic professional privileges and become anything resembling an industrial proletariat. Yet the forces that are intent on applying industrial concepts of efficiency to health care could so change the circumstances of their work as to rob it of its intrinsic rewards. Should this occur, patients as well as doctors would lose something precious.

TWELVE

The Reorganization of the Medical Profession

It requires no special perception to see that health care is going through massive changes in the United States. Before World War II it was largely a cottage industry composed of self-employed physicians working primarily in their own offices and sometimes sending their patients to hospitals where nurses and members of a few other health care occupations cared for the patients according to the doctors' orders. It was, furthermore, financed largely by charitable contributions and by the patients themselves. And while it did require machines and other tools of the trade that even then were too expensive for individual physicians to own themselves and use in their offices—making physicians somewhat dependent on hospitals for access to capital equipment as well as beds and paramedical services—health care technology was not sufficiently developed to support a large manufacturing industry. Finally, in those days the role of government was essentially passive, protecting the institutions of health care by licensing, tax, and other laws but remaining otherwise uninvolved.

Much has changed since then, and change has accelerated since the passage of Medicare legislation. Most physicians still work in their own offices, but they have become less able to deal with their patients' ailments without the aid of services and goods that are outside their own control. Health care occupations have multiplied in large numbers and form an ever more complex division of labor. More than anything else the hospital has changed, with consequences for all producers and consumers of health care. Hospitals no longer exist merely for the convenience of "attendings," and they have developed a complex administrative structure to coordinate the division of labor. Furthermore, after the federal government began financing health care, they had to develop elaborate medical record systems and complex accounting schemes. The massive expansion of health care technology, with its train of consequences for capital costs, new specialized occupations, and even new legal and ethical problems, has added to the complexities of hospital administration.

What do these changes mean? Do they have a distinct direction and are they likely to continue in that same direction indefinitely? What are their consequences for the consumers of health care? And what are the consequences for the producers? All of these questions cannot be answered here, but surely we can gain some insight into answers by focusing on the medical profession. In the past, physicians were clearly the key producers of health care. Thus, if we focus our attention on them and on the way the changes of the past decades have affected them, we may be able to gain an especially strategic view of what has been happening. Indeed, most prophecies of the future shape of health care have emphasized changes in the role of the medical profession.

MAJOR THEORIES

In this paper, I shall review several major theories concerning the position of physicians in the health care system and their future status. I shall argue that those theories are flawed, taking too little into account to be useful guides for our understanding and distorting our view of what is happening. I shall then discuss some important but often overlooked changes in the medical profession and go on to suggest my own way of making sense of the changing position of physicians. Finally, I shall discuss some implications of that theory.

Professional Dominance

A useful way to grapple with the various theories that predict radical changes in the status of the medical profession within the health care system is to contrast them with the position, asserted not long ago, that the medical profession dominates the system. My phrase "professional dominance" (Freidson, 1970a) was later taken up by Illich (1980) and others. However, "professional dominance" is merely a phrase and thus masks a number of different facets of the profession's position in the health care system. My usage was drawn from ecology rather than from politics, and it referred primarily to the relation of the medical profession to most other health care occupations in the division of labor. Other occupations existed under medicine's shelter, and while these occupations gained their protection from outsiders, they had to exist only on what medicine allowed them and had to give up the capacity to be independent and grow large and strong. In such ecological usage, the primary emphasis was on the legal subordination of nurses, pharmacists, inhalation therapists, and others to medical orders, sustained by the licensing system. The medical profession was portrayed as dominant in a division of labor in which other occupations were obliged to work under the supervision of physicians and take orders from them. With its exclusive license to practice medicine, prescribe controlled drugs, admit patients to hospitals, and perform other critical gatekeeping functions, the medical profession is portrayed as having a monopoly over the provision of health services, a monopoly that Berlant (1975) has emphasized at some length.

Other writers, however, have gone well beyond those limited economic and occupational aspects of the health care system in characterizing the position of the medical profession. The most sweeping characterization of the professional dominance of physicians is certainly that of Illich (1976), though Foucault and his followers (for example, Arney, 1982) imply even more. Illich asserts that the medical profession creates the needs that lead people to seek their services, that it in effect influences consciousness itself so that people think of their problems as medical in character and as requiring the aid of health professionals. This power is much more than what Starr (1982) calls the "cultural authority" of medicine: it might more appropriately be called ideological or cultural hegemony, a pervasive form of intellectual dominance that controls the way people think. A somewhat less sweeping but related characterization of such hegemony is found in work by McKinlay (1973), Zola (1972), and especially Conrad and Schneider (1980) on "medicalization."

Deprofessionalization and Consumer Dominance

In contrast to those characterizing the medical profession as dominant in the health care system—on the one hand controlling access to critical aspects of health care, including the use of a variety of other occupations in the division of labor and protected by an economic monopoly, and on the other asserting control over the way people think about themselves and their problems—there are others who believe that the medical profession is in decline (for historical views, see Starr, 1978, and Burnham, 1982). One theory is that medicine is losing its professional status. The theory of deprofessionalization is most closely associated with the work of Haug (1973, 1975, 1977), who spoke about professions in general, even though one might guess from the substance of her analysis that she had medicine in mind more than, say, law or accounting. Betz and O'Connell (1983) advance a similar, though less complex, analysis of medicine in particular (see also Toren, 1975).

The major emphasis of the theory of deprofessionalization is on the relations between professionals and consumers. Professional status presupposes that consumers have some special trust in professionals that they do not have in mere specialists. In the case of the latter, consumers actively question, even challenge those offering specialized services: they do not accept them on mere faith. Trust or faith, however, seems to depend in part on the general prestige of an occupation. It also depends in part on the degree to which the occupation has a genuine monopoly over a particular body of knowledge and skill, that is, the degree to which consumers feel they do not know enough to be able to judge the specialized service themselves and to make their own choices. According to the deprofessionalization theory, consumers' unquestioning trust diminishes as the "knowledge gap" between the medical profession and the consumer diminishes. Today's consumer is better educated and thus likely to know more about medicine, which closes the knowledge gap. Furthermore, the computerization of knowledge has made it more accessible to all, and new specialized occupations have arisen around bodies of knowledge and skills that physicians themselves are not competent to employ.

All these trends lead to the deprofessionalization of medicine—the reduction of physicians to mere secular specialists, dependent on rational, well-informed consumers who approach their services with the same questioning attitude they bring to other commodities in the marketplace. According to this theory, consumers, not physicians, will dominate health care in the future, and medicine will become just another health occupation.

Proletarianization and Managerial Dominance

Finally, there is the theory of the proletarianization of the profession, drawn from Marxism. One basic tenet of Marxism is the assumption that eventually all participants in the capitalist economy will be drawn into one of two opposing classes: those possessing capital or serving as the agents of capital, the bourgeoisie, and those who perform the basic productive labor of the economy but who are exploited for the cause of profit and the accumulation of capital, the working class. Marxist theorists differ in their view of the place of the professions in the present class system, some seeing them to be allied with capital and others seeing them in "contradictory class locations." Still others, however, see them as eventually joining the working class, or proletariat, losing control of their work, and becoming subject to the exploitative discipline of the managers who serve the ultimate interests of the capitalist class (Oppenheimer, 1973; Larson, 1980). In the case of the American medical profession in particular, McKinlay is the most recent proponent (1982), with Coburn, Torrance, and Kaufert (1983) doing much the same for the medical profession in Canada.

It is a bit difficult to be entirely clear about the application of the theory of proletarianization to the medical profession, because proletarianization itself remains unarticulated as a concept and because there is so much equivocation (McKinlay, 1982: 37–38) about the degree to which the process has already occurred and the pace of change itself. Those who employ the theory, however, seem to emphasize above all the overriding importance of two changes in the position of the medical profession that have already begun.

First, they point out that more and more physicians are salaried rather than self-employed. Thus, they are losing their economic independence and assuming the wage-labor status of the proletariat. Second, more and more they practice in bureaucratically organized institutions, their work thereby becoming subject to the control of management. A similar change in status is suggested by Starr's notion of medicine's loss of "professional sovereignty" (1978), though he does not draw on Marxist theory or terminology.

EVIDENCE FOR THE THEORIES

Described in such a compact fashion, it is easy to see that the theories do not really address each other, that is, they do not look at the same evidence and interpret it differently so much as they look at different evidence and assert that it is the key to understanding the changing position of the medical profession. In some cases, the evidence itself is too weak to rely on as support for the theory. In other cases, the evidence is ambiguous enough to be amenable to more than one reasonable interpretation. And most important of all, a great many analytically important conditions affecting the position of the medical profession in the health care system are completely overlooked. Let us turn to examining the evidence that is relevant to assessing the theories.

The theory of professional dominance emphasizes two quite different kinds of phenomena—cultural or ideological on the one hand, and economic and legal on the other. It can be argued plausibly that they are interdependent: that the special, privileged, and authoritative position of the medical profession could not be obtained in the first place and maintained subsequently unless the profession had some "cultural authority," unless its orientation to health and illness and its knowledge and skill were widely respected. Thus, some degree of respect and trust is essential to gaining a legally supported economic monopoly from the state. However, the degree of respect and trust must be great, compared to what other occupations receive, if that monopoly places other health care occupations in a subordinate position.

Respect and trust are one thing and cultural hegemony another. The capacity to control how people think of themselves and their problems is a far more profound form of dominance than the capacity to be dominant in a division of labor. The concept of hegemony is such that it is difficult to specify (or even imagine) the evidence one would need in order to demonstrate its presence and document its operation. Should it be asserted that one manifestation of such hegemony lies in the way that human problems are "medicalized," that is, interpreted as medical problems or diseases, the evidence available shows that there is no consistency of source—that lay groups are as prone to medicalize their problems and urge a reluctant medical profession to take jurisdiction over them as the medical profession is eager to do so on its own. This is true in part because of the social, political, and economic structure surrounding the ideology: in the nineteenth century one gained at least social and political benefits by being considered "sick" rather than "bad," and in the modern welfare state one stands a chance of getting economic benefits as well.

On balance, I do not believe that the thesis of cultural hegemony in its full-blown form can be settled by anything other than faith, which I lack. It is an idea to play with rather than a concept to address systematically and use analytically. Occupational dominance and monopoly are much easier to deal with empirically. It is clear that medicine remains the key occupation in health care: it is dominant in the health care system's division of labor, and its position is sustained by an elaborate tissue of licensing laws and quasi-legal systems of institutional licensing and accreditation of health problems. "The AMA cooperates . . . in the accreditation of over 3000 educational programs, at more than 1700 institutions, for the 26 allied health professions it recognizes" (Havighurst and King, 1983: 149).

This is not to say that all in the health care system are under the doctor's orders, for dentists, optometrists, podiatrists, chiropractors, and others have operated independently of medicine in the past while others have emerged more recently. But in every case those who are licensed to practice independently of medicine in health-related matters practice in a carefully delimited sphere of activity, whether surgical, pharmacological, or technological. (For an examination of the positions of physicians' assistants and nurse practitioners, see Kissam, 1975). While the medical profession has never been completely successful in preventing independent practice in areas that border on or even compete with it, it remains successful in limiting it and preserving its own strong monopoly. There is no evidence of a trend toward weakening that monopoly, though there is a literature that urges action to do so. It would be a mistake to regard such literature as evidence of actual change instead of desire for change.

That statement contradicts the implication, if not the actual assertion, of the theory of deprofessionalization, that medicine has become or is clearly on the road to becoming just one of a multitude of health-related occupations, without a special position among them. It rests on the objective evidence of licensing laws and accreditation practices and the continued failure of efforts to change them significantly. For example, various states have passed "sunset laws," which automatically terminate "a board, commission or agency unless reauthorized or reestablished by the legislature" (Roederer and Palmer, 1981: 2). In many instances, licensing boards were prime targets of sunset laws, the hope being that new licensing legislation would be written to reform the system. But as Lippincott and Begun (1982: 477) conclude, sunset laws have been a "dismal failure" in changing the situation. Thus, we find little evidence that the medical profession's legally sustained position in practice and in the division of labor is being changed so significantly as to become just one of a number of health care occupations.

If that is so, then we should expect the profession to have some position of respect and trust in the public's eye. The deprofessionalization theory asserts that there has been a loss of such a position, and indeed some evidence of a decline does exist (Betz and O'Connell, 1983). If that decline really does exist, why have there not been greater changes in the medical monopoly? The answer is that the decline is only relative and has not been of sufficient magnitude to sustain any serious attacks on the profession's monopoly.

A recent comprehensive review of surveys of public "confidence" in American institutions has shown that all major American institutions, not just medicine, have suffered a decline in public confidence over the past decades. Medicine, however, has remained the institution in which the *greatest* amount of confidence exists (Lipset and Schneider, 1983). Furthermore, the public continues to be overwhelmingly "satisfied" with the quality of the medical care it receives from doctors (Health Insurance Association of America, 1982: 14). None of those findings supports the idea that there has been a decline in trust of such magnitude as to support deprofessionalization processes.

Other evidence to sustain the deprofessionalization thesis is equally weak. The notion that the population has become on the average better educated than in the past is true enough, but the assumption that this reduces the "knowledge gap" between medicine and the health consumer is valid only if medical knowledge and technique have stagnated and not increased. Like science and technology, however, medical advances have been increasing exponentially, far faster than the rate of increase in lay knowledge. If anything, one should expect the "knowledge gap" to increase rather than decrease, with the computerization of new knowledge having little to do with the capacity of lay people to use or understand it. Indeed, Langwell and Moore (1982: 12) review findings that consumers exercise direct choice over less than half of the health services they consume and that only in the use of routine pediatric and obstetrical care are consumers well informed.

In all, the deprofessionalization theory makes far too much of the potential of the consumer movement. It is conceivable that consumers can keep up with medical advances, but only if they, too specialize. This in fact is what has occurred. Various health consumer groups specialize in particular issues such as childbirth and women's health care, particular chronic illnesses or disabilities, and the like. Such groups are small, composed primarily of educated, middle-class women, and often their members are transient. The consumer movement in any case has no broad grass-roots base in the population. It is less a function of organized activities on the part of numerous consumers than it is of organized political actions by "program professionals" (McCarthy and Zald, 1973; Walker, 1983) who lead public interest groups. Without deprecating the value and importance of the consumer movement, one should not exaggerate its capacity to change drastically the position of the medical profession in the health care system.

It seems, then, that the evidence that the medical profession is losing its position of relative public trust, its relative supremacy in the occupational division of health labor, and its command over truly esoteric knowledge and skill is quite poor and unpersuasive. Change has indeed been taking place in each of those areas, but it has been of insufficient magnitude to have had critical effects and of insufficient duration to sustain the idea of a steady, unilinear trend into the future. As yet, we must take those characteristics of relative public trust, exclusive command over a body of specialized knowledge and skill, and dominance in the division of labor as givens and ask how other changes qualify or limit them. This is what the proletarianization thesis, if true, can answer.

The theory of proletarianization points out that there is a distinct trend toward physicians' being salaried rather than self-employed, a trend that may accelerate over the coming decades (Friedman, 1983). However, an important proportion of salaried physicians is not actually in practice, instead serving as administrators, researchers, teachers, and the like, and another proportion collated in labor statistics is salaried only in the technical sense of being employees of their own professional corporations. Thus, the magnitude of this trend is certainly exaggerated in official statistics. However, there is no doubt the trend exists, even though it remains to be seen whether it will continue indefinitely until all physicians become salaried workers.

The question is what the trend means. Certainly it cannot mean loss of professional status as such, for the majority of all professions has always been employed rather than self-employed. It does mean loss of what Marxists call petit bourgeois status—a purportedly anachronistic survival of early or precapitalist times—but that is not synonymous with professional status. The assumption of the proponents of the proletarianization thesis seems to be, however, that loss of self-employed status means loss of control over the economic terms and conditions of work, which is one characteristic of the working class's relationship to capital. But in fact employment status does not, in and of itself, mean loss of economic independence. If one's position in the labor market is strong, one can specify the terms and conditions of one's employment, granting little power to the employer. Similarly, if one's position as a self-employed entrepreneur in the marketplace is weak, one is at the mercy of the consumer's terms and conditions, a position of vulnerability that the history of medicine has often documented for self-employed physicians in bad times. The mere status of being employed or self-employed tells us much too little to be analytically useful. Even if the trend toward employed status continues, it does not, in itself, imply anything of importance about the changing status of physicians. The nature of their monopoly, the supply of competitors, and the available economic resources are much more important.

The other major element cited in the theory of proletarianization is the nature of the organizations in which physicians, employed or self-employed, work. They are called bureaucracies and their operation characterized by Max Weber's ideal type of rational-legal administration. These are organizations governed by an elaborate set of written rules, keeping meticulous records, differentiated into specialized positions or offices, each with carefully defined responsibilities and organized into a pyramidal hierarchy with ranks of officials and supervisors whose function is to coordinate and control the work of those below them. Work is fragmented into small, highly specialized tasks, and discretion is minimized. In the case of medicine, it is the hospital that is invoked as such an organization, though it is noted that there is also a trend for clinics, some Health Maintenance Organizations, and other forms of potentially large-scale practice to replace individual office practice and extend bureaucratization into the community outside the hospital. The consequence of this bureaucratization is said to be the loss of professional autonomy, reducing the physician to a mere cog in a machine.

In all, there can be no doubt that there is a trend toward larger and more complex hospitals and practice organizations and toward the greater rationalization of all services, medical and otherwise. Both governmental and private pressures to reduce costs—or to prevent further rises in cost—serve as the motor for such rationalization, as do governmental regulations themselves. The basic issue is the degree to which rationalization is instituted and the form that rationalization takes, not the mere fact of rationalization. Does Weber's model actually describe that form or does it serve a special, nondescriptive function? Giddens notes that Marxist writers "characteristically accept too much of what Weber has to say about the nature and consequences of bureaucratization . . . while declaring bureaucratic domination to be a specific outcome of the class system of capitalism" (1982: 200), and he goes on to deny that individual autonomy is impossible in bureaucracy, that organizations in fact conform to the ideal type and operate accordingly, and that the worker is powerless (202–05). Indeed, even economists, who have had a notorious appetite for ideal types or abstract models, have discovered that hospitals are hardly fully rationalized organizations (Harris, 1977; Pauly and Redisch, 1973).

Current organizational theorists have suggested that open-system and loosely coupled system models that fit organizations such as schools and hospitals would also suit hospitals far better than Weber's ideal type. This is not to deny the value of the ideal type but rather to caution against forgetting that it *is* an ideal type and assuming instead that it describes empirical reality.

At the foundation of the concept of proletarianization is the notion of completely alienated workers, without control over their economic circumstances, without any important voice in the policies of the organizations that employ them, subject to close and oppressive supervision, and unable to exercise significant choice in the work they do and the way they do it—in short, the stereotype of the industrial blue-collar worker. Without reference to those concrete conditions to provide focus for the collection of evidence, proletarianization is not a concept so much as a slogan. What we must ask, then, is how closely the position of physicians conforms to those characteristics in large practice organizations in general and in the hospital in particular.

Looking at the evidence on the place of the medical profession in the hospital, we must note that in the United States, trends toward employment notwithstanding, most fully qualified physicians are not employees but "attendings." They are dependent on the hospital for the care of some of their patients and the performance of some of their work, but the hospital is also dependent on them to provide patients. It is only the physician who has the right to admit patients to the hospital and to choose and take responsibility for their modes of treatment, so it is no accident that the new, for-profit hospitals actively court physicians who serve a well-insured clientele to join their staffs. Furthermore, the standards of the Joint Commission on Accreditation of Hospitals, on which both state and federal authorities generally rely, require that the medical staff of hospitals, unlike the nursing staff or any other occupation in the hospital, be *directly* responsible to the governing board rather than to the chief executive officer (Christoffel, 1982, 108–10; somewhat dated but still relevant is Southwick and Siedel, 1978).

In American labor law, professional employees, among whom are employed physicians, are assigned a special craft status and marked off from ordinary employees by the special characteristic of having the legitimate right to exercise discretion on an everyday basis in the conduct of their work. Thus, physicians are in a fairly strong economic bargaining position in the hospital because they have a monopoly over the right to admit, determine treatment, and discharge patients, and it is assumed that they exercise discretion in the course of their work. Furthermore, they have direct access to the policymaking governing board, and there is in fact at present a distinct trend toward more and more hospital governing boards' including medical staff among their members (Noie, Shortell, and Morrisey, 1983).

Save for the matter of supervision and control, which I shall discuss in more detail shortly, I think it can be said without fear of contradiction that the present position of physicians in hospitals and other organizations in which they work is in no reasonable way analogous to that of the blue-collar or white-collar worker in factory or firm. Most are not even employed by the governing board, and whether employed or not they have a special, policy-relevant relationship with the board. They have a large amount of control over the tasks they undertake and the way they perform them. It is true that they are not wholly autonomous, but when one takes into account the operation of the invisible hand of the market in constraining the self-employed, putatively "free" professional, they never were. Neither the facts of employment nor of working in large, complex organizations constitute in and of themselves sufficiently persuasive evidence to support the use of the concept of proletarianization to characterize the position of physicians in a truly analytic fashion.

PROFESSION — AGGREGATE OR ORGANIZATION?

On the whole, I think it fair to say that all the theories I have discussed are too grand and sweeping to have much more than rhetorical and possibly political value. They are casual about providing the evidence to support their validity, and as often as not when they do provide evidence it is of dubious relevance to the analytic implications of the concepts. I suggest that at bottom their flaws stem from an inadequate conception of what a profession is in the United States, particularly the medical profession. They tend to conceptualize the profession implicitly as an aggregate of individual practitioners and not as an organic social entity. Thus, dominance is defined by the relations between individual physicians and other health care workers, or by the doctor-patient relationship; deprofessionalization by the relationship between doctors and demanding consumers; and proletarianization by the relationship between doctors and employers and managers.

While the profession is indeed composed of individuals doing their daily work with others, it is also corporate in character. The profession is organized by formal associations whose officers negotiate licensing laws, accreditation standards, and the like that establish the framework within which its individual members work. Furthermore, some important segments of the profession are not engaged in everyday practice. And finally, the profession is stratified: elite members of the profession perform special roles in professional associations and institutions and engage in critical negotiations with legislators and government officials in shaping laws and administrative procedures as well as with the governing boards of hospitals and other institutions. Other elites, as we shall see, establish, advance, and communicate the body of knowledge and skill claimed by the profession.

Thus, to conceive of the profession as a mere aggregate is to be insensitive to critical forms of functional and hierarchical differentiation within the profession and the institutions that are responsible for insulating practitioners from some of the changes that are taking place and reorganizing their relationships with each other in adaptation to other external changes. It is that organized character of the profession and the connection of its organization to state policymaking and institutional chartering that pose a major barrier to actual deprofessionalization or proletarianization. Potentially critical pressures have been cushioned by adaptive changes in the organization of the interrelations among members of the profession, changes intended to satisfy the demands of consumers, politicians, and third-party payers without sacrificing overall professional control.

CHANGES IN THE NORMS AND PRACTICE OF PROFESSIONAL CONTROL

The significance of two changes in the formal and informal rules governing economic and professional relations within the profession has not been adequately recognized. First, while competition between other occupations and the medical profession has remained seriously limited, open and public competition among practitioners *within* the profession is now possible through advertising. Previously discouraged as "unethical," advertising became possible when a Federal Trade Commission order of 1979 barred the American Medical Association from exercising formal bans against advertising. Its order was upheld on appeal by the U.S. Court of Appeals for the Second Circuit in New York and affirmed by the Supreme Court in 1982. An effort to pass federal legislation to exclude the medical profession from the jurisdiction of the Federal Trade Commission and the Sherman Antitrust Act also failed in 1983. While antitrust action to increase competition between physicians and other health practitioners seems of limited potential in spite of Dolan's (1980) enthusiasm, the increase of overt competition within the profession itself is of some importance, breaking as it does a tradition that has helped sustain the cohesion of the medical profession during its twentieth-century prime.

Competition in health care has received a great deal of attention over the past ten years, during which the ideology of classical economics has been revived and reasserted as the key to solving the fiscal crisis of health care in the United States, so I need not address it in any detail here. (For a review of research on competition, see Langwell and Moore, 1982.) Advertising is one form of such competition. What is more, it *publicizes* competition. Advertising is a public claim of superiority that, explicitly or implicitly, denigrates competitors. Furthermore, it appeals to the lay criteria of potential patients rather than to professional criteria. Public statements denigrating competitors were not uncommon among physicians before the twentieth century: in earlier days it was not unheard of for one physician to deprecate the diagnosis and treatment recommended by another. Nor was it uncommon to advertise that one did *not* employ unpopular cures such as bleeding or dosing with cathartics.

Open, public competition for patients inevitably means strained collegial relations. Advertising lower prices than another physician implies that the other physician charges too much. Advertising elaborate credentials such as board certification in a specialty, for example, maligns the competence of physicians without them, even though specialty boards disclaim any intent to make invidious distinctions. (See Havighurst and King, 1983: 141, and Stevens, 1971: 43 for a discussion of the way specialization was considered to be invidious and divisive, an issue still exercising the legal profession in the United States.) While competition for desirable patients always goes on among both employed and self-employed physicians serving the same population, with some being considerably more successful than others, professional norms that control advertising minimize invidious comparisons, prevent open warfare, and preserve a modicum of harmony and decorum within the profession.

It is too early to tell just how far the use of advertising will go in health care. Given constraints on "misleading" advertising that did not exist in earlier times, extensive advertising campaigns are far more likely to be useful to relatively large and specialized health care organizations than to individual physicians. If that should be the case, individual members of the profession will not be in public competition with each other and their relations will not become especially strained. Eliminating some of the restrictions on advertising is therefore primarily of symbolic importance, representing the collapse of one of the traditional devices the profession has used to preserve its nominal solidarity. Of far more immediate importance to the solidarity of the profession is the second of the two changes—the collapse of the norms governing the way colleagues evaluate and control each other.

An important tradition bearing on the cohesion of the profession is the norm of suspending overt, public judgment about the competence, conscientiousness, and ethicality of colleagues even though privately one may feel they have made serious errors or have been negligent (Freidson, 1970b, 1980; Bosk, 1979). A related norm discourages taking any action to control the behavior of errant colleagues. These norms have been displayed in a variety of situations in the past. In the courts, when malpractice suits were brought against physicians, it has often been noted that it was difficult to find physicians who would testify as experts against their colleagues. This "conspiracy of silence" has been attacked and seriously weakened over the past twenty years, and it is far more common now for physicians to testify against each other.

A related phenomenon is to be found in the activities of local and state medical association disciplinary committees and state licensing boards. In the past, they were notorious for their reluctance to pursue complaints against physicians (Derbyshire, 1969). Publicity and political pressure have forced them to be considerably more active in investigating, judging, and censuring the conduct of colleagues. Indeed, in some states "informer laws" have been passed that require physicians to report gross negligence on the part of colleagues to disciplinary boards on pain of being accused of "unprofessional conduct," a charge that can lead to the suspension or loss of the license to practice.

Finally, and most importantly, we may note the implication of the establishment of a series of formal review procedures, some required by federal legislation and administrative law and some strongly encouraged by large private health insurers. For some time all hospitals accredited by the Joint Commission on Accreditation of Hospitals have been required to have committees that review aspects of the care provided by the medical staff, but neither the way committee reviews were conducted nor their findings were subjected to very close or critical scrutiny, and accreditation requirements left great leeway in their modes of operation. Indeed, it was their inadequacy in discovering and dealing with errant colleagues that led to the publicity that sparked informer laws and other review requirements imposed by the state.

Medical research was the first target of federally mandated institutional committees that required formal review of the protection of the welfare and rights of "human subjects" (Barber et al., 1973; Gray, 1975). In the late 1960s, the first federal effort to control increasing costs required hospitals to establish formal utilization review committees to assess the propriety of the decisions of physicians to hospitalize their patients, followed later by legislation requiring the more elaborate Professional Standards Review Organizations. Since that time, a variety of other committees has been required, committees that focus less on the logistics of medical decisions than on their complex social, psychological, and ethical implications; the Infant Care Review Committees, which monitor the life support of deformed newborns, is a recent example. In all these review and disciplinary committees, active members are either exclusively or predominantly medical doctors.

It is not necessary to go into exhaustive detail in order to make the point that various formal mechanisms have developed to examine, judge, and, if necessary, correct and control the technical and ethical standards employed by physicians in the conduct of their work. They now exist primarily in the hospital, but they are also found in large-scale ambulatory care Health Maintenance Organizations and public clinics. Their operation has certainly been facilitated by the use of computers to record and collate large masses of information that were difficult to deal with systematically in the past. Working in such committees, it is no longer possible for physicians to say, There but for the grace of God go I, or, Who am I to judge? and, save for some covert gossip with trusted colleagues, be silent. Physicians are now required to judge and take action through such committees. Furthermore, this action is *formal* in character, that is, official supervision and control of individual practitioners' decisions. And since their activities must be on the record they cannot be merely informal, private, and advisory—indeed, they are always potentially public.

While it would be false to claim that practitioners are now stripped of all the protection that collegial relations used to provide, it can be claimed that the rules of the game have changed sufficiently in medicine to have introduced important changes in the relationship that members of the medical profession have with each other, both in the way they compete with each other in the marketplace and in the way they interact with each other at work, particularly in large, complex institutions subject to financing by the state.

Superficially, these changes might be interpreted as bureaucratization in Weber's ideal-typical sense, for they are accompanied by an increase in hierarchical positions as health care organizations grow in size, records become more and more elaborate, specific standards govern the formal evaluation of more and more work, supervision in the form of evaluation of work becomes more and more widespread, and hierarchical positions of responsibility increase in number and variety. However, in all circumstances involving the work of medicine, it is members of that profession who are in charge of setting standards, reviewing performance, and exercising supervision and control. Thus, those changes do not affect the position of the profession as a corporate body in the social as well as institutional division of labor so much as they affect the *internal* organization of the profession, in the relations among physicians. In essence, I suggest, they are creating more distinct and formal patterns of stratification within the profession than have existed in the past, with the position of the rank and file practitioner changing most markedly.

We can gain better insight into the peculiarities of that emerging position by contrasting it to that of the classic industrial proletariat. In what is now a classic though historically overdrawn portrait of proletarianization, Braverman (1974) emphasizes the process by which capitalist management "expropriated" the skills of workers. Nonworkers—that is, managers and more particularly industrial engineers—studied the production process as the workers performed it, developed new methods of selecting and performing production tasks designed to make these tasks more amenable to supervisory control, and then required the workers to do their jobs in the new way. The workers thus became mere passive tools of management, the proletariat: they were supposed to do exactly what they were told to do.

That condition is superficially analogous to what I have described for medicine today, but with a critical difference that destroys the pertinence of what is analogous. In the case of medicine, both supervision and control and the creation of "production standards" are carried out by members of the same profession as those who perform the basic, productive medical work. In the case of supervisory and managerial authority over medical work, a variety of legal and quasi-legal devices in the United States requires that the supervisors and managers of physicians also be physicians. The professional corporation, for example, is a legal form in which it is required that shareholders be only those who are practicing members of the corporation; shares, furthermore, cannot be transferred to or even inherited by lay people.

To take another example, state laws against the "corporate practice of medicine" may not prevent lay investors from owning shares in for-profit health care enterprises in many states, but if the chief executive officer of the practice unit is not a physician, then the head of the medical staff must be. In factories, a truly analogous situation would be the requirement that no supervisor or manager of production could hold the position without first having received the training of an industrial worker.

It is the same for the standards that are being established to order the work of rank and file physicians. They are established by members of the profession, and not by outsiders who develop their own standards for their own reasons. Two methods of establishing standards may be noted. One is fairly common and, in fact, has a long tradition of use in negligence or malpractice suits: if a physician hospitalizes a patient for a condition that most other physicians do not believe requires hospitalization, the physician is asked to justify the deviation from the standard. The same method is employed in assessing the individual's decision to keep a patient in the hospital. This method establishes a standard for evaluation by democratic professional consensus, by invoking the most common practice of all the physicians in an institution, community, region, or even nation as the criterion by which to judge individual practices. Individuals are no longer free to do whatever their idiosyncratic judgment suggests, but the constraint on their judgment is generated by collective *collegial* practice and not by "outsiders."

A rather different method is likely to be more important over the long run, however—deriving standards for supervising and controlling practice from professionally authoritative knowledge and practice. For example, at outpatient pediatric clinics at two New York City hospitals, computers monitor the treatment of children in light of mandated treatment procedures that have been specified for 85 percent of the patients' complaints. If the computer shows that a physician has not followed them, then he or she must justify that deviation to medical superiors (Sullivan, 1984). It is not that a physician cannot deviate, but that deviation must be formally justified by reference to a common body of practice that is considered to be a legitimate norm. It is conceivable that the deviant was correctly exercising discretionary judgment in an individual case, and the opportunity is provided to demonstrate its propriety. This opportunity is provided to physicians in every review context with which I am familiar. The rank and file practitioner thus has virtually statutory opportunity to use discretion in following standardized procedures and to deviate from them.

In that same New York City program of pediatric practice, it was noted that since the system was instituted there has been a sharp drop in the prescription of antibiotics for the treatment of colds and the like—a prescribing practice that has long been common among physicians and long deplored by medical authorities. If the standard procedure were to be determined by widespread medical custom, the prescription of antibiotics to treat upper respiratory infections could conceivably be a formal rule. Instead, the rule was based on the authoritative opinion of elite practitioners and the scientific findings of medical researchers.

Increasingly, the precepts of elite practitioners and researchers rather than the common customs of rank and file physicians establish the standards for medical work, much the way the standards of industrial engineers do for industrial work. Unlike the engineers, however, those authorities are members of the same profession as the rank and file, sharing the same basic professional training but afterward going on to a different postgraduate training and a different career line within the profession. Working primarily in medical schools and teaching hospitals, they cannot be said to be outsiders expropriating the skills of practitioners. Rather, they are the ones who teach those skills and who create, expand, screen, and revise them. Their position within the medical profession as authorities who set the standards by which the work of the rank and file practitioner is evaluated and controlled becomes considerably more formal than it was in the past.

THE REINFORCEMENT OF STRATIFICATION IN MEDICINE

In essence, these new modes of evaluating and exercising control over the work of physicians are created by reinforcing and formalizing the positions of medical administrators or supervisors and of medical researchers. There is nothing new about the positions themselves. After all, chiefs of staff and heads of services or departments have existed in hospitals for as long as there have been medical staffs, and medical researchers and professors have existed as long as there have been medical schools. Originally they held part-time positions in the United States, but over the past century the trend has been toward their becoming full-time, salaried positions. More important, until recently both positions were advisory rather than authoritative. As Goss (1961) showed, while the physician-administrator's authority in such "housekeeping" matters as scheduling would be accepted by those in his or her unit, in matters involving the practice of medicine itself such authority was only advisory.

The same could be said for the recommendations of researchers and other cognitive authorities: while in their teaching and in their journal articles they may have condemned the prescription of antibiotics for upper respiratory infections as both ineffective and potentially dangerous, practitioners were free to ignore their conclusions. Now, however, in hospitals and other large practice settings, the authority of both the physician-administrator and the physician-researcher has become more extensive and definite and has become more binding on the practitioner. Formal administrative authority and formal cognitive authority analogous to "line" and "staff" authority in industry become much more definite, leaving rank and file practitioners with considerably less freedom of action than existed in the past. This does not mean that they are no longer professionals with a significant degree of discretion; rather, it means that their discretion must take into account the authoritative norms laid down by other members of their profession, that they become in some sense subordinate to a select group of their own colleagues.

In most writing on medicine, stratification within the profession has been approached largely in terms of the relative prestige and income of the specialities (Abbott, 1981). But neither prestige nor, for that matter, income tells us anything about the authority relations among members of either the profession as a whole or the specialty. The literature has largely neglected the position of academics and administrators. Indeed, the tendency has been to see them as in some sense separate professions and not "real" doctors. Alford (1975), for example, sharply distinguished practitioners as "professional monopolists" from administrators and medical school teachers and researchers, whom he clustered together with industrial, institutional, and governmental agents to constitute the "corporate rationalizers" (see also Brown, 1979: 204–07). He was right to distinguish them from practitioners in that there are important differences in their aim and orientation but wrong to separate them, because all three are essential parts of the same organized profession.

Those in medical schools, teaching hospitals, and the like control, codify, refine, communicate, and augment the profession's body of knowledge and skill: their activities maintain control by the profession over knowledge and technology and discourage "expropriation" by outsiders. Those in administrative positions in practice organizations balance the necessity to carry out the collective ends of a governing board, municipality, state, firm, or whatever against the needs and desires of those who do the medical work, thereby buffering the practice of medicine against the political and economic pressures of the environment. Without physicians serving in both roles, the profession could only sustain a position that is at best like that of the crafts, dependent on its organization but at the mercy of others' technological innovations and administrative practices. Nor could it sustain the plausibility of that part of its ideology that claims to be concerned with the collective, public good.

But both researchers and administrators do have a different perspective than that of everyday practitioners. They are certainly more committed to the rationalization of practice (Scott, 1982a: 225, 1982b) in the interest of scientific or therapeutic knowledge, on the one hand, and of more adequately serving a population or organization within the limits of available resources on the other. As Scott (1982a: 222) points out, both researchers and administrators are oriented to the "macro care" of populations, while practitioners are oriented to the "micro" or clinical care of individuals. There is therefore bound to be tension if not conflict between the practitioners of the profession and the administrators who supervise them by employing the standards that are created by the researchers (Scott, 1982a: 229).

These are the major lines of cleavage within the profession, with far deeper implications for the unity of the profession as a whole than mere differences of specialty, prestige, or income. Where once all practitioners could employ their own clinical judgment to decide how to handle their individual cases independently of whatever medical school professors asserted in textbooks and researchers in journal articles, now the professors and scientists who have no firsthand knowledge of those individual cases establish guidelines that administrators who also lack such firsthand experience attempt to enforce. Where once all practitioners were fairly free to decide how to manage their relations with patients, now administrators attempt to control the pacing and scheduling of work in the interest of their organization's mission, which may regard the collective interests of all patients (or of investors or insurance funds) to be more important than the interests of individual practitioners and their relations with individual patients.

Even though there are significant escape clauses in the form of offering the practitioner an opportunity to justify deviation from administratively imposed norms, it is not hard to imagine the potential for conflict. Nor is it hard to see the organized division of interests that arises between practitioners as a whole and physician-administrators, policymakers, and researchers.

TRENDS IN THE IMMEDIATE FUTURE

Where, then, is the medical profession going? I will not hazard prophesying the far future, but I will suggest probable directions for the next decade or two. In brief, I can say that the medical profession is going where health care in general is going—toward greater rationalization and formalization. Rationalization of financing and accounting for care is fairly well advanced already and is likely to continue. Rationalization of the organization of care, however, has been slower to develop, and given both the nature of health care itself and the place of the medical profession in the division of labor it is not likely to advance so far.

But there can be no doubt that it will continue, particularly in relatively large-scale settings such as hospitals, clinics, and Health Maintenance Organizations but also in more specialized units such as urgent care centers that are part of continuing efforts to control costs—whether to maintain profits for investors or to prevent increased demands on public funds. Rationalization will also be an important part of continuing efforts to control the quality of care and the accountability of those who provide it.

Rationalization of matters bearing on cost and health care itself is, of course, interconnected and is expressed through the social arrangements by which care is organized. Rationalizing social arrangements in health care organizations means formalizing the relationships among its participants. The health care division of labor among the various participating occupations has already been formalized. It is the medical profession that alone was able to resist formalization until recently, thereby preserving the appearance of a unified profession.

Perhaps because it resisted so successfully in the past it is likely to have to go through even more changes than other health care occupations in the immediate future. Given cost control efforts and increases in the number of physicians, it is likely that the profession's average income will decline. It is possible that the profession's prestige will decline as well, though certainly not precipitously and only modestly in relation to other professions. And it is likely that changes will continue to occur, as they have been doing during this entire century, in the periphery of medicine's jurisdictional boundaries in the health division of labor. But there is no reason to believe that medicine's basic position of dominance, its key position in the health care system, will change. It will have considerably less control over the economics of health care, however, and will have to struggle to maintain its strong voice in policymaking and in the governance of the organizations in which its members work.

I do not see changes that will actually transform rather than merely alter the position of the medical profession in either the nation or the health care system. Many of the changes to which the profession is adapting are to be welcomed as long-overdue methods of providing greater protection to patients and to the public treasury, but even in those cases members of the profession formulate the standards and staff the formal positions created to administer them. While there can be no doubt that nonphysician administrators have increased in importance and will continue to play more important roles in the emerging system, there is no sign that they will gain legitimate authority to formulate standards for, supervise, and control health care. That remains in the hands of medicine and its "allied health occupations."

What is far more seriously contested is control over the allocation of resources to health care. That is what lay administrators in hospitals and other large practice organizations are likely to control, in conjunction with their governing boards, and that is where the medical profession will find its greatest challenge, both in the particular institutions in which its members work and in the legislatures where politicians ultimately determine the amount and type of resources to be made available to the health care system.

To meet that challenge requires effective political organization, however, and there is the real possibility that medicine is losing its cohesion and thus its capacity for effective political organization. The formalization of professional control has led to formal distinctions between the judges and the judged, the authoritative researcher and the compliant practitioner, the superordinate and the subordinate. And even among rank and file practitioners, that large minority, if not majority, who will continue to work in small, private settings will have interests quite divergent from those working in large organizations, so that not even they may be able to act as a body. While all may be expected to join together for common action to increase the resources made available to the health care system as a whole, on which they all depend, their differences and lack of a common sense of profession may prevent them from being as effective as they were in the past.

REFERENCES

Abbott, A.
   1981.   Status and status strain in the professions. *American Journal of Sociology* 86:819–35.
Alford, R.
   1975.   *Health care politics.* Chicago: University of Chicago Press.
Arney, W. R.
   1982.   *Power and the profession of obstetrics.* Chicago: University of Chicago Press.
Barber, B., J. J. Lally, J. L. Makarushka, and D. Sullivan.
   1973.   *Research on human subjects.* New York: Russell Sage Foundation.
Berlant, J.
   1975.   *Professions and monopoly.* Berkeley: University of California Press.
Betz, M., and L. O'Connell.
   1983.   Changing doctor-patient relationships and the rise in concern for accountability. *Social Problems* 31:84–95.
Bosk, C. L.
   1979.   *Forgive and remember.* Chicago: University of Chicago Press.
Braverman, H.
   1974.   *Labor and monopoly capital.* New York: Monthly Review.
Brown, E. R.
   1979.   *Rockefeller medicine man.* Berkeley: University of California Press.
Burnham, J. C.
   1982.   American medicine's golden age: What happened to it? *Science* 215 (March 19):1474–79.
Christoffel, T.
   1982.   *Health and the law.* New York: Free Press.
Coburn, D., G. M. Torrance, and J. M. Kaufert.
   1983.   Medical dominance in Canada in historical perspective: The rise and fall of medicine. *International Journal of Health Services* 13:407–32.
Conrad, P., and J. W. Schneider.
   1980.   *Deviance and medicalization.* St. Louis: C. V. Mosby.
Derbyshire, R. C.
   1969.   *Medical licensure and discipline in the U.S.* Baltimore: Johns Hopkins University Press.
Dolan, A. K.
   1980.   Antitrust law and physician dominance of other health practitioners. *Journal of Health Politics, Policy and Law* 4:675–90.
Freidson, E.
   1970a.   *Professional dominance.* New York: Atherton Press.

————.

1970b.   *Profession of medicine.* New York: Harper & Row.

————.

1980.   *Doctoring together.* Chicago: University of Chicago Press.
Friedman, E.

1983.   Declaration of interdependence: More and more physicians find
salaried status attractive. *Hospitals* 57 (July 1):73–80.

Giddens, A.

1982.   *Profiles and critiques in social theory.* Berkeley: University of
California Press.

Goss, M. E. W.

1961.   Influence and authority among physicians in an out-patient
clinic. *American Sociological Review* 26:39–50.

Gray, B. H.

1975.   *Human subjects in medical experimentation.* New York: John
Wiley & Sons.

Harris, J. E.

1977.   The internal organization of hospitals: Some economic implications. *Bell Journal of Economics* 8:467–82.

Haug, M. R.

1973.   Deprofessionalization: An alternative hypothesis for the future.
Sociological Review Monographs 20:195–211.

————.

1975.   The deprofessionalization of everyone? *Sociological Focus*
3:197–213.

————.

1977.   Computer technology and the obsolescence of the concept of
profession. In *Work and technology,* ed. M. R. Haug and J.
Dofny, pp. 215–28. Beverly Hills: Sage Publications.

Havighurst, C. C., and N. M. P. King.

1983.   Private credentialing of health care personnel: An antitrust perspective. *American Journal of Law and Medicine* 9:131–201,
263–334.

Health Insurance Association of America.

1982.   *Health and health insurance: The public view.* Washington,
D.C.: HIAA.

Illich, I.

1976.   *Medical nemesis.* New York: Pantheon Books.

————.

1980.   *Toward a history of needs.* New York: Bantam Books.
Kissam, P. C.

1975.   Physician's assistant and nurse-practitioner laws: A study of
health law reform. *Kansas Law Review* 24:1–65.

Langwell, K. M., and S. F. Moore.

1982.   *A synthesis of research on competition in the financing and deliv-*

204   THE PRESENT STATUS OF THE PROFESSION

ery of health services. DHHS Publication no. (PHS) 83–3327, Research Report Series. Washington, D.C.: National Center for Health Services Research.

Larson, M. S.
1980.   Proletarianization and educated labor. *Theory and Society* 9:131–77.
Lippincott, R. C., and J. W. Begun.
1982.   Competition in the health sector: A historical perspective. *Journal of Health Politics, Policy and Law* 7:460–87.
Lipset, S. M., and W. Schneider.
1983.   *The confidence gap.* New York: Free Press.
McCarthy, J. D., and M. N. Zald.
1973.   *The trend of social movements in America: Professionalization and resource mobilization.* Morristown, N.J.: General Learning Press.
McKinlay, J. B.
1973.   On the professional regulation of change. *Sociological Review Monographs* 20:61–84.

———.
1982.   Toward the proletarianization of physicians. In *Professionals as workers: Mental labor in advanced capitalism,* ed. C. Derber, pp. 37–62. Boston: G. K. Hall.
Noie, N. E., and S. M. Shortell, and M. A. Morrisey.
1983.   A survey of hospital medical staffs—Part I. *Hospitals* 57 (December 1):80–84.
Oppenheimer, M.
1973.   The proletarianization of the professional. *Sociological Review Monographs* 20:213–27.
Pauly, M. V., and M. Redisch.
1973.   The not-for-profit hospital as a physicians' cooperative. *American Economic Review* 63:87–99.
Roederer, D., and P. Palmer.
1981.   Sunset—expectation and experience. Louisville, Ky.: Council of State Governments.
Scott, W. R.
1982a.   Managing professional work: Three models of control for health organizations. *Health Services Research* 17:213–40.

———.
1982b.   Health care organizations in the 1980's: The convergence of public and professional control systems. In *Contemporary health services: Social science perspectives,* ed. A. W. Johnson, O. Grusky, and B. H. Raven, pp. 177–195. Boston, Auburn House.
Southwick, A. F., and G. J. Siedel III.
1978.   *The law of hospital and health care administration.* Ann Arbor: Health Administration Press.

Starr, P.
    1978.   Medicine and the waning of professional sovereignty. *Daedalus*
                107:175–93.
———.
    1982.   *The social transformation of american medicine.* New York:
                Basic Books.
Stevens, R.
    1971.   *American medicine and the public interest.* New Haven: Yale
                University Press.
Sullivan R.
    1984.   City expanding use of computers to monitor pediatric care. *New
                York Times,* February 29, B24.
Toren, N.
    1975.   Deprofessionalization and its sources. *Sociology of Work and
                Occupations* 2:323–37.
Walker, J. L.
    1983.   The origins and maintenance of interest groups in America.
                American Political Science Review 77:390–406.
Zola, I. K.
    1972.   Medicine as an institution of social control. *Sociological Review*
                20:487–504.

THIRTEEN

The Medical Profession in Transition

The past two decades have brought change to most professions in the United States, but the medical profession alone seems to be undergoing extensive changes. Some writers have characterized those changes as the decline of the medical profession (Burnham, 1982), others as the "waning of professional sovereignty" (Starr, 1978, 1982), and still others as "deprofessionalization" (Haug, 1975) and "proletarianization" (McKinlay, 1982). Elsewhere I have discussed those characterizations at length and criticized them as overgeneral, without any reasonably close relationship to the truly critical changes that have been taking place, and without the conceptual resources that allow adequate analysis of the consequences of change (see chapter 12). Here I should like to identify the events that have precipitated changes in the environment of medical practice, the barriers that have channeled their implementation, and the consequences they are likely to have for the medical profession and its members over the next decade or so.

THE PRECIPITATING FACTORS OF CHANGE

Medicare and Medicaid legislation was the single most important factor of change for the health care system in the past two decades. These programs committed vast federal funds to pay for the health care of the elderly and the indigent, in the former case largely on the same permissive terms that private insurers had been paying for a large proportion of the working population. This commitment made the cost of health care more visible than it was in the past and politicized it, making it a topic for public consideration and debate and a subject for remedial legislation.

As we all know, a variety of other events were leading to an increase in health care costs. Continuous innovation in medical research and technique, fueled by new technology, led to the capacity to treat health problems that were previously treated far less expensively if treated at all. The new technology required increasingly larger sums of capital but at the same time, unlike many other kinds of technology, did not substitute for labor: health care remained labor intensive. Furthermore, labor costs themselves increased greatly when collective bargaining for previously low-paid hospital workers became legally possible, and in some areas fairly strong unions were formed. Of the professional workers in health care, nurses were especially conspicuous in unionizing. Labor costs were also increased by the trend toward licensing and certification among technically trained health occupations, many of which were developed to deal with the new health care technology.

Even before Medicare and Medicaid legislation was enacted, a series of other events influenced the general climate of public opinion within which public discussion of health care takes place and by which it is politicized. The public's traditional ambivalence toward science in general and medicine in particular moved from fairly uncritical approval and trust to a considerably more qualified and concerned (but by no means wholly critical) attitude. In the 1960s, regulations were written requiring all research programs financed by the government to be reviewed in advance for their method of protecting the rights of "human subjects." During the 1970s, public preoccupation and debate grew, fed by the media, on the issue of the ethics of medical and other research involving human beings. At the same time concern for the pollution of the natural environment grew, as did concern for the safety of drugs and processed foods. Part and parcel of this shift in concern was a growth of suspicion about the competence and ethicality of physicians. Malpractice suits swelled, and the profession's reputation was damaged by publicity about the way its average income increased much faster than the rate of inflation during the years following passage of Medicare legislation.

More recently, the very success of advances in medical technique and medical technology added to public concern with the work of the doctor. Perhaps the Quinlan case can typify the issue—namely, that it had become possible to intervene medically into what was heretofore only natural uncontrolled processes leading to death, and this power raised questions about the physician's role in the process. The successful movement to legalize and commercialize contraception and, later, abortion, and the women's movement, which pressed for the right of a woman to control her reproduction, also raised a host of ethical and legal questions. In all those issues the role of the physician was central, the lightning rod for unprecedented questioning. The abuse of medical authority was not so much the question as what authority a physician should have and what rights the patients and their families should have.

Most commentators have grievously exaggerated the consequences of this shift in the climate and focus of public opinion about health care. A recent, careful analysis of public opinion poll data has shown that there has indeed been a distinct decline in public confidence in American medicine. That decline is part and parcel of a decline of confidence in all American institutions, however. Compared to other American institutions, confidence remains highest of all in medicine (Lipset and Schneider, 1983); polling data indicate that the vast majority of all Americans have been and remain satisfied with their health care (Health Insurance Association, 1982). Neither medicine itself nor the health care institutions in which its members work are the objects of widespread and deep hostility or doubt, but they have become the objects of more questioning and challenge.

Another major phenomenon that has precipitated changes is rather difficult to characterize simply. I refer to the growth of an emphasis on competition, which stemmed from two distinct sources. If one can speak of the consumers' movement as a monolithic entity, some of its activities were concerned with gaining more stringent government regulation of the health industry so as to assure the safety and quality of its products and services. Others of its activities have been concerned with gaining for consumers more useful and complete information about the services and goods available to them and providing them with better criteria for choice—a concern that has on occasion led to legislation. Another part of the consumer movement, however, has been in favor of decreasing government regulation and increasing competition among health care providers, partly by removing or tempering restrictions on practice posed by licensing laws and partly by reducing professional restraints on advertising prices, competitive bidding, and so forth. That "procompetitive" pressure also grew from an entirely different source—exponents of the nineteenth-century economic ideology of laissez-faire, who emphasize consumer activism in a free market. Understandably it came from representatives of industries that have been subject to government regulation, but it also came from economists, lawyers, political scientists, and policymakers.

RESPONSES TO CHANGE

A variety of factors have had an important impact on the traditional institutions of medicine: continuous and unexpected rise in health care costs at the same time that financing became a public issue; an increasingly questioning attitude toward medicine and health care issues; and increased tendencies to challenge both government regulation and conventional methods of organizing and controlling the provision of health care.

It did not take many years after Medicare legislation for health care costs to be seen as out of control. Just a few years after the initial legislation there was political pressure to slow the rise. The initial target was primarily the largest source of expense—the hospital. The method of control developed by legislation was formal review. Each decision on the part of a physician to hospitalize a patient and, after hospitalization, the number of days the patient was hospitalized were to be reviewed in light of the primary diagnosis by a medically constituted committee in the hospital. A series of subsequent legislative efforts tinkered with the organization, mode of operation, and sanctioning powers of such review committees, the general trend being toward greater standardization of the criteria by which medical decisions to hospitalize and treat patients are evaluated.

This development was very significant in that the principle of mandatory, formal review of medical decisions was established and given legitimacy. Some sort of collegial evaluation of physicians' decisions has probably always existed wherever they worked in proximity to each other and most particularly in hospitals. The Joint Commission for the Accreditation of Hospitals has required for some time the existence of some form of committee to review facets of the medical care provided in hospitals. In all teaching hospitals, furthermore, some form of supervision and evaluation is routinely exercised down the hierarchy of the medical staff. But rules were not laid down to govern procedure from one institution to another, and records were not complete nor consistent nor systematic. Nor were formal sanctions specified. At present, some observers have charged that the Peer Review Organizations (PRO, which is the latest in the series of changing review systems) do not function in a truly effective manner. However, they represent a sharp break with earlier times in that they constitute a formal system for the review of the propriety of physicians' decisions, which is much the same everywhere. Furthermore, the system, presently limited to hospitals, can be extended into ambulatory settings where most physicians now are subject solely to claims review.

In addition to those general utilization review mechanisms devised to control the cost of care, a number of other, more specialized review groups have been constituted, primarily in hospitals, in response to public concern with the ethical, social, and medical issues created by developments in sustaining life artificially, transplanting organs, implanting artificial organs, performing fetal surgery, and the like. In some cases, as in the Infant Care Review Committees created to monitor the life support of deformed newborns, such formal review activity is mandated by governmental regulation, while in others it is voluntary. The PRO and other formal methods of reviewing medical decisions in hospitals do not exhaust movement toward closer surveillance, evaluation, and discipline over medical acts. In the past the disgruntled patient had recourse to the law of torts and the courts, where it was possible to sue a physician for malpractice and gain financial recompense. But financial penalties are one thing and losing one's very license to practice is quite another. Licensing boards and the disciplinary committees attached to them can revoke or suspend licenses. But when Derbyshire (1969) published his examination of the activities of such boards, he documented their lethargy. Political pressure, fed by well-publicized scandals, has led to much greater activity since that time. Some states have passed "informer laws" that require physicians and others to report to the licensing authority the name of any physician they believe to have acted in a grossly negligent fashion. By 1983, when Derbyshire reported again on the activities of state agencies, the picture had changed considerably (Derbyshire, 1983). Formal procedures for the systematic review and evaluation of boh the ethical and technical quality of physicians' performance have been reinforced and extended, though their effectiveness should not be overestimated.

Taken together, it is appropriate to say that while many of those formal physician review enterprises had roots in past institutions, the emerging situation has been genuinely new for the profession. Where once a physician could bury his mistakes with no one the wiser, so private was his practice, where once judges denounced physicians for their "conspiracy of silence" in refusing to testify against colleagues being tried for malpractice, and where once the hospital was the physicians' workshop in which they were free to follow their own variable inclinations without serious interference, now a variety of groups review both the technical propriety of the everyday decisions of physicians and the moral acceptibility of their activities. Those groups, furthermore, are formally constituted, and thus are required to function in such a way as to keep systematic records and develop standardized procedures.

The imposition of formal review is one important step toward restructuring the milieu in which medicine is practiced. Another step stems from quite different sources that are more directly concerned with reducing the cost of health care in general and the level of physicians' charges in particular. Early in the 1970s federal legislation was passed to facilitate the formation of health maintenance organizations (HMOs) that could offer consumers prepaid service contracts—taking care of most of their needs for medical service and consultation in return for a fixed annual sum, instead of charging them or their insurers on a piece-rate or fee-for-service basis. HMOs are quite varied in form, some being loosely organized aggregates of physicians working in their own offices, others being partnerships among physicians working together, and still others being organizations with a staff of salaried physicians. What joins them all together, however, is the common condition of physicians entering into a contractual relationship with consumers and insuring organizations. In that contractual relationship, the physician has a formal obligation to provide specified services over a given period of time to eligible patients, an arrangement which is quite different from the traditional fee-for-service relationship between physician and patient that was constrained by the barriers of a fee to be paid for each visit.

HMOs expanded considerably once federal legislation both neutralized state laws that handicapped their development and provided them with economic aid, but even now they cover less than 7 percent of the population. While they may be expected to grow further, in light of the varied forms of health insurance available, the persistent attraction of traditional forms of practice to many consumers, and the development of new, specialized forms of competitive ambulatory care, HMOs are unlikely to become the prototypical method of practice. But the contractual relationship with patients that they embody is likely to extend into other forms of practice and become more widespread than HMOs themselves. It can be extended into individual office practices by use of the recent "preferred provider" arrangements that are being explored by insurance organizations, hospitals, and employers seeking to reduce their costs for providing health benefits to their employees. Insofar as the number of physicians has been growing in relation to the population, many more may be interested in salaried practice (Friedman, 1983) than has been the case in the past, while others may be interested in entering into service contracts out of their own offices. Such contracts, like salaries, could assure both that they have patients and that they get paid.

With both public and private financing agencies seeking to reduce costs, service contracts can be attractive insofar as there is sufficient competition among physicians or groups of physicians to lead to economic terms that are desirable for insurers and patients. Until recently, such competition could only be muted and covert and was significantly handicapped by the codes of ethics of medical and other professional associations. A series of Supreme Court decisions in the 1970s, however, concerned specifically with law, pharmacy, and engineering, destroyed the barrier that organized professions have traditionally raised against overt price competition among their members and against advertising price and other features of their services. Aggressive antitrust enforcement on the part of the Federal Trade Commission, sustained by the courts on appeal in 1982, extended the requirement to medicine. Now, physicians and health care organizations are free to advertise both the prices and the character of their services within as yet uncertain limits of truth and propriety, and they are free to participate publicly in competitive bidding for clients or contracts with clients.

Another competitor for clients and the public and private insurance funds that pay for much of their care has emerged in the growth of for-profit health care enterprises financed and owned by lay investors. Traditionally, such enterprises have been financed and owned by physicians— the proprietary hospital being the best-known example, though some medical groups or clinics may also be mentioned. Given the recent climate of opinion that emphasizes the virtues of free competition, deprecates the motives and competence of public agencies, raises questions about the disinterestedness of physicians and representatives of the traditional non-profit, voluntary health care institutions, deplores the cost of care, and resists the generation of investment capital for hospitals through taxation, many stimuli for the expansion of private investment exist. Apart from hospitals and nursing homes, home care, kidney dialysis, "urgent" (or more precisely, casual) ambulatory care, and numerous other services have grown up as for-profit enterprises, some owned by lay investors and some by physician-entrepreneurs.

Few of these for-profit enterprises would have been initiated if there were not some large, reliable "third party" to pay their charges either directly or by reimbursing the patients who paid out of pocket. Even more attractive to for-profit enterprises was that initially, before costs came to be considered intolerable, little constraint was placed on the sums that could be charged for health care services. Most recently, however, large employers who bear the cost of health care benefits for their employees, health insurance companies themselves, and state and federal authorities have reinforced efforts to restrict the rise in health care costs by placing ceilings or "caps" on what they will pay. It is much too early to tell whether or not the effort will succeed and what its concrete consequences will be for particular health care enterprises, but it seems certain to put competitive pressure on traditional medical practices in both the private consulting room and the hospital floors. Many physicians are likely to be drawn into some contractual agreement with large organizations able to advertise effectively and otherwise attract insured patients, and to rationalize payment and administration so as to restrict their operating costs. Other physicians are likely to be drawn into salaried and otherwise rationalized and limited economic arrangements. And medical decisions in hospitals are likely to receive even closer scrutiny and critical evaluation in light of their implications for hospital income.

CONSTRAINTS ON CHANGE

The changes that have been taking place seem to have revolutionary implications for the medical profession. Instead of being free to exercise their own clinical judgment, physicians become subject to systematic and formal review of their decisions by increasingly standardized criteria. Instead of being protected by their monopoly over practice, they are thrown into a highly competitive marketplace in which price cutting and advertising may make the difference between success and failure. Instead of administering the affairs of their own practices in their own way, they become drawn into and dependent upon a highly rationalized and bureaucratic system of purportedly efficient management practices drawn directly from large business enterprises. They become subject to economic pressures that they cannot deal with on their own terms, in their own way, not the least of which is produced by entering into formal contractual arrangements with a large and powerful organization. If we take these changes at face value, without qualification by the social and legal context within which they occur, and if we assume that the trend will continue at the same pace into the future, the position of the medical profession might very well be characterized appropriately as declining. Even the extreme characterization of proletarianization may be accurate.

However, none of the changes I have described is thus far free of some very basic constraints that for the moment preclude the assumption that they will realize to the full their intrinsic logic in the near future. The medical profession retains its basic, legally enforced monopoly over the key functions of health care and, the consumer movement notwithstanding, retains its basic "cultural authority." At its edges, competitors have made some inroads on medicine's monopoly, but every inroad has been carefully limited by law, providing no hint of the possibility that the basic monopoly of medicine is seriously threatened.

Nonetheless, a monopoly does not necessarily have the consequence of situating the profession so well in the marketplace that economic returns to its members are inevitably handsome. Indeed, given the new competitive arrangements designed to reduce costs it is quite likely that the American medical profession will finally join the other professions of the advanced industrial nations and like them suffer a decline in income, monopoly or no (Scitovsky, 1966). But its monopoly is more than a device to maximize income: it is also a device to control work. While the monopoly is no longer able to contain competition among its members, it is still able to control some of the terms and most of the conditions, content, and goals of health care. In antitrust actions, as Kissam (1980) has noted, the courts have typically limited themselves to economic issues, leaving technical or scientific issues in the custody of the profession itself. Physicians continue to be the key people with the sole authority to legitimately diagnose and carry out the treatment of health problems. They are the ones who officially certify illness, who can admit to and discharge from hospitals, and who direct and coordinate the specialized activities of the varied health care occupations that are part of the health care division of labor. Their strategic location in the health care system cannot fail to provide practitioners with a strong lever for continuing to control much of what goes on in health care, even though their economic position has weakened.

A series of legal and quasi-legal requirements and practices sustains the capacity of the profession to retain a strong if not wholly determinative position in the health care system. Some may be seen in the federal and state staffing regulations governing the licensing of health care institutions and the designation of eligibility for reimbursement by health financing agencies, as well as in state laws governing the "corporate practice of medicine." Others may be seen in the regulations and practices governing the composition and operation of the official boards or committees that review medical decisions in health care organizations or that review consumer complaints against individual physicians. In a variety of ways, those legal and quasi-legal customs require that only physicians supervise the work of other physicians, review it, and evaluate it. The criteria by which the technical work of physicians is judged must be established by physicians. And in the formal review bodies in which the ethical and social issues of medical work are considered, physicians routinely predominate over lay members.

Because of the physicians' strategic position in the operation of the health care system, and the lack of any evidence that their position is changing in any marked way, one can understand why hospitals remain concerned with being attractive to physicians who can fill their beds with well-insured patients. Indeed, it seems no accident that something of a trend has been observed recently to include members of the medical staff on the governing boards of hospitals (Noie, Shortell, and Morrisey, 1983). This trend is a reversal of past practices, when the medical staff had direct access to governing boards (instead of being represented by the chief executive officer) but were not often members. Furthermore, whenever for-profit hospitals are organized, they are reported to go to great lengths to attract physicians to their staff, in some cases coopting them as shareholders who have a financial stake in the hospital's fortunes. Physicians have somewhat less leverage in ambulatory settings, but it is a frequent legal requirement that in health care enterprises outside the hospital, the chief executive officer be a physician. In the case of laws governing professional corporations, most states require that none but the working professionals themselves can own shares, and that those shares cannot be transferred to lay persons. Thus, professional control over the evaluation of medical work is mandated, as is control over the administration of medical work.

THE CONSEQUENCES FOR THE MEDICAL PROFESSION

I have noted a variety of important changes in the fiscal, administrative, and social environment of health care that on first glance appear to have devastating consequences for the medical profession. I then noted a number of circumstances connected with the legal and quasi-legal position of the profession that have not changed markedly from the past and that exercise important constraints on change. These constraints should not be considered barriers to change so much as devices that channel change. Taken together, the interaction between the changing environment of medical practice and the relatively unchanging legal position of the profession in the system seems to produce the continued strength of the profession as a corporate body, for members of the profession administer and perform the new functions of control pushed onto it by external forces. At the same time the profession becomes divided internally as the brunt of change is born by the everyday practitioner.

Consider the matter of the proliferation of formal groups or agencies charged with the official duty to review systematically the medical and ethical practices of working physicians. Those review groups subject everyday practitioners to unprecedented surveillance and evaluation, and they are empowered to impose concrete economic sanctions, in some cases so severe a sanction as suspending the license to practice. Although the review groups are staffed by members of the medical profession, a division is created between those serving on such review groups as judges and those they judge.

Similarly, as the organization of many practices becomes more complex, those physicians serving in the legally mandated positions of supervisor, staff director, or chief executive officer become superordinates and the practitioners subordinates. Remembering that physicians themselves have been active participants in the new, for-profit enterprises in health care; we may also assume that in a growing number of cases a cleavage will develop between physicians as owners or shareholders of health care businesses and other physicians as their employees and profit producers. Finally, the likelihood being that standards for evaluating technical practices will shift away from common usage toward standards established by academic researchers, the division between authoritative experts and mere practitioners will also deepen and intensify.

The profession as a corporate body, then, remains in control of the basic processes of the health care system by having its own members serve in the supervisory and standard-setting positions demanded by the forces of change. By competing and innovating or collaborating as entrepreneurs in the marketplace, by assuming administrative responsibility for reviewing and guiding if not actually dictating the performance of practitioners in complex systems, and by formulating defensible technical standards by which the competence and conscientiousness of their performance can be judged, the profession remains in charge, but it also intensifies divisions within itself.

Division and formalization of function are being organized into specialized roles around which develop specialized career lines and from which emerge distinct, organized interests. Whereas physicians serving in administrative or managerial roles were relatively uncommon and inconspicuous in the past, the number of organizations requiring their services has increased and they seem on the way to emerging as a self-conscious segment within the profession. Indeed, an American College of Physician Executives was formed not long age. Like deans of medical schools and directors or chief executive officers of hospitals, their concern is negotiating with and accommodating to the external forces on which the prosperity of their organization depends. This means striving to fulfill the demands for efficiency and accountability made by public and private financing agencies and sustained by political pressure and the climate of public opinion. To fulfill those demands requires maintaining working conditions to which practitioners are not accustomed and for which their preconceptions do not prepare them.

COPING WITH NEW WORKING CONDITIONS

Rank and file physicians confront all those changes from a different vantage point than that of the physician executive. Like all workers, they need to develop methods of tempering the pressures of their work environment. Traditionally, physicians kept their own medical records however they chose, and in hospitals were notorious for their recalcitrance in making entries and keeping the record up to date. In addition, they considered themselves free to follow their own clinical judgment, willing to consider the advice of colleagues but ultimately making their own decisions. In a health care organization like a hospital or a clinic they were willing to concede the legitimacy of the authority of lay and professional administrators over such housekeeping issues as scheduling hours, assigning space, and providing equipment, supplies, and supportive personnel but insisted on their sole right to make their own individual diagnostic and therapeutic decisions (cf. Goss, 1961). Their diagnostic and therapeutic decisions were in turn used to strengthen and legitimize their demands for space, time, equipment, supportive personnel, and the like. Once cost became a pressing concern, however, and formal methods of accountability and review instituted, the capacity of the practitioner to maintain past attitudes, values, and behaviors was seriously weakened, and relations with those in administrative positions as well as with their colleagues were changed.

By and large, it is in ambulatory care settings where the greatest tension between practitioners and administrators is likely to develop because in such settings the workload is subject to wide fluctuation. Periodically—as during the flu season in regions with cold winters—practitioners will experience an extremely heavy workload and may receive little or no relief in the form of additional supportive personnel or physicians. As one study found (Freidson, 1980: 55–85), practitioners may cope with this overload by refusing service, by cutting corners in their physical examinations, or—something facilitated by a prepaid service contract—by referring their patients to consultants or sending them out for tests or X rays after perfunctory examination. And certainly the records they keep—always a bone of contention between administrators and practitioners—will suffer. Each of those methods of coping with overload poses problems to the organization—possibly violating contractual agreements, raising its expenses, shifting the boundaries of the jurisdiction of primary practitioners and their consultants so as to lead to heavier use of consultants, and risking both legal and financial difficulty by virtue of inadequate records. Since all practitioners in ambulatory settings work in the nominal privacy of consulting rooms, and since all have a significant degree of discretion in their work in spite of formal review processes, administrative efforts to reduce or eliminate such methods of coping are unlikely to be fully successful. The tension between practitioner and administrator, therefore, is likely to be endemic, increasing in intensity during recurring periods of overload.

The service contract creates new problems with patients, which cannot be dealt with easily by traditional methods. With a service contract, physicians, or their practice organizations, agree to provide services to patients who themselves can realize the benefits of their insurance only if they consult those who have agreed to the contract. In the past, patients and physicians rarely had formal commitments to each other. If patients were dissatisfied and had other alternatives available, they could switch to them. By the same token, if physicians thought a patient too difficult to be worth dealing with and they could afford the loss of fees, they could use a variety of devices, including raising their fees arbitrarily, to encourage the patient to seek care elsewhere. In a contractual relationship, however, it is not easy for either practitioner or patient to withdraw without desirable costs or inconvenience (cf. Freidson, 1980: 41–54). They are both, in a sense, trapped by the contract and must work out some way of coping with each other rather than merely avoiding each other. Neither is able to act as an individual in a free market, for the contract is likely to prevent the doctor from raising a fee barrier and to discourage the patient from seeking care from someone else because it would cost money out of pocket.

Not all patients will pose many problems, however. From members of the affluent middle-class, physicians should expect the fewest overt difficulties, for the middle class are likely to have very generous and flexible health benefits that allow many options. And even when not, members of the middle class are less likely to find out-of-pocket costs burdensome in light of their total income. (For a recent study of physicians in HMOs and an up-to-date bibliography of others, see Barr and Steinberg (1985). From the poor and from blue- and white-collar workers physicians should also expect to meet few difficulties, particularly if the agency paying for the poor is passive and if the employed have no union that negotiates their benefits, educates them about their contractual rights, and intervenes on their behalf. It is primarily the large and growing group of college-educated, middle-income professional and technical workers—sometimes called the new middle class—that has the greatest potential for creating difficulties for physicians working under contract. They are well educated enough to consider themselves capable of understanding medical matters, well enough exposed to the media to consider themselves well informed about up-to-date diagnoses and treatments, and of high enough status to wish to be treated as equals. Furthermore, they are likely to have a fairly detailed understanding of their contractual rights and, being articulate as well as familiar with bureaucratic procedures, inclined to seek bureaucratic satisfaction from the insurer if they cannot get it from the physician. Their moderate income discourages them from the option of exiting and paying out of pocket. They have little choice but to stay and voice their complaints and desires within the system itself.

It would not be wise to exaggerate the number of such patients in everyday medical interactions, for most encounters are routine and most patients cooperative. But even a small proportion of patients who are troublesome can so color the quality of physicians' experience as to transform their perception of their practice as a whole and of the appropriate role to play in it. How physicians learn to cope with that minority of patients in contract practice has profound implications for the spirit in which service is provided to all and at least some implications for the substance and cost of services (cf. Freidson, 1980: 86–98). It is possible for physicians to guide their methods of coping by employing the criteria of traditional "free" practice—resenting contractual constraints, manipulating what they can to their financial advantage, and seeking opportunities to leave the system to become independent entrepreneurs. (For a rare study of physician entrepreneurs, see Goldstein, 1984a, 1984b.) Physicians can also adopt a bureaucratic stance toward their patients and their work. In cases of doubt or challenge they would go by the book, providing patients with what they ask as a contractual entitlement no matter what their personal judgment of its medical necessity or propriety. It is easier to dispense the benefit than to argue. A quite different and more desirable possibility is for physicians to adopt a purely professional stance of holding to their own medical judgment when the evidence supports it and refusing to satisfy inappropriate demands from patients while at the same time attempting to teach why they are inappropriate.

Which of those alternative ways of coping with work problems under the new conditions of contractual practice is adopted depends less on the particular variation in the contractual arrangement that is employed than on the way collegial relations in practice are organized and on the degree of financial stringency imposed on the system as a whole. The professional stance is time consuming and thus expensive in the short run. It is, furthermore, virtually impossible to adopt in times of overload and too vulnerable to official reproach if "quality" standards employed by official review bodies are narrow and mechanical. If the system becomes "efficient" enough that overload is endemic and standards precisely calculable, then those who cannot leave it to become entrepreneurs and managers are likely, as rank and file, to have no other way to cope than to adopt the techniques of the bureaucratic official, going by the book in dispensing contractual benefits and in making medical decisions that are subject to formal review.

THE ORGANIZED PROFESSION IN TRANSITION

In most discussions of professions such as medicine and law, the professions are characterized as divided primarily along specialty lines. Specialization has in fact been the major source of segmentation in medicine during most of this century (cf. Stevens, 1971). Less conspicuous and, until recently, less important have been the divisions of function that organize the way professional practice is carried out, no matter what the specialty. When the bulk of practice was carried out as an individual enterprise on an uninsured fee-for-service basis, individual practitioners themselves carried out the functions of administration and review, and individual clients were obliged themselves to undertake evaluative and sanctioning actions. In medicine today, however, even individual practitioners in their own offices are bound into reimbursement and review systems in which others become full-time specialists devoted to performing the functions of administration, evaluation, and sanctioning.

On both analytic and pragmatic grounds these growing divisions between the managers and the managed, the judges and the judged, the employers and the employees, and the standard-setters and the standard-followers are emerging to be a good deal more important than specialty in the segmentation of the profession as a whole. They cut across all the specialties, and they represent the hierarchical organization of economic, administrative, and cognitive authority over everyday practice no matter what the specialty. Furthermore, their growth creates a far more serious challenge to the political strength of the organized profession than the growth of specialty associations created in the past. Organized medicine in the United States has already lost through antitrust action some of its capacity to control the economic behavior of its membership. It is also in danger of losing its political position as the most effective representative of the profession as a whole.

While some very illuminating studies of the American Bar have been conducted recently (e.g., Halliday, 1982; Cappell and Halliday, 1983), the activities of the American Medical Association (AMA) have not received detailed analysis for some time, and I am not in a position to do so here. It is my impression, however, that while the AMA remains fairly influential on matters of licensing and on technical or scientific issues, the organization has lost much of its influence on economic and social policy. Part of that loss no doubt reflects the general decline in public confidence as well as the rise in importance of other sources of influence that combine to outweigh that of the AMA.

Even though the AMA carries on important joint activities with the American Hospital Association (AHA) and the Association of American Medical Colleges (AAMC), the AHA and AAMC seem to have more frequently taken different positions than the AMA on policy issues; at the same time the AHA and AAMC have become more influential than earlier. This also appears to be the case with at least some specialty associations and the associations representing medical scientists or researchers. Indeed, while many of the latter participate in those activities of the AMA involving the communication of research findings, their associations are more closely allied with the AAMC. The AAMC, after all, and the AHA, insofar as it speaks for teaching hospitals, represent the institutions in which medical researchers and academics work and upon which their fortunes depend.

If the analysis of this paper is accurate, we should expect the growth in size and influence of other health-related associations that represent the interests of the expanding, new, or renovated forms of organized practice—HMOs, urgent care centers, ambulatory surgical centers, and the like. As is the case for hospitals and medical schools, representation in such associations is institutional in character, embodied in the directors, deans, or chief executive officers responsible for the institution as a whole. Their orientation is toward overall policy in light of the larger political and economic environment that provides the legal and economic resources upon which the institution depends. The needs of the rank and file practitioners in their organization are only one and perhaps not the major factor they take into consideration in guiding their institution and protecting its interests. Theirs is a "macro" or policy-oriented perspective (cf. Scott, 1982: 222), which is quite different from the "micro" or clinical practice perspective of rank and file practitioners trying to cope with everyday problems of work. And in controlling the allocation of resources they have a direct impact on the way everyday medical work can be carried out.

In the past, like all professional associations, the AMA has attempted to be an umbrella association, representing the entire medical profession. Naturally, this policy has meant that, on issues that are deeply controversial among significant segments of the profession, it has had the choice of being silent, temporizing, adopting a very vague position, or adopting one of the contending positions and risking the alienation of those members who espouse the other. This problem, of course, is common. But if the issues become too important to evade and if perspectives on them are so distinctly different as to polarize large numbers of members, then it becomes impossible to exercise influence over their resolution without alienating one of those major segments and even splitting the association.

Thus far the AMA has tempered the winds of change by successfully maintaining professional control over the administrative, review, and sanctioning functions connected with health care. But it has not yet faced the implications of that short-term success for the creation of stronger divisions among its membership that will threaten its unity. The distinct possibility is that, as more physicians are drawn into organized systems of practice and become subordinate to other physicians who are employers, administrators, reviewers, and standard-setters, the satisfaction of their needs may run head-on against the needs of the system as conceived by those speaking for it. If the AMA is not successful in gaining agreement on some balance between the two needs, it may very well suffer the historic fate of schoolteaching, which is now divided into a large association for the rank and file alone and separate associations for their colleagues who are researchers and administrators. Sometimes these organizations are joined together on policy issues and sometimes they are bitterly opposed. The outcome of efforts to accommodate these different and equally legitimate interests will affect not merely the future of the profession as such but, more important, the spirit and substance of the profoundly essential human service it provides to the public.

REFERENCES

Barr, J. K., and M. K. Steinberg.
1985.   A physician role typology: Colleague and client dependence in an HMO. *Social Science and Medicine* 20:253–62.
Burnham, J. C.
1982   American medicine's golden age: What happened to it? *Science* 215 (March 19):1474–79.
Cappell, C. L., and T. C. Halliday.
1983.   Professional projects of elite Chicago lawyers, 1950–1974. *American Bar Foundation Research Journal* (1983):291–340.
Derbyshire, R. C.
1969.   *Medical licensure and discipline in the U.S.* Baltimore: Johns Hopkins University Press.
———.
1983.   How effective is medical self-regulation? *Law and Human Behavior* 7:279–90.
Freidson, E.
1980.   *Doctoring together.* Chicago: University of Chicago Press.
Friedman, E.
1983.   Declaration of interdependence: More and more physicians find salaried status attractive. *Hospitals* 57 (July 1):73–80.
Goldstein, M. W.
1984a.   Abortion as a medical career choice: Entrepreneurs, community physicians, and others. *Journal of Health and Social Behavior* 25:211–29.
———.
1984b.   Creating and controlling a medical market: Abortion in Los Angeles after liberalization. *Social Problems* 31:514–29.
Goss, M. E. W.
1961.   Influence and authority among physicians in an out-patient clinic. *American Sociological Review* 26:39–50.
Halliday, T. C.
1982.   The idiom of legalism in bar politics: Lawyers, McCarthyism,

and the civil rights era. *American Bar Foundation Research Journal* (1982):911–88.

Haug, M. R.
1975.   The deprofessionalization of everyone? *Sociological Focus* 3:197–213.

Health Insurance Association of America.
1982.   *Health and health insurance: The public View.* Washington, D.C.: HIAA.

Kissam, P. C.
1980.   Antitrust law, the First Amendment, and professional self-regulation of technical quality. In *Regulating the professions,* ed. R. D. Blair and Stephen Rubin, pp. 143–83. Lexington, Mass.: Lexington Books.

Lipset, S. M., and W. Schneider.
1983.   *The confidence gap.* New York: Free Press.

McKinlay, J. B.
1982.   Toward the proletarianization of physicians. In *Professionals as workers: Mental labor in advanced capitalism,* ed. C. Derber, pp. 37–62. Boston: G. K. Hall.

Noie, N. E., S. M. Shortell, and M. A. Morrisey.
1983.   A survey of hospital medical staffs—part I. *Hospitals* 57 (December 1):80–84.

Scitovsky, T.
1966.   An international comparison of the trend of professional earnings. *American Economic Review* 56:25–42.

Scott, W. R.
1982.   Managing professional work: Three models of control for health organizations. *Health Services Research* 17:213–40.

Starr, P.
1978.   Medicine and the waning of professional sovereignty. *Daedalus* 107:175–93.

———.
1982.   *The social transformation of American medicine.* New York: Basic Books.

Stevens, R.
1971.   *American medicine and the public interest.* New Haven: Yale University Press.

PART FOUR

Health Care in the Future

The Prospects for Health Services in the United States

Whatever the facts are, as many words as dollars have been in circulation during this decade, the words declaring that there is a crisis in health care in the United States and the dollars symbolizing the crisis. There are hundreds of technical monographs, many issued by federal agencies, bristling with statistics on the use of health services, on charges to Medicare and Medicaid funds, on the coverage of various health insurance programs in the United States and abroad, on the cost and coverage of commercial insurance plans, on the substance of varied legislation being proposed, and the like. There has been a steady increase in the number of technical monographs devoted to various facets of health care research, administration, planning, and policy. And a great many of the new books issued by commercial publishers each year are devoted to some aspect of health care. The number and variety of words are so great that no individual can possibly keep abreast of them any more. Overwhelmed with information, we must rely on impressions based on only a sample of what is available. My own impression of what I have seen of all those words is that virtually all agree on the basic symptoms. All seem to agree that the central problems in health care today are those of, first, excessive costs, second, the highly uneven and inequitable distribution and availability of adequate services, and third, the uneven quality of health care.

But while almost all agree on the nature of the symptoms, analyses of their etiology and prescriptions for their care run a range that is virtually logically exhaustive. The most obvious range of opinion refers to the *amount of change* necessary to remedy the crisis. At one extreme we find claims that while some minor difficulties exist, fairly simple measures of relaxing governmental pressure are all that is necessary to rectify them: the system will take care of itself. In the center we find the bulk of opinion, contributing a multiplicity of suggestions, concrete and abstract, for various reforms in the financing of health care, assuring access to it, and modifying the organization of services. At the other extreme we find opinions that assert the hopelessness of reform and, implicitly or explicitly, call for the construction of a totally new system.

A complete range of opinion is also to be found in proposals concerning the *kind of services* to be made available to the population. Some, at one extreme, seek to assure access to everyone of all services now available and yet to be invented. Most in the center seek to limit access to only "necessary" or "efficacious" services. Some, at the other extreme, seek to eliminate the availability of most, if not all, of the presently available "therapeutic" armamentarium of physicians.

And finally, one may note that the same broad range of opinion exists in discussions of the *kind of health personnel* to be made available to the population. At one extreme are those who merely wish to assure that physicians are available to serve all who need services. In the center are those who would continue to employ physicians but who wish to allocate segments of the physician's present work to less expensive, more briefly trained health workers, thereby increasing the variety of occupations engaged in health care. At the other extreme are those who wish to dispense with the physician entirely as a direct health care provider.

Clearly, it is impossible that all of the prescriptive proposals are politically, economically, and socially viable. Indeed, as they are stated, some of the more extreme proposals, such as Ivan Illich's recommendation to "demedicalize" society and Milton Friedman's proposal to "delicense" professions, may be taken seriously only as statements of principle that, by the interest and conviction their rhetoric attracts, can influence the *direction* of the outcome of the practical compromises by which change takes place in ordinary times. They would never be adopted in their pure form.

However, the more radical or outrageous proposals have one very important merit: by their nature, they produce a very clear picture of their basic assumptions about the essential dynamics of social systems. This is why they can have as much force as they do and also why they will never be considered practical. But their very transparency allows them to be understood and assessed in ways that are not possible for the purportedly practical proposals with which we have been inundated. Indeed, I would argue that none of the available proposals can be assessed with very much profit unless we understand the logic of their underlying assumptions. Without that understanding we are not able to guess at the content and direction of the unanticipated outcomes that always result from the operation of the concrete institutions that new programs establish. Such understanding is all the more important because of the fact that we really have very little reliable and valid information about the way present-day health care systems actually work.

It may seem odd to say that we really have very little reliable information about the way the health system works, just after it was noted that billions of words have been written about it. Nonetheless, we do lack data obtained by direct, firsthand observation carried out systematically by trained investigators. The data we have in bewildering profusion are primarily indirect, secondhand data collected for administrative and accounting purposes but treated as if they represent what actually goes on in health care settings. We also have documents produced by the participating members and institutions of the health care system, which are at best only a partial and inevitably biased representation of what goes on. And we have reports of dubious accuracy produced by task forces, commissions, and other tourists after they have visited some country or institution, been led on officially conducted tours, and chatted briefly with officially selected informants under institutionally controlled conditions. By far the smallest proportion of all the words available report systematic and direct study designed and carried out independently of the institution by skilled researchers, and even there most of them are surveys long on representativeness and reliability but short on validity. In all, the primary resource on which we rely in order to make sense of health services is not so much sound information as our sense of plausibility, which varies by our personal experience and our theoretical, moral, and political prejudices.

The key to the variety of proposals, then, is not so much the "facts," which are inadequate, as the implicit theoretical, moral, economic, and political positions of their proponents. And those basic positions are more often than not unstated. It would help the debate a great deal if those positions were presented clearly and arranged alongside each other for scrutiny, and this is what will be done here. However, mere presentation is not enough. For some, it seems sufficient to deal with systems in their conceptually pure and morally ideal form. But conceptual clarity is not compatible with empirical reality, so that if one wishes to take any responsibility at all for the confused muddle of the real world, one should feel obliged to be concerned with the particular directions in which ideal models are altered in the course of attempting to realize them. Thus, after sketching the logic of the various models implicit in the many schemes for reorganizing health care, it is necessary to discuss the pathologies characteristic of each when attempts are made to institutionalize them. The logic of the alternative given, and the dangers of their pathological forms specified, it then becomes possible to assess the characteristics of the current system to see what models or blend of models are compatible with it, and therefore what the immediate future is likely to be.

FOUR MODELS FOR THE PRODUCTION AND DISTRIBUTION OF SERVICES

At the bottom of all the proposals, in various mixes and blends, are four logically pure, ideal models for organizing the production and distribution of goods and services. As models, they are guides for reasoning about the real world without themselves ever being more than highly selective, and perhaps wishful, abstractions. In considering them we must remain constantly aware that they are only consistent ways of thinking and that they do *not* represent the real world. Indeed, as abstractions, they can never be real.

The best known of these models is that of the classical *free market* of capitalism. It is unconstrained by deliberately organized controls, and people participate in it primarily as individuals competing with each other on the basis of the pursuit of their individual interests, measured primarily by material gain. In the free market, productive work is motivated fundamentally by the desire for material gain. What work people do, how they do it, what they produce from their work, and how they assign value to it are essentially functions of market demand.

Essentially calculative of advantage, the worker competes with all others for the limited gainful work available in the marketplace. He is expected to be physically, psychologically, socially, and legally free to shift from one kind of work to another as demand or supply shifts. Demand sets the tone: workers supply what is demanded because that is the route to gain. The workers' personal judgment of and concern for the quality of their product is essentially irrelevant to the process, since it is the market and demand that set value, and it is only money that measures it. Workers cooperate with others only when it is to their material advantage to do so and, in theory, do not develop any sense of solidarity with each other or any collective organization.

The free market model also makes certain assumptions about the consumers of the production of the worker—customers. If anyone is the controlling agent of a genuinely free market, it is the customer and not the worker, the entrepreneur, or the capital investor. In order for this to be true, and the outcome socially defensible, the model must assume that consumers are capable of judging the value of available products and services reasonably accurately, and capable also of calculating their own material advantage so as to be able to choose intelligently and parsimoniously among competing products and services in the marketplace. By calculating relations among cost, quality of product, and their own needs, consumers will contribute to an aggregate market demand that eschews products of high cost or low quality or both. Such a selective, calculating demand is assumed to require workers to produce and supply goods at low cost if they are to survive. In consequence, more products and services at low cost will be available to all consumers, distributed widely, and society will thus reach what Adam Smith called "universal opulence."

The free market gains its coherence by the unplanned compatibility of the aggregate of material interests of producers and consumers engaged in exchange in the marketplace on the basis of rational calculation of advantage. In contrast, the coherence of the second model, *rational-legal bureaucracy,* stems from the deliberate planning and control of work on the part of a limited, elite group of government officials of a nation or managers of particular productive enterprises. What workers do and how they do it are a function of the systematically drawn-up plans and rules both created and enforced by the administration, which is itself in theory controlled by rules specifying the limits of its powers. The product itself—the volume of production and the quality of the product to be produced and distributed—is determined in advance by formal planning.

Different tasks are deliberately created with some stated, productive end in mind, and they are arranged into jobs coordinated by supervisory officials. Since the aim is predictability of production, the thrust of rationalization is toward the standardization of tasks and work roles. It is assumed that the tasks necessary for gaining a given productive end can be reduced to rules and thus that only minimal discretion on the part of workers will be necessary for them to perform their work. For both productive workers and managers, the assumption is that the material security and predictable career prospects provided by the plan, in conjunction with the legitimacy ascribed to the plan and its functionaries, will lead them to perform in accordance with the rules and therefore produce in a predictable manner. Supervision and quality control are built into the system. As to customers, it is assumed that they can both learn and understand their rights under the rules and thus that they can and will seek and gain the goods and services they are entitled to.

Whereas the thrust of work in the free market is toward a gainful product and the thrust of work in a rational-legal bureaucracy is toward a standardized, predictable product, the thrust of the work in the third ideal model, the *collegium of workers* or the professional model, is toward a qualitative product. Since they claim that only they possess sufficient knowledge and skill to evaluate their work, workers claim also that the intrinsic value of the product they produce can be legitimately judged only by them, not by the customer or the manager. Thus, workers must assume responsibility for the nature of their own product and also for the welfare of the customer and the public in general. Neither equity adjudicated by a set of legitimate rules nor a favorable position in the marketplace can adequately protect the client. Cost, distribution, and quality are thus to be determined by the workers' decisions, based on their own notions of quality and the public good. Insofar as the work is produced by only one kind of worker—one occupation—relations among workers are equalitarian and based on occupational solidarity. Where a division of labor is required, the various kinds of work are coordinated by the workers themselves, using functional criteria to establish the grounds for the exercise of authority by the member of one occupation over those of another.

Neither market advantage nor the authority of office is granted legitimacy in coordinating and directing effort in the worker-control model. Influence and status are based on superior skill and knowledge rather than money or official position. Consistent with that criterion, the relation of workers to each other and to their customers is one based on the persuasive demonstration of the value of the skill or knowledge embodied in the work. The clientele are led to use the products or services of the worker because they have gained faith in their value, not because the products or services are bargains or are an official entitlement or right.

The fourth model, socialism, or *cooperative equalitarianism,* is the most difficult to delineate, for the word has meant many different things to many different people over the past century or so, and unlike the others, it has been presented less often as an explicit model than as something implicit in socialist critiques of the capitalist model. Thus, the characteristics of socialism as an ideal model for the organization of production and distribution must be inferred more often than read directly from some expository text.

From what I am able to guess, the model seems to cancel out the essential terms of all the others. Instead of being built around the notion of individuals competing with each other for personal gain, it emphasizes the cooperation of all for the good of all. Instead of allowing cost, distribution, and quality to be determined by impersonal market forces, it emphasizes the preeminence of social need over all else and the collective determination of that need. Instead of being built up around the idea of a rationalized hierarchy of differentiated jobs planned, established, and coordinated by some superior planning or managerial authority to produce and distribute goods or services at a given cost, it is equalitarian and makes no provision for hierarchical organization. Instead of being built up around the idea that particular groups of workers with specialized skills organize themselves around particular tasks in order to control them and claim authority over their own production by reason of their esoteric occupational skill and knowledge, it emphasizes the equality of all workers as a class, regardless of their different skills and functions in the process of production and consumption: subordinating one group of workers to another is antithetical to the model.

Thus, as I see it, the ideal model of socialism is hostile to the idea of hierarchical control by either private owners of capital or by the state, hostile to the idea of a stable division of labor and its implications of authority based at the very least on skill and function, and hostile also to the idea of the impersonal working of the market. It seems to imply the theoretically fluid division of labor suggested by the free market model, but without the motivation of calculated individual self-interest on the part of its participants and without the mechanism of the market by which cost, distribution, and quality may be determined without authoritarian planning. Indeed, it seems to me that it makes no real provision for a division of labor of sufficient complexity and magnitude to produce enough goods and services to provide a reasonably comfortable standard of living for all. Even on the level of an abstract model, it seems to be either incomplete or self-contradictory.

CHARACTERISTIC PATHOLOGIES OF THE MODELS

As I have already noted, the models are ideal and not real. They do serve as ideals and guides for political decisions, and stated or unstated, have served as at least partial guides for all of the proposals currently confronting us. But since they are ideals that cannot be realized in their full purity, they must be assessed by the forms they take in reality. This is not to say that past realities preclude better future performance on the part of any of the models, but it would be irresponsible to make proposals based on an ideal and ignore the characteristic ways by which that ideal has been corrupted by its realization, notwithstanding exculpatory explanations by its adherents. Let us turn to the real pathologies of those ideal models.

The vulnerability of the free market ideal to reality has been well publicized, from Adam Smith down to Milton Friedman today. Both have deplored organized conspiracies against the consumer in the interest of assured profit or wages, and both have deplored the frequent intervention of the state into the operation of the market. Over and over again individual self-interest has found advantage in cooperating with others in order to gain a monopoly in the market and to control both price and profit, and the state has been called in to rectify or control the results. Furthermore, consumers have often not been able to evaluate the nature of the goods and services being offered them, or their cost, sufficiently well to allow them to choose in such a way as to exercise effective control over price or quality. Neither cost nor distribution nor quality tends to serve public need adequately because each is influenced too much by the desires of investors, managers, and workers for their own gain. Human services are especially vulnerable to such pathology.

The pathologies of the bureaucratic model have also been well publicized. Rules and procedures of bureaucracy, intended to be guarantees of both predictability and fairness, come to be ends in themselves, displacing the goal of producing goods or services. Thus, bureaucratized workers may become so concerned with their records and procedures that they may never provide customers with what they ask or else may send them along tortuous and useless paths in the course of passing the buck. Formal accountability encourages passing the buck. Furthermore, economically secure in their positions and unmotivated by devotion to service, bureaucratic workers may resist customer requests unless accompanied by a flattering, deferent manner or the intervention of an influential person, a bribe, or a gift. Political or economic privilege may further interfere with impartial functioning by the rules. Cost, distribution, and quality are all controlled, but in a fashion that falls considerably short of the expectations of those responsible for the system. True costs—including the bribes, tips, and gifts that are the analogue of the black market that always accompanies a fully planned economy—never get specified. Distribution and quality meet nominal but not impressive standards. Human services become standardized, perfunctory, and dehumanized.

The pathologies of the craft-professional model also require little discussion here. It is a deliberate restraint on free competition among occupations for customers, without external administrative or industrial control of the labor market. That restraint is justified by reference to a body of skill and knowledge too complex and dangerous for consumers to be trusted to judge and control. The workers' conduct of that monopoly, however, has tended to disappoint reasonable expectations: the collegium becomes more concerned with its own welfare than that of its customers; it expands the scope of its monopoly well past its capacity to serve public needs; it actually resists efforts at rationalization that would reduce the cost of its work and the range of its jurisdiction and control, and practices featherbedding with impunity; it becomes preoccupied with refining its knowledge and skill for their own sake, irrespective of public need; stratification develops internally, dividing its members. Cost, distribution, and quality are virtually uncontrolled by the regulatory processes that the collegium claims it exercises. Quality varies widely—from extraordinary virtuosity to perfunctory routine and even negligent incompetence.

Finally, there are the pathologies of the socialist model. Perhaps because of the model's lack of any social mechanisms for organizing production and distribution, empirical efforts to realize socialist goals of distribution seem prone to employ various versions of the bureaucratic model, which defeat its goals of equality. In democratic socialist nations, which have mixed economies, this is routinely the case, tempered by efforts to include consumers in the decision-making process. In revolutionary or state socialist nations, the hierarchical organization of production is such that within or alongside it there is a separate party organization designed to exercise ideological control over the motivation and functioning of managers and productive workers. For a variety of reasons—perhaps its dysfunctional concern with minimizing hierarchy and the differentiation of labor, perhaps the intrinsic difficulties of centralized planning, perhaps the "political interference" of party cadres in productive enterprises, perhaps the hostility of the international economic and political environment produced by capitalist nations—revolutionary socialist nations have characteristically had difficulties in reaching an adequate level of production and in controlling the quality of what is produced. Minimal resources are often made available to all consumers by virtue of state control of cost, distribution, and quality—an important achievement not to be deprecated—but the quantity and quality of the goods and services produced have been questioned by both friendly and unfriendly critics. Democratic socialist nations have shown fewer of those pathologies, though some have shown that they have done rather less to reduce inequality among their citizens than might be expected from their ideologies.

From what has been said, it should be apparent that the most marked empirical deviation from theoretical and ideological purity is to be found in the case of the two most logically extreme models—the free market and socialism. Both models seem to specify forms of motivation and organization that have, in all known historical instances, been too fragile to survive intact for long. Both, in their empirical forms, seem prone to revert to versions of the bureaucratic model, in which policy is controlled either by private monopoly capital or by the state. Much less frequently, and in only special industrial sectors, do we find the worker-controlled model. The influence of both the free market and the socialist models seems most marked in determining not so much how the organization of production and distribution takes place as who are the public or private agents who control that organization and what is the policy governing its productive and distributive goals.

In the case of health care, the American system has been, historically, primarily a mixture of two of the models—the free market and the collegium of workers. Since the early twentieth century, physicians have had a state-licensed occupational and institutional monopoly within which a partial free market, limited by rules against advertising and other forms of "unfair" competition, has been used to determine cost, distribution, and quality. The failure of that system is the issue today. But since the possibilities for peaceful change are inevitably limited by the essential characteristics of the various segments of the system, no matter that we might wish it otherwise, we must assess the characteristics of those segments in order to assess the kinds of change that are most likely to take place in an effort to improve the cost, distribution, and quality of health care.

THE SEGMENTS OF THE HEALTH SYSTEM

One important and often ignored segment of the system is composed of those firms that manufacture health-related goods—the drug, appliance, and health technology *manufacturers*. As part of the private sector, their aim must of necessity be to return a profit to those who invest in them—a profit sufficiently high, compared with competing investment opportunities, to both attract and hold investment capital. In theory, their method of producing profit should be to improve their products, invent new ones, and increase the efficiency of manufacture so that prices are competitively low. Such methods are not so easily accomplished for a variety of reasons, so instead, a great deal of energy goes into new kinds of convenience packaging, attractive product and packaging design, new combinations and mixes of old products with new brand-names, the development of disposable products and, permeating the market, extensive reliance on advertising and other forms of promotion.

Given the nature of the health system, the prime target for promotion is not the ultimate consumer, the patient, but rather the physicians and hospital functionaries who order and use the products on behalf of the consumer. Merchandising pressure is for continuous turnover or replacement of products, and for expansion of consumption irrespective of the functional value of the products. So long as this sector depends on increasing its profits in order to continue to attract investment capital, there will be a continuous proliferation of products, extensive advertising pressure to expand consumption and thus expand the proportion of the total cost to the health system accounted for by health-related manufactured goods. If stringent limits are placed on the total expenditures of the health system so that the pie to be divided cannot increase in size, it is quite likely that there will be massive efforts by manufacturers and their lobbyists to encourage the use of manufactured goods as substitutes for the use of health personnel.

The manufacturing sector is distinct in the health system by virtue of its orientation toward yielding profits for the private investors who provide its capital. The *service sector* does contain some institutions with the same foundation, and while they have increased in number since Medicare and Medicaid have reduced their economic risks, my guess is that they will continue to be marginal and atypical because of their political vulnerability and the competitive advantage that so-called nonprofit status confers. Most of the service sector is likely to remain "nonprofit." But the service sector has its own kind of expansionist tendencies. Health-related institutions are headed by people who are ideologically as well as materially committed to the importance of their activities. Their tendency toward expansionism has often been explained by imputing economic motives to them, but while there is no doubt that successful expansion advances administrative careers and managerial perquisites, it does not directly increase profits to capital investors. The issue of expansionism and imperialism in health institutions and health occupations is far too complex to be explained successfully by imputing "capitalist" motives of profit to their leaders.

The officials of health institutions are more often than not tied in closely with the medical profession, likely themselves to be physicians by training. While they do represent an interest group separate from the profession, they also constitute an increasingly influential stratum within the profession. Like colleagues who are practitioners, they have a deep-seated belief in the importance of medical knowledge and skill in health affairs. While they may attempt to rationalize or bureaucratize their institutions by seeking to gain more power to determine who performs what jobs in their institutions—institutional licensing being one way of doing so—they are commited both ideologically and by their careers to the preservation of their health institutions and the expansion of their responsibility into ambulatory care. They differ from practitioners less in their conviction that medicine and its practice are of foremost importance for the public good than in their notion of how health policy and service delivery should be organized and who should have the power to control it.

Academics, health institution administrators and researchers, and government health officials do not compose a monolithic group. On balance, nonetheless, their perspective is at odds with the practitioner. They differ with the practitioners on the standards to be used to assess quality of care, on the method to be used in organizing services, on the methods to be used in determining the services to be paid for, on the method and amount of payment for goods and services, and on the methods of accounting for payment. The overall thrust of what they stand for is toward the bureaucratization of both ambulatory and residential health services, that is, the creation of administrative mechanisms by which institutional costs can become manageable, the distribution of resources orderly, and the quality of service standardized and predictable. Thus, their pressure is toward the bureaucratization of health care, but *within a framework of medical ideology and the ideology of expertise,* sometimes tempered by a concern for more democratic and humane modes of providing that care.

The medical school–hospital–state agency segment of the health system is concerned with creating an administrative, legal, and fiscal framework by which to organize the financing, distribution, and quality of services. Those who actually do the work, however—physicians, nurses, technicians, and the like—constitute a separate segment that is being pressed toward at least nominal bureaucratization. This aggregate of health occupations is fractured into both functional and hierarchical divisions, which compete with each other for legislative support of their jurisdictions. Within the aggregate is a primary service system composed of a stratified division of labor dominated by the authority of physicians. The structure of that medical dominance is very clear in hospitals, where the work of dozens of subordinate occupations is organized around the doctor's orders. Separate from that primary division of labor, largely independent of it and uncoordinated with it, are a series of other relatively autonomous specialists—dentists, podiatrists, optometrists, chiropractors, Christian Science readers, and the like. By and large, excepting the lower strata in which clerks, typists, receptionists, orderlies, security guards, and other such workers are to be found, occupational licensing and certification establishes and maintains both jurisdictional boundaries and the hierarchy of occupational authority. It also provides a modicum of job stability and security to the workers involved. But as the institutional licensing and the "new careers" movements suggest, such job security is obstructive to managerial rationalization and efficiency, and to the occupational mobility of those who wish to move up from one occupation to another.

As everyone knows, medical practitioners have been a powerful force obstructing change over the past fifty years. Once given protection by the state against serious competition from other occupations in the early twentieth century, they have attempted to maintain their freedom to exercise their own economic, organizational, and clinical judgment without the intervention of patients or third parties. While they have become weaker as a political force, they still have considerable influence and are likely to continue to have it so long as they are the sole or major experts on the diagnosis and treatment of illness and discomfort, and so long as health care remains organized around their skill. Health as a human value has powerful political appeal, particularly when associated with immediate, concrete and dramatic curative or ameliorative benefits to individuals. In contrast, the preventive services, which administratively oriented professionals properly emphasize, have little immediately perceptible benefit and are too abstract to draw widespread political support away from curative practice. Thus, while there may be increasing divergence in the positions of the administrative, research, academic, and governmental wing as it moves toward preventive measures and of the practitioner wing that gains its strength from curative or repair measures, the latter is fairly well entrenched and cannot be expected to be shifted easily.

The final major segment of the health system is the health consumer. The true universe of consumers is composed of the entire population of the nation, for everyone was, is, or will be involved in using some health service at some time. But in the vast majority of cases, consumer contact with the system is only occasional. Thus, the national universe of health consumers is an unorganized and fragmented population, with little communication, interest, and coordination joining it together. Some segments of the population are, as volunteers, actively engaged in work addressing particular health problems. But one segment of interested and involved persons has little or no relationship to any other segment. And what is true on the national level seems true also on the local community level. Very few members of the average community are continuously and deeply concerned with health care problems, and of those that are, most are special interest groups preoccupied with the particular problems or illnesses that happen to affect or interest them. Most health consumers are thus difficult to mobilize for participation in the affairs of a health program for any extended period of time, and those who are mobilized are likely to be concerned with specialized rather than community-wide problems.

But while the universe of health consumers is unorganized and largely passive, it does, nonetheless, constitute a political force of a special kind. We must remember that they are subjected to massive stimuli from the media. They see feature articles or television programs about particular health hazards. They hear of new drugs or modes of treatment that provide magical benefits. They are taught early warning signs and symptoms. They are exposed to countless patent medicine advertisements promising chemical relief from pain and embarrassment. And they are appealed to by well-organized national foundations concerned with gaining support for their own campaigns against their chosen diseases or health problems. In this light, there should be little wonder why consumers are deeply concerned with health care in general and why many worry about the cost and accessibility of health care. Polls show that well over a simple majority is in favor of some form of government health insurance program that will reduce their out-of-pocket costs when they need care. Since lack of organization does not preclude voting by individuals, this widespread concern has not been overlooked by politicians.

THE PROSPECTS FOR HEALTH SERVICES

This, then, is the level and direction of the pressures built into the present American health system. The profit-making sector promotes forcefully and ubiquitously the value of its constantly changing products to both the consuming public and its professional purchasing agents, seeking to expand consumption. In turn, health institutions, health occupations, and private interest groups, not to speak of government campaigns, promote the value of health and of their own services, while being divided on the methods of financing, distributing, and controlling them. The public is unorganized but as an aggregate prone to medicalize its problems and to press for increasing the availability of health services while reducing the out-of-pocket cost. The government discovers that there is a point of demand for health services past which present methods of public financing become politically impossible. Obviously, something must and will be changed. What is the substance of that change likely to be?

In order to answer that question, it is necessary to be aware that the programs and plans established by the use of political and economic power lay down the limits of action on the part of those who perform the productive work, insofar as those actions are dependent on those resources. The limits to available resources being given, how they are used is determined by the participants. The outcome of any plan or program is therefore determined by the interaction between the limits they set and the available alternatives for action that the participants happen to choose in order to advance their own ends. It is at the very least naive and wishful to assume that we can predict the performance of the participants of a scheme by reference to the legislation or the formal organization alone. It is equally naive and wishful to assume that administrative records and accountings reflect more than the most gross elements of performance. No form of organization—not even so extreme a form as a concentration camp or a maximum security prison—has ever succeeded in preventing its participants from turning some of its resources to their own ends and for their own purposes. Knowing of their ends and purposes, as well as the process by which they seek to gain them, is essential for anticipating the outcome of their actions.

The organizational framework for health care that seems to be emerging in this decade is one that is gradually forsaking the free market model, restricting the worker-controlled model, and extending the bureaucratic model. The various sectors participate in these changes in different degrees. The organization of manufacturing is highly bureaucratic, while the environment in which it attempts to sell its goods is competitive, though collusion to divide up markets and fix prices is a constant possibility, and government licensing and regulation are constantly increasing. The institutional sector may be expected to move further toward bureaucratization, though occupational licensing remains a serious obstacle to extensive movement. If the unionization of health workers increases, so will bureaucratization of those sections of the institutions in which they work. Those of the health occupations whose members are characteristically employed full-time in health institutions are likely to undergo increasing bureaucratization. The weaker of the occupations will see their qualifications and tasks defined and supervised by management; the strongest will have to keep better and more detailed records of their decisions and performance. Those of the health occupations whose members can work independently self-employed, will escape bureaucratization of their immediate work setting, but not of their service and financial records. Consumers also will not escape the process of bureaucratization: instead of being customers in a free market, entitled to shop around, to buy or not, with no long-term contract with anyone, they become clients with entitlements or rights to service defined by specific legislation and insurance contracts. They must both learn and cope with the rules, and must deal with the bureaucratic procedures established by those organizing the provision of services.

The issue of interest, however, is not bureaucratization in and of itself as an ideal model but rather the particular qualities it will assume in reality. There is no logical reason why it cannot be efficient, reliable, high quality, and protective of the rights of its clients: logically, it is designed to be so. In order for it to actually be so, one of course needs first of all a well-designed framework, with adequate resources; one also needs workers who are adequately trained and motivated, a social milieu for work that operates as a continuous, positive reinforcement to conscientious performance in the spirit of the plan, and effective methods to correct inadequate performance.

While it might be argued that performance and credential-based criteria for the recruitment of health personnel are, in conjunction with well-designed job descriptions and systems of supervision, sufficient guarantees of performance, I would disagree in general and disagree most particularly in the case of health care. The basic tasks of health care are not yet so well rationalized and mechanized that discretion can be reduced to an insignificant level, and the physical and personal milieu in which many basic tasks are performed are such as to preclude close supervision without serious infringements on both the privacy and needs of the patient. Complete bureaucratization is no more possible than it is desirable. Bureaucratic frameworks are possible and perhaps desirable for ensuring a modicum of accountability and control, but within these frameworks there must be heavy reliance on the regulatory processes carried out by the participants themselves. The system is most vulnerable here, for if their purposes deviate from those assumed by the policy establishing the bureaucratic framework, the framework can be used by the participants to protect and advance their own ends at the expense of the intent of policy, even if not at the expense of the letter of its formal requirements.

All the financing schemes of the past, from the Blues and other private plans to Medicare and Medicaid, have suffered grievously from the consequences of that vulnerability, and I do not see any prospect for more than minor change over the next decade. In the past, financing schemes have been passive in character, assuring payment to hospitals and practitioners without any serious effort to assess either the propriety of the charges or the quality of service, and with at best spotty attempts to improve the community and regional distribution of services. In the case of more active schemes initiated by the government, the institution of special financial incentives intended to direct activity to desired goals has encouraged the invention of ingenious methods of getting around the intent while at the same time gaining financial reward. That is the profound weakness of neoclassical economic assumptions: financial incentives tend to subvert policy goals by stimulating the efforts of those most inclined to put gain before any other end and discouraging the others.

Throughout the process of formulating health policies, the presumption has been that self-interested motives are in some way tempered and constrained by professional values of service and craftsmanship: no one could possibly consider employing fee-for-service payment without assuming that professional behavior is directed by other than economic motives. And while noneconomic motives no doubt guide some individuals and institutions some of the time, little in the organization of service down at the grass roots level has been available to assure that it is mostly the case. The administrative immunity of physicians in practice institutions and the dominance of the protective norms of professional etiquette over the professional norms of service have allowed wide variations in the quality of performance. It is very unlikely that the requirement of more meticulous reporting and accounting schemes and of formal review procedures—some of which have already been instituted, and others certain to come—can do more than require better administrative records and control over costs, without much positive impact on the actual services provided. Indeed, one might guess that as the demands of the emerging system increase, it is the patient who will suffer the most. As more time is spent in required committee meetings and in keeping required record systems complete, the quality of care will become more perfunctory, more mechanical, and more dehumanized. Cost pressures are also likely to encourage the substitution of drugs and manufactured goods for human contact and care—a substitution understandably encouraged by profit-oriented manufacturers, their political lobbyists and salesmen, and, for different reasons, by administrators. This, too, will contribute to the further dehumanization of care.

However, while a variety of devices at any given point in time can reduce costs, including the politically dangerous device of restricting eligibility for services of various kinds, the intrinsically expansionist character of all segments of the system is likely to lead, sooner or later, to a renewed growth in costs past the level of political acceptability. Then the cycle of the past will be repeated again, with new legislation created in order to at least reduce the pace of escalation but without making any significant impact on established profit margins and incomes on the part of the producers and providers of the system. Attempts at the containment or reduction of cost have, under such circumstances, no other option than to rely on bureaucratic accounting and control techniques.

Since there are no important grounds for believing that the spirit of compliance to such essentially external methods of containment will be positive, there is little reason to believe that there will be any change in the processes that have produced the professional and bureaucratic pathologies characteristic of the past. Thus, the cycle of the past is likely to be reproduced over and over again, a cycle of legislative reform, accumulating difficulties and scandals, new reform, and so on. Only basic changes in the very foundation of the system seem likely to lead to real improvement in the cost, distribution, and most particularly the quality of health care. Perhaps our experience with several of those already familiar cycles will develop the political climate necessary for the institution of basic change before the end of this century.

FIFTEEN

Industrialization or Humanization?

In the previous chapter I speculated on the near future of health services in the United States in light of what I believe to be the characteristic interests and political processes shaping them. I suggested that change is likely to be cyclical, spurred by successive crises created by inadequate, partial solutions to the problems of quality, cost, and distribution that have always plagued the American system, even before centralized third party payment dramatically exposed them. And in the preceding chapters I speculated about the consequences of changes that are taking place in the differentiation of the members of the organized medical profession. Here I wish to pick up some of the themes that have recurred throughout this book and discuss not what I think *will* occur but what I think we should try to attain in the future.

The suggestions I shall make are not truly radical, but neither are they so conservative as to be realized easily. They are somewhere in between—policies grounded in the institutions of the health care system today, but requiring changes that offend the sensibilities of some and the material interests of others. If we desire them, we will have to struggle for them. Furthermore, I shall stress principles more than concrete policies for attaining them. If principles are clear and firmly established, there are usually a number of ways to realize them.

THE SOCIAL REGULATION OF HEALTH CARE

In all complex societies health care has been treated as a special kind of service and given protected status. This is due to three special characteristics. The first is that it deals with one of the most elementary human needs—relief from suffering, disability, and at times the threat of death or permanent incapacitation. It is thus a very precious service. Today it is all the more precious because it can go beyond merely salvaging human capacities to enhance and expand them. Second, poor or incompetent health care can have disastrous consequences, including permanent disability and even death. While it is precious, it is also potentially dangerous. Third, most of those who seek health care are not sufficiently knowledgeable or detached to be able to evaluate adequately either the competence of those offering it or the quality of the care they give. While they may be able to evaluate the results of their care in some cases, in others damage may be hidden or may not become apparent for some time.

For these reasons health care is not allowed to be just another commodity in the marketplace. Those who are believed to be competent and conscientious are given special privileges that provide them with considerable advantage over others in offering their services, sometimes even giving them a monopoly over the right to do so. Some people who may believe themselves competent are prevented from offering their services, and consumers are prevented from trying them out. The consumer may choose only those who are approved by the authorities.

As I have shown in chapter 11 and elsewhere in this volume, in advanced industrial nations like the United States regulation is pervasive. The labor market for health workers is structured by occupational licensing that in critical cases provides a legal monopoly on the performance of particular tasks. The market for health services is structured by institutional licensing that provides approved organizations like hospitals with a legal monopoly over the possibility of providing care. Neither over-the-counter and prescription drugs nor an enormous number of both consumer and capital goods may be offered for sale or used in health care settings without the approval of government agencies. Many medical goods are not commercially viable unless government agencies agree to reimburse charges based on their purchase and operation.

There are few if any other areas of the economy that are so heavily regulated. Nor is there any significant inclination to have it otherwise. Leaders of particular occupations may wish to modify medicine's monopoly over services; midwives and nurse practitioners, for example, want more autonomous practices. But neither they nor others wish to eliminate occupational licensing and registration. They want a more advantageous position for themselves in the regulated system, including reimbursement for their fees by third-party payers.

Similarly, those who speak in favor of for-profit enterprise in health care institutions have not attacked the institutional licensing system or the centralization of payment by insurance companies and the state. Indeed, without the protection from truly free competition provided by regulation and the assurance of receiving payment for their goods and services from reliable third parties, health care would lose much of its attraction as an investment for private capital. Some of those engaged in the manufacture of health-related goods have deplored delay in gaining government approval, but without major changes in the civil law governing product liability it is doubtful that even they would want anything more than modifications in regulation.

A truly free market for health services and goods is not really contemplated by most participants in policy debates, even though some of their rhetoric implies its desirability. This is true not only of the ideologues whose stock-in-trade is the universal panacea of a free market, but also, in a more complicated and contradictory way, those who speak for the consumer movement and even so-called radical critics. But the intrinsic characteristics of health care are such that regulation is virtually inevitable. To introduce wishful images of a free market into policy debate is to obscure and confuse the real issue, which is the status of participants in the health care system as beneficiaries of its regulation.

In light of the regulated character of the system, an appropriate principle to guide change is that *all participants in the system should be considered in the public service rather than engaged in private economic pursuits.* This includes not only those who organize and provide health services but also those who manufacture and distribute health-related goods and those who insure payment for them. We should conceive of health care as analogous to a public utility even when the provision of services and goods is in private hands. And since the economic rewards gained by those in the system are a consequence of public regulation, they can and should be determined by deliberate public policy even while remaining in private hands.

EQUITY AND HEALTH CARE

Because health care is so unusually precious, dealing both with what is essential for life itself and with enhancing capacities for living, it should be available to all in need regardless of economic status. The viability of pursuing this principle of equity in health care has been called into doubt by estimates of its intolerable cost. However, those estimates take as a given the social and economic arrangements of today, the very arrangements of a system that, large and expensive as it is, still fails to provide adequate care to tens of millions of Americans.

The first and most important step toward a principled health care policy is to forsake the self-serving fiction that the high cost of health care is inevitably, necessarily, and rightly what it is today and to struggle for strategic if not revolutionary changes in the arrangements that produce it. Present-day costs reflect the privileged legal, economic, and political position of those organizing and producing goods and services in the health care marketplace. As free market ideologues point out, they are costs created by present forms of public regulation. Thus, they can be reduced by public regulation. And if we reduce the cost of individual services and goods, there are more to go around for the same total sum. Before we consider reducing the total sum devoted to financing health care, we should make more care available for that sum in order to be able to serve those who are now unserved.

TECHNICAL AND HUMAN STANDARDS OF CARE

One danger of relying on monetary cost as the primary criterion by which we evaluate health care is that it tends to become an end in itself. Cost is a practical reality that cannot be waved away, but to have any meaning it must be associated with some minimally acceptable standard of the quality of goods or service. There is, however, more than one kind of standard. In the case of health care, *the standards for determining what is minimally acceptable should be heavily but not entirely qualitative.*

In earlier chapters I distinguished between the somewhat remote bureaucratic system of control which relies on indirect, formally structured sources of information about performance and employs fixed criteria to evaluate it, and the collegial system, which derives its information from direct observation and work records and employs many qualitative criteria to evaluate performance. The pursuit of efficiency and cost reduction in the health services has led to the massive growth of the bureaucratic method of control and the decline of the collegial method. This has meant that more and more fixed *technical* standards are being employed to evaluate health care at the same time that it has become possible to mechanize care.

For perhaps the first time in the history of humanity it is possible to conceive of a health care system that is thoroughly rationalized and extensively mechanized. New knowledge and technology have developed computers that can diagnose complaints and prescribe treatment alternatives. Machines can monitor and substitute for body functions and adjust their activities accordingly. Furthermore, standard classifications of complaints and diagnoses have been established, along with requirements that standardized techniques be employed for all cases falling within them. Standardization defines what is minimally acceptable in terms that allow mechanization and reduce the cost of producing services. The techniques of industrialization are being applied to health care.

The Industrial Revolution of the nineteenth century reorganized the work force, mechanized its tasks of shaping physical materials into goods, and standardized the goods it produced. An analogous process has been developing in the service sector of our economy. It might be called the Second Industrial Revolution: the first industrialized the way workers dealt with materials, and the second industrializes the way workers serve people, so that people themselves become standardized industrial objects.

The use of technical standards to evaluate and control the quality of care dehumanizes both those who provide services and those whom they serve. Workers lose much of their discretion and work mechanically and inflexibly, like machines. Patients lose their uniqueness as individuals and become anonymous members of an abstract category or class. It is true that some standardization and dehumanization is inevitable in any kind of service work, for even if no single case may ever be exactly the same as any other, it is impossible to approach each afresh, without guidance from categorization and routine. But mechanization, the apotheosis of routine, eliminates all judgment or discretion and thus, while reliable, efficient, and cheap, eliminates the possibility of adapting to individual cases and circumstances.

The difference I am emphasizing is, in the case of the production of goods, the difference between the mass-produced, standardized object and the custom-made object adapted to individual desires or circumstances. Most of the time the far lower cost of mass-produced goods outweighs the loss of individuality, but health care is too important to the quality of human life to treat the same way. In the pursuit of equity in health care, industrialization of services is a tempting alternative because of its capacity to reduce costs. But that tactic devalues the very conception of human need and human potential that equity is predicated on.

A health care system worthy of a decent society should sustain the responsible exercise of discretionary judgment, a judgment aimed at the treatment of individuals rather than of ciphers defined by their bureaucratic or diagnostic classification. Diagnostic and treatment standards employed during the course of reviewing the quality of care should not be permitted to become narrow and mechanical. Care must be evaluated on qualitative grounds. Only by that means can truly human health care be preserved.

THE MAXIMIZATION OF CONSUMER CHOICE

The final principle that should guide policy in creating a better system is one that limits and qualifies the principles I have already suggested. It concerns the role of those for whom such a system is intended—the people who seek care for their complaints. Constraints on their freedom to choose whatever care they wish are justified by the assumption that health services are potentially dangerous and difficult for lay people to evaluate. But not all services are potentially dangerous and not all consumers are unable to evaluate all available services. *Policy should be guided by the principle of maximizing the individual's freedom by minimizing professional restrictions on the choice of goods and services.* All services and goods that are neither potentially harmful nor especially complex and esoteric, and all that can be controlled by impersonal means to prevent harm to users, should be freely available to consumers at their own convenience.

The rhetoric of the consumer movement recognizes few if any

limits to the empowerment of the consumer. It often represents the consumer as a kind of "universal man," capable of being knowledgeable about anything he wants to consume and fully rational and active in evaluating and choosing it. As I indicated in earlier chapters, some believe that the knowledge gap between prospective consumers and physicians has so narrowed that consumers are in fact assuming the imperious role in the medical marketplace that is implied by the idea of the free market. But I reject the plausibility of that belief because of its implicit assumptions that medical knowledge has not increased while public knowledge has and that present-day medical knowledge is something one can easily learn. In fact, I argued in chapter 1 that one source of the fundamental asymmetry in the doctor-patient relationship stems from differences in knowledge and skill.

While we recognize that expert opinion must limit consumer choice in health care, we should nonetheless closely examine the present limits to identify additional instances where customers can dispense with professional services and diagnose and treat themselves. What can be purchased over the counter could probably be increased without serious risk to the consumer's well-being. For items requiring a greater degree of control than those now sold over the counter, though not so great as those requiring a prescription, it is possible to create an intermediate category of drugs, appliances, and the like that can be freely bought by the consumer but whose purchase must be recorded.

Consumers could also make use of mechanized, professionally programmed services that do not require human contact. While I have just deplored the possibility that in the drive toward cost reduction health care can become mechanized and standardized, it would be unwise to romanticize the human encounter connected with medical care. Sometimes people are not deeply worried and would prefer low-cost convenience and simplicity to solicitous human contact. Indeed, for those seeking merely a routine checkup, one can imagine a credit-card-operated diagnostic and treatment computer: the consumer could punch in answers about history and symptoms in response to questions on the screen, even have vital signs read, perhaps blood and urine taken and tested. In no longer time than it takes a subway photomatic to develop and dispense its portraits, the consumer could receive a medical self-portrait and fortune in the form of a diagnosis and evaluation. Standard prescriptions could drop out of the machine already formulated and packaged, like Raisinets or Milk Duds; while for other patrons there would be no prescriptions, only an urgent appeal to see a physician.

I have suggested a few ways by which more choices of both goods and services could be made available to consumers. Such a policy maximizes the possibility that, within regulated limits, patients can care for themselves if they wish to do so, without an expensive and inconvenient consultation with a professional. Certainly there are many other ways by which people can care for themselves and, for that matter, can be cared for by those who care for them. Such self-care and mutual care should be voluntary, however, and not a forced substitute for professional care. Furthermore, those who engage in it should not be penalized by being denied at least some of the financial benefits that would have been available had professional services been used instead.

Finally, I might note that even after everything possible is opened to free consumer choice, there still remains much that must be dealt with by professionals. In this area, too, there is greater room for choice than has been allowed by the present health care system—namely, choice between physician services and those of, for example, midwives and nurse practitioners. It is naive to expect that those "paramedical" practitioners can be as truly independent of medical supervision as, for example, dentists. And it is equally naive to think that they will bring much more responsive, human qualities than do physicians to the relationship they have with their patients once their practices stabilize and move toward greater professionalization. Still, the permissible scope of their services should be extended as far as possible and made more freely available to consumers.

However, after everything has been done to widen the range of the consumer's freedom to choose services and goods, there will remain a great many circumstances in which the use of medically controlled services will be necessary. And there, regardless of good intentions, the fact is that patients will often be treated as objects rather than as individuals, and that care will become routinized. After all, day after day health workers see people who present similar problems that must be dealt with in similar ways and identified as members of a general diagnostic and/or management class. Though good manners preclude addressing Mr. Jones as "the gall bladder in Room 10F," patients inevitably are seen as gall bladders, not individuals. Such categorization is unavoidable. What is avoidable is bad manners, insufficient respect for patients to explain and allow them to choose alternatives, and the use of standard diagnoses and treatments without taking into account the patient's individual characteristics and circumstances.

PATIENT POWER

In earlier chapters of this book I discussed the intrinsic asymmetry of the doctor-patient relationship, as well as the way that imbalance is reduced when patients have high status and great power. In order to compensate for that asymmetry patients must have power. Patients with power can expect to be treated as individuals, not to speak of good manners, explanation, and choice. However, history teaches us that when patients have overwhelming power, the care they get may be what they want rather than what physicians believe to be appropriate. This, of course, destroys the whole point of a professional or expert service. The power of the patient should be limited, yet some kind of dependence on patient good will must be built into the system of health care. *The patient's perspective and interests should be represented on the governing boards of all institutions providing health care.* It is also appropriate to have consumers' interests represented on the boards of private insurers and health-related manufacturers, and in the corporate programs formulating employee benefits.

Broad consumer participation is desirable, but because most people's contact with health care is limited and episodic, taking place on occasions when they may be incapacitated emotionally as well as physically, representation is a more viable possibility. It may be vulnerable to the danger of cooptation, particularly in the case of those serving as paid ombudsmen in large institutions, but it is better than no representation at all.

Patient representation is no panacea, however, and may even have mischievous results if it is merely adversarial. Pressed too aggressively, practitioners can defend themselves by retreating behind technical standards that are difficult to question. This would defeat the purpose of patient representation by dehumanizing care. Further, since there is an increasing number of health care institutions in which practitioners are employees with no representation on governing boards, there is also a real danger that in response to aggressive patient representation the institution itself may impose a variety of dehumanizing formal bureaucratic requirements on medical work.

PRACTITIONER POWER

In considering how to organize health care so that patients can have a strong voice in determining how they are treated, we must never forget that no matter how informed and active the patients, no matter what personal wealth and power or representation they have, the permanent working staff has irreducible advantages merely by virtue of being staff. Its members have special expertise, they know the ins and outs of the organization and its procedures, they have alliances with others on the staff, and they create the selective records that portray the organizationally salient characteristics of both their clients and their own performance to the managers of their organizations and to the system outside. It is they who shape what goes on and what, without firsthand study, we know about what goes on.

Crude bureaucratic, political, or economic pressure can force changes in their behavior and their records that may seem desirable, but it is likely also to change the spirit in which they do their work. Retreat behind the protection of bureaucratic form and purely technical norms reflects such change, as does manipulation of the system in order to maximize economic reward. And staff may tolerate, even encourage the convention of bestowing special attention in return for tips, gifts, or outright bribes. Indifference, passivity, formalism, and venality are the adaptations of those who have no important voice in the policies of the organizations in which they work, most particularly when they feel oppressed and embattled by those policies. In order to avoid such an adaptation, *staff as well as patients must have power in all health care institutions,* no matter what their ownership status. Like patients, their perspective and interests must have strong representation on governing boards. And their voice must be organized.

Given a system in which patients are empowered and there are stringent efforts to reduce costs, it is quite possible that at the same time as patient pressures increase, the resources available to the staff become inadequate for doing good work. To counteract those demoralizing possibilities, practitioners should have a voice in determining the policies of their institutions, including the allocation of resources. The traditional American model of collective bargaining, which leaves to management the prerogatives of constituting and scheduling tasks, setting the standards for the evaluation of performance, and allocating resources, is inappropriate for them. So is that of the professional association, insofar as it is organized primarily for shaping legislation and policy remote from individual work settings. New forms of work-site organization for practitioners will be needed to provide them with collective defense of their economic and professional interests. And because the Supreme Court's *Yeshiva* decision removed professionals who participate in the governance of their work settings from the protection of American labor law, the law must be changed to recognize the intrinsic difference between professional and industrial work.

DISCRETION, COLLEGIAL CONTROL, AND THE ORGANIZATION OF PRACTICE

The prime purpose underlying all my suggestions for change is to create circumstances that encourage the provision of health care that is devoted to the flexible service of individual needs. This means that while it is essential to establish and enforce high standards by which to evaluate medical work, they cannot be so narrow and mechanical as to leave little room for exercise of the discretionary judgment that is essential for truly human care. If the expansion of external review organizations employing bureaucratic methods of control is prevented, however, and their standards kept broad enough to allow a significant amount of discretionary judgment, there must be other means available to review and evaluate that judgment. The best and most desirable means lies in the principled interaction of the physicians themselves. This is so because they can examine each others' patients and see the medical charts that record directly the salient events, observations, and findings of their colleagues' work. They can also share the vicissitudes of practice and know the extenuating circumstances created by the character of the local community, the patients, the work load, available personnel and equipment, and the like.

Such shared experience is not possible in all forms of practice, however. Insofar as the collegial method of reviewing and influencing performance is desirable, therefore, we must follow the principle that *practice must be organized in such a way as to provide the conditions of observability that make direct review of performance possible.* Those conditions are more likely to be established in the collective or group form of organization, but it is also possible to knit solo practices together in such a way as to share patients and to maintain and circulate the complete medical record among all those in the network.

However, as I noted in chapter 5, the mere possibility of observability is not enough. Its potential cannot be realized unless it is accompanied by a process of active individual and collective critical review and discussion of both problematic and questionable clinical decisions. It is conceivable that such a process can be part of the informal interaction between colleagues, but the requirement of formal review meetings insures that they will meet periodically and engage in review of each others' performance.

TOWARD A NEW PROFESSIONAL ETIQUETTE

It is a truism to observe that virtually any formal requirement can be met by ritual conformity that defeats its purpose. This is also the case for requiring formal review. How such review is carried out is as important as the fact of review itself. Medicine in particular and the practicing professions in general have long held to an etiquette designed to minimize conflict among colleagues by tempering review. It dictates that one should be slow to judge and that even when one does deplore a colleague's action, one does so privately. Unless there is some pressing reason to do so, it is not proper to confront the offender, even in private. And public criticism, even before a group of colleagues, is anathema.

No collegial method for controlling performance can succeed unless that etiquette is changed. Its technical justification in medicine stems from an earlier day when there was little reliable knowledge and technique and when practice was far more art than science. Without denying that medicine still remains something of an art and will continue to be so as long as it deals with cases in the discretionary manner I am advocating, its body of knowledge and technique has become precise enough to make the traditional etiquette anachronistic and self-serving. If this etiquette continues to dominate colleague relations during the course of review, it leaves social policy no option but reliance on bureaucratically imposed, mechanical review and discipline. *The etiquette of colleague relations must change if practitioners are to be relied on to control their own performance.*

A more appropriate etiquette can be drawn from science, and, for that matter, humanistic scholarship. It requires that one's evidence and sources be open to the close examination of colleagues and assumes that critical discussion either in print or at public forums is an essential and virtually routine part of practice. It can be developed among practitioners if, during the course of medical school and postgraduate internship and residency, it is emphasized as a principle without which the integrity of the craft is lost. And it should be a routine expectation in work settings. This, of course, is much easier said than done, for it introduces a source of tension in collegial relations that most people want to avoid. Still, if discretionary work is to be preserved, it *must* be done.

MAXIMIZING PROFESSIONAL INCENTIVES

The introduction of this new etiquette would be greatly facilitated if there were a change in the balance of the practitioner's incentives. As I have noted in earlier chapters, present-day policies appear to rely solely on economic incentives to change the doctor's practices, but in reality they make the covert assumption that the doctor is also influenced by moral and professional values. In fact, more than one incentive figures in human conduct, and the relative strength of each varies. While economic incentives can certainly have some place in motivating physicians to participate in an acceptable collegial review process, I believe that greater emphasis on professional values—pride in the quality of one's work and the respect of colleagues and clients—would facilitate that development. Indeed, I think that considerably less emphasis on economic incentives would greatly improve the spirit in which practitioners approach their work.

Short of taking holy vows, and even that is becoming more and more rare, no one can be expected to disregard income. This is especially the case in a capitalist society where every effort is made to lead people to increase their consumption, whether of the latest fashions in clothing or the latest advances in medicine. However, it is one thing for people to be concerned about their income in a general way and quite another to tie it to the number and type of individual tasks they perform each day—that is, to be paid on a piecework or fee-for-service basis. I have no illusions that any formal method of payment by itself produces a simple, predictable result—indeed, I have taken issue with those who advance such a view. Nonetheless, I suggest that, on balance, if the fee-for-service system of compensation were replaced by either salary or a limited number of capitation fees, physicians would be far more likely to provide truly human care and to adopt the etiquette essential to collegial control of the quality of that care. I believe that when expectations of income become stabilized as an annual salary, professional incentives can play a larger role in the way work is performed, and the cooperative behavior essential to effective peer review can be facilitated.

This assertion will no doubt be met with hostility and skepticism, in part because of its implication that the income of physicians be capped, in part because self-employment and fee-for-service are traditional in medicine, and in part because of thoughtless stereotypes about the behavior of those who work on a salaried rather than self-employed basis. On the matter of income, like it or not, it is now fairly clear that the combination of an increasing number of physicians and a revolt by powerful public and private third-party payers against further cost increases is already slowing the growth of physician income and may even lead to decline. Furthermore, given the virtual disappearance of the traditional individual patient who pays out of pocket, the freedom of negotiation implied by self-employment and fee-for-service payment has also disappeared. The golden age has passed.

There is no reason to assume that a salaried health service will lead to poor care. Only tradition and a selectively blind ideology deprecates the way those on salary do their work. As I noted earlier, professors, engineers, priests, and scientists have traditionally been employees with modest salaries, but this has not prevented them from truly extraordinary accomplishments in service, research, and scholarship. They have shown no more and probably less incompetence, indifference, and venality than have the traditionally self-employed professions of medicine and law. Indeed, it may be no accident that in the United States it has been these two professions—which characteristically work with the incentive of fee-for-service or analogous payment—that have most often been accused of venality.

To have a reasonable salary in a reasonably secure position is to be in some sense more free than one is when one depends on the day-to-day increment of fees received for individual tasks. One is also more free to exercise personal judgment rather than follow the dictates of the individual demanding service. Of course, it could be answered, this protected independence is precisely what allows salaried professionals to be unresponsive to individual clients and to either dictate the service to them or withhold it unjustifiably. The common custom in state socialist health services for patients to give gifts, tips, or bribes to physicians in order to receive service is rightly held up as an example of the pathologies that can occur in a salaried service. The irony, of course, is that what is a "pathology" to exponents of fee-for-service payment is nothing but a supplementary fee-for-service payment scheme.

SOURCES OF COST REDUCTION

In my suggestions for the future I have presented a picture in which consumer self-diagnosis and treatment are maximized, the use of non-physician health workers encouraged, and every effort made to preserve the disciplined exercise of discretionary judgment so that health care does not become mechanized and dehumanized. Within the delicate restraints of a larger bureaucratic framework of accountability, I have suggested that in health care work settings both patients and practitioners should participate in determining policy, no matter who the legal owner. And I have recommended that in every health care institution control over the quality of care be in the hands of its practitioners, who alone are able to evaluate and when necessary correct the discretionary behavior that is essential to truly human care.

How would these policies affect the cost of health services? If all were realized, the consequences would be mixed. Certainly cost is reduced when consumers do more things for themselves and consult professionals less often. It is also reduced when some of what physicians now do for patients is performed instead by other, less costly health workers. Furthermore, there would be a significant reduction in the cost of administering the system were fee-for-service payment eliminated. On the other hand, my suggestions for a collegial method of controlling the quality of care entail arrangements that could increase costs, for these oversight procedures reduce the time available for service itself, thereby requiring more practitioners.

But when we remember that the system is publicly regulated and that cost is a function of that regulation, we can find additional sources of savings. Current efforts by the state to restrict increases in physicians' fees and even decrease fees by determining differential values for various specialty services will reduce the cost of physician's services, as will contractual arrangements being negotiated by private insurers. In those cases, cost reduction is at the expense of physicians. But why stop at physicians? Equity alone should justify pressure to cap or reduce the rapidly growing level of compensation for the managers and executives of health care institutions.

Finally, I may note that significant savings can be gained by limiting the profits for capital. A commonly mentioned source of cost reduction lies in drugs. The evidence is that brand-name drugs are not superior to their generic counterparts, but they are generally much more expensive. Both public and private insurers should refuse to pay for more than the cost of generic drugs. Assuming a private, investor-owned pharmaceutical industry, and taking into account recently revised patent laws highly favorable to the proprietary rights of that industry, there is every reason to believe that it more than recoups the cost of its research and development programs during the period over which it holds its patents. Excessive profit on brand-name drugs gained after generic drugs can be sold in the marketplace should stem solely from the free choice of consumers to pay more for them out of pocket or it should be taxed as windfalls. Indeed, all those who gain so much from the advantages of regulation—insurance companies as well as manufacturers of medical products—should be closely scrutinized to determine whether or not they profit too much at the expense of the nation. The health industry, manufacturers as well as those providing services, must bear some of the burden of reducing cost so that more is available for those in need.

THE CRITICAL CHOICE

Finally, I wish to reiterate the major assumption underlying the choices I believe are desirable for the future—that because health care has the capacity to enrich the possibilities of human life it should be given a special value in the political scheme of things that is not measured by cost alone. It is true that much more effort should be devoted to the prevention of illness by protecting and renovating the physical and social environment in which we live, but that does not mean that curative, rehabilitative, corrective, and reconstructive health care loses its importance. The benefits from clinical medicine and the medical model of illness and its treatment are too great to ignore. The issue can only be to make them available to all as well as to undertake more individual and community preventive measures.

A fundamental choice faces us now. We can passively accept a health care system that, in the interest of cost containment, slowly moves toward mechanizing and bureaucratizing services. Or we can actively choose to struggle for a system that, while striving to be as inexpensive as possible, insists on organizing health care as a discretionary service designed to do everything it can to improve the unique lots of all those who need help. In the first case, physicians and other health care workers will be expected to follow elaborate rules of procedure that have been laid out for them by their bureaucratic and professional superiors. Patients will become standardized objects, their individual needs defined by Procrustean classifications and their treatment and virtually mechanized.

Should the industrialization of health care be the outcome, both physicians and patients will have lost something precious. Physicians will have lost the opportunity to do autonomous, challenging, and creative work. And patients will have lost the opportunity to regain and expand their full individual potential. Clearly, even though tension is intrinsic to their relationship, the fate of patients is tied to the fate of doctors. One may hope that their common interest in a truly human health service may lead them to struggle for it together.

NAME INDEX

Abbott, A., 198
Alford, R., 198
Andrews, L. P., 31, 41 n., 151
Arney, W. R., 180

Baird, L. L., 90
Balamuth, E., 88
Balfe, B. E., 130, 131
Barber, B., 111–12, 114, 193
Barr, J. K., 220
Bechhofer, F., 141
Becker, H. S., 17
Begun, J. W., 184
Ben-David, J., 33 n., 111
Berlant, J. L., 77, 180
Betz, M., 181, 185
Blau, P. M., 113
Bonner, T. N., 37 n.
Bosk, C. L., 192
Braverman, H., 195
Brown, E. R., 198
Burnham, J. C., 181, 206

Caplow, T., 95, 127 n.
Cappell, C. L., 222
Carlin, J. E., 80
Carr-Saunders, A. M., 31
Cellini, B., 15–16
Chen, E., 16
Christoffel, T., 189

Clark, M., 16, 22
Cobb, S., 16
Coburn, D., 182
Cohen, J. M., 19 n.
Cohn-Haft, L., 86
Coleman, J., 31, 83, 88
Colombotos, J., 90
Conrad, P., 180

Denson, P., 88
Derbyshire, R. C., 193, 210–11
Dittrick, H., 37 n.
Dolan, A. K., 191

Egdahl, R., 85
Eliot, G., 26
Elliot, B., 141
Etzioni, A., 124 n.
Evans-Pritchard, E. E., 37 n.

Foster, G. M., 31
Foucault, M., 180
Freidson, E., 16, 40, 80, 89, 90, 145, 180, 192, 218, 219, 220
Friedenwald, J., 37 n.
Friedman, E., 186, 212

Giddens, A., 188
Glaser, W. A., 90
Goldstein, M., 131 and n., 133

SUBJECT INDEX